TILT

TILT: Teaching Individuals to Live Together

By
Kalman J. Kaplan, Ph.D.
Michael Reese Hospital and Medical Center
Chicago, Illinois

Wayne State University
Detroit, Michigan

USA	Publishing Office:	BRUNNER/MAZEL *A member of the Taylor & Francis Group* 325 Chestnut Street Philadelphia, PA 19106 Tel.: (212) 625-8900 Fax: (212) 625-2940
	Distribution Center:	BRUNNER/MAZEL *A member of the Taylor & Francis Group* 47 Runway Road Levittown, PA 19057 Tel.: (215) 269-0400 Fax: (215) 269-0363
UK		Taylor & Francis Ltd. 1 Gunpowder Square London EC4A 3DE Tel.: 171 583 0490 Fax: 171 583 0581

TILT: Teaching Individuals to Live Together

Copyright © 1998 Brunner/Mazel. All rights reserved. Printed in the United States of America. Except as permitted under the United States Copyright Act of 1976, no part of this publication may be reproduced or distributed in any form or by any means, or stored in a database or retrieval system, without the prior written permission of the publisher.

1 2 3 4 5 6 7 8 9 0

Printed by Edwards Brothers, Ann Arbor, MI, 1998.

A CIP catalog record for this book is available from the British Library.
∞ The paper in this publication meets the requirements of the ANSI Standard Z39.48-1984 (Permanence of Paper)

Library of Congress Cataloging-in-Publication Data

Kaplan, Kalman J.
    TILT: teaching individuals to live together/by Kalman J. Kaplan.
      p. cm.

    1. Psychoanalysis. I. Title.
BF173.K35   1998
158'.9—dc21
                                                                                          98-25595
                                                                                          CIP

ISBN 0-87630-927-9 (case)
ISBN 0-87630-928-7 (paper)

To Moriah, who has taught me much of what I have attempted to conceptualize in this book.

The Jewish sage Hillel used to say:

If I am not for myself, who will be for me?
If I am only for myself, what am I?
If not now, when?
(Avot 1:14)

Contents

Foreword by John Parr	*xi*
Acknowledgments	*xv*
Preface	*xvii*

Part One
Definitions and Measurement

Chapter 1   **The Problem of Psychological Distance: A Distinction Between Walls and Boundaries**   3

A Definition of Interpersonal Distance	3
Two Distancing Patterns	4
Individuation and Attachment	6
Walls and Boundaries	12

Chapter 2   **The Individuation–Attachment Questionnaire: A Bidimensional Measurement Approach**   17

Conceptual Underpinnings	17
Directions for Administration	18
Directions for Scoring	19
Interpretation of Scores	21
Reliabilities	31
Divergent and Convergent Validities	31
External Validity	34
Summary	42

Part Two
TILT for Individuals

Chapter 3 **Developing a Model: Distinguishing Developmental and Clinical Axes** — 47

Need and Fear Energy — 47
Patterns of Interpersonal Distancing — 54
The TILT Therapy — 58

Chapter 4 **Psychotherapy Illustrations for Individuals** — 65

Developmental Cases — 65
Clinical Cases — 70

Chapter 5 **TILT Across the Lifespan: From Mistrust to Trust** — 85

Erikson's Eight Stages — 85
TILT Across Life Stages — 87
*TILT*ing Erikson: Through a Stage Vertically — 89

Part Three
TILT for Couples and Families

Chapter 6 **TILT for Couples: Helping Couples Grow Together** — 119

Unidimensional Versus Bidimensional Views of Family Cohesion — 119
Need and Fear Energy in Couples — 126
Cohesion and Couple Type: A Bidimensional Distancing Analysis — 131
TILT for Couples: A Program for Responsive Couple Growth — 145

Chapter 7 **Psychotherapy Illustrations for Couples** — 155

Developmental Cases — 155
Clinical Cases — 164
Implications for Children — 185

Chapter 8	**TILT for Families: A Family Study on Adolescent Suicide**	**187**
	Parents and Children: A Theoretical Extension	187
	The Developmental (BED) Axis	188
	The Clinical (AC) Axis	189
	Family Factors in Adolescent Suicide	191
	A Taxonomy	193
	An Empirical Study	195
	Implications for TILT	201
	Implications for SAFE	204

Part Four
TILT for the Clinician

Chapter 9	**A Developmental Guide for the Clinician**	**209**
	The General Problem	209
	Within-Stage Dynamics	213
	Between-Stage Dynamics	214
	The Life-Stages	216
	Summary	232
Chapter 10	**Conclusion: Applications to Other Areas**	**233**
References		*235*
Index		*255*

Foreword by John Parr

> Love is a universal migraine,
> A bright stain on the vision
> Blotting out reason.
>
> Symptoms of true love
> Are leanness, jealousy,
> Laggard dawns;
>
> Are omens and nightmares—
> Listening for a knock,
> Waiting for a sign:
>
> For a touch of her fingers
> In a darkened room,
> For a searching look.
>
> Take courage, lover!
> Can you endure such grief
> At any hand but hers?
>
> —Robert Graves, "Symptoms of Love"

If you have ever wondered why you seem to react unfavorably to change or why your seemingly satisfying relationships sometimes fail, if you fear being alone or find intimacy scary, this book is for you. It offers a diagnostic tool for understanding and a map to help you find a path toward gaining secure attachments and satisfying self-reliance.

Dr. Kaplan's book is a stimulating mix of well-researched theory and practical application. This model can be understood at a multiplicity of levels, from that of self-help to complex psychoanalytic theory and practice.

Throughout the development of psychoanalytic thought, theorists have attempted to equate idiosyncratic adult human behavior and relationship conflict with childhood developmental deficits. Pioneers such as Klein, Fairbairn, Piaget, Bowleby, Mahler, Erickson, have provided us with excellent, if occasionally conflicting, constructs that offer insight to the pain and interpersonal conflicts of daily life and relationship stress. Therapists explore issues of trust vs mistrust, of object relationships or of maternal deprivation, while many of their lay clients ask themselves, "What is this all about?," "How do I relate to this?," "How does this help me to understand and solve my problem?" While theory may be helpful and even stimulating to the professional, much of it is inaccessible to their clients and patients. Perhaps at the worst, theory may become an alienating factor in the therapeutic relationship. The TILT model, however, is an exciting schema for understanding human behavior—the intricate 'dance of life'—in which we all regularly engage. In the hands of the skilled professional it can be used as a precision tool, for working with the broad spectrum of psychological problems presented in the consulting room. It is helpful to couples who can readily understand the concepts after a brief description and begin at once to apply their knowledge to bring healing to their relationship difficulties. It is helpful in relationship counselors' work to facilitate understanding and growth within interpersonal relationships. It is useful in industrial settings for examining blocks to successful teamwork and for finding methods of combatting corporate stress. And it can be used by social psychologists to interpret and unravel the complexities of international politics.

Dr. Kaplan cleverly interlinks child development theories of Individuation and Attachment, incorporating them on one healthy axis. He shows how clear self–other boundaries develop and how these replace defensive walls. This occurs when we are provided with the necessary safety to leave our significant others to explore our environment. With an understanding of Dr. Kaplan's model, we discover a clear explanation for those times in our adult lives when as a result of social stressors we again experience archaic insecurity around change that reactivates our natural response which is defensiveness. On the pathological axis, in contrast, our boundaries and walls are not so coordinated. Often we take down walls too early (before boundaries have been established). Grave's poem illustrates the divine torture some individuals and couples experience in "loving" relationships. You will have heard or experienced the tension of "I can't live with him or her and I can't live without him or her." Kaplan neatly explains the dynamics underpinning this kind of relationship torture, the early warning symptoms, and how to get to a healthy resolution so we can enjoy our relationships without the loss of our autonomy or sanity.

The simple yet profoundly illuminating model described in this book sheds light on these complex issues. We begin to understand our fellow humans as we

Foreword by John Parr *xiii*

learn about our own unique "dance steps." If I Tango while you Morris Dance our disharmony is readily apparent, at least to observers. However, the nature of and solution to our problem may remain hidden from us, especially if we are dancing to music in the ear phones of our personal stereo systems (i.e., heard only by us and not by our partner). Our competitiveness may cause us to misunderstand each others' signals: "You're just not hearing me!"

If I Salsa while you Rhumba the difference may be less apparent: "Well, we're both doing Latin American, aren't we? It's just that your timing isn't so good." Our walls and boundaries relate respectively to individuation and attachment issues; knowledge and understanding help us to value and respect each other's needs and to take appropriate steps to coordinate the dance. We can agree on which dance band we will listen to together and get to enjoy the rhythm of our relationships. You can have attachment without loss of identity; you can be yourself without losing your relationships. This book demonstrates how.

Acknowledgments

The author would like to acknowledge the help of Oren Uziel, Kristin McTigue, Mithun Nallari, and Eve Bratman, my research assistants at Michael Reese Hospital in Chicago, in the preparation of this book. Their tasks ranged from theoretical discussions to cutting out paper figures in various distancing positions. In all this, their friendship, loyalty, and commitment has been very important. I would also like to thank a number of students and associates at Wayne State University who have shown interest and support along the way, including Nader Saderghiani, Helen Linkey, Nancy O'Connor, Lisa Thomson Ross, Tom Figurski, Susan Weldon, Lisa Berry, Marshall Maldaver, Shirley Worth, Flint Lachenmeier, Sandy Joseph, Vic Wooddell, and Brian Tabaka, and to Al Bochenek of Visual Aids who helped me conceptualize and design many of the figures in this book. Special thanks are due to Doug Clyde, Nancy Capace, Christine Jensen, and John Parr, all four practicing therapists who saw immediately the implications of the TILT concepts for interpersonal therapy, and to my son, Daniel Kaplan, who helped me chase colored ping-pong balls representing different TILT positions around the floors of various delis and restaurants. Finally, this work has benefited from the devoted labor of past and present staff of Taylor & Francis Publishers, especially Elaine Pirrone, Bernadette Capelle, Alison Howson and Thaisa Tiglao, and to Eleanor Umali at TechBooks.

Preface

Ask any group of people what their major problems in relationships are and you will be deluged with complaints of the following order: "She doesn't give me enough space." "He has commitment problems." "I don't have time for myself with him." "I feel I have sacrificed everything for my career." The present book will explore what people seem to want and what they really want. The confusion lies in the way in which interpersonal distance has been viewed in our society—as a unidimensional concept ranging from far or remote distance at one end to near or intimate distance at the other. The near end offers intimacy but carries the danger of loss of self. The far end offers space for one's self but is accompanied by the sensation of loneliness and isolation. Health seems to lie somewhere in the middle: not too much closeness and not too much aloneness.

The TILT program presented in this book offers an alternative to this bipolar choice between "nearness" and "farness." It suggests that interpersonal relationships can be understood in terms of the *dance* between the parties. Different dance steps are described: reciprocal, compensatory, enmeshed or clinging, disengaged or aloof, static or inert, and conflicted. The particular couples described in this book come from the specific patients seen clinically by the author. Names and some specific facts have been altered to protect anonymity. However, the concepts offered in TILT can reasonably be applied to all types of individuals involved in interpersonal situations, regardless of culture, age, gender, or sexual orientation. It is applicable in both personal and public situations. This novel way of looking at "distance" should be helpful to therapists and counselors who are attempting to facilitate understanding and growth in interpersonal relations, whether they are working with families, schools, organizations, or governments.

Part one of this book deals with definitions and measurement issues. Chapter 1 divides the concept of distance into two dimensions: distance from the other (i.e., attachment–detachment) and distance from the self (i.e., individuation–deindividuation). Boundaries (i.e., individuation) are often confused with walls (i.e., deindividuation), and a lack of boundaries (i.e., deindividuation) with an absence of walls (i.e., attachment). Boundaries can be said to "keep the self in," walls to "keep the other out."

Chapter 2 introduces the Individuation–Attachment Questionnaire, which has been designed to measure these separate tendencies and to unconfound our traditional definitions of "near" and "far." A behavioral tendency toward interpersonal nearness (i.e., an approach response) potentially contains both a desire for attachment and a fear of individuation. Likewise, a behavioral tendency toward interpersonal farness (i.e., an avoidant response) potentially contains both a need for individuation and a fear of attachment. The IAQ, in contrast, yields four scores: (1) need for individuation (for independent thought, feeling, and action), (2) fear of individuation (of independent thought, feeling, and action), (3) need for attachment (for cooperation with other in thought, feeling, and action), and (4) fear of attachment (of cooperation with others in thought, feeling, and action). Different scores on these subtests correspond to different TILT positions.

Part two of this book deals specifically with the implications of TILT for individuals. Chapter 3 differentiates two axes: a developmental axis and a clinical axis. On the developmental axis, individuation and attachment go hand in hand. In other words, walls become more permeable as boundaries become more articulated. On the clinical axis, individuation and attachment are inversely related, fixation and vacillation occurring between enmeshment and disengagement. Enmeshment (deindividuated attachment) describes a weak boundary-porous wall combination. Disengagement (detached individuation) describes a strong boundary-rigid wall combination.

Chapter 4 provides clinical illustrations of eight positions emerging from the TILT model. Patients at three developmental positions (regressed, emerging, and advanced) and five clinical positions (two neurotic, two borderline, and one psychotic) are described. Critical in all these descriptions is a distinction between immaturity and pathology. One may outgrow immaturity, but without some outside intervention, is often trapped in a cycle of pathology.

Chapter 5 extends the TILT model across the life span. This multistage, multilevel model of interpersonal development defines successful growth as the gradual replacement of walls by boundaries. Healthy and pathological axes are differentiated, and appropriate intervention is suggested to tilt an individual off of the clinical axis onto the developmental axis. The TILT therapeutic program is described as accomplishing three goals: (1) "backward regression" off of the clinical axis back to the first level of the developmental axis, (2) integrated progression along the developmental axis, and (3) advance to the next developmental stage with the regression in level such growth entails (i.e., "forward regression").

Part three of this book extends this analysis to couples and families. In chapter 6, the TILT program is applied to couples. Healthy couple development is defined as mutually integrated increases in levels of intraindividual individuation and attachment. Healthy couples can be described as progressing from "falling in love" to "loving"; in other words, from a regressed reciprocal position to one of emerging reciprocity to one of advanced reciprocity. Couple pathology is defined as incongruency between individuation and attachment. Enmeshed, disengaged, and rejection–intrusion couple types are defined on the neurotic level as are paranoid, depressed, and mixed borderline couple types. Finally, a psychotic level couple type is described. TILT for couples is described as a method to tilt pathological couples onto the healthy axis of couple development.

Chapter 7 provides examples of a number of couple types seen clinically by the author. Couples on the developmental axis are described first, examples provided of regressed, emerging, advanced, and the anomalous parent–child couples. Next, couples on the clinical axis are discussed. On the neurotic level, enmeshed, disengaged, and rejection–intrusion couple types are described. On the borderline level, the paranoid, depressed, and mixed borderline couple types are discussed. Finally, a psychotic couple is described in TILT terms.

Chapter 8 attempts to test these ideas in a description of an original study linking parental marital structure and adolescent suicidal activity. Parental types showing incongruency between individuation and attachment are more highly associated with adolescent suicidal activity than are those showing congruency between these two life factors. At the same time, the study shows no relationship between adolescent psychopathology and suicide. Some pathological defensive behaviors on the part of the adolescents growing up in disturbed families (e.g., hostile withdrawal) actually may serve a suicide-preventive function by removing the adolescent from the pathological family dynamics.

Part four of this book is addressed specifically to the clinician or counselor and to the individual attempting to help him- or herself. In chapter 9, a life-span model is introduced for the clinician to help alleviate the stress inherent in individuation–attachment conflict and to teach individuals how to live together with others in a way that expresses rather than inhibits their own identities. This chapter specifically applies TILT to Erikson's stage theory of human development. A life event is seen as offering the individual a chance for integrative growth or posing the threat of self-destructive disintegration. Such life events often provoke pseudo-resolutions between the pathological polarities of enmeshment and disengagement rather than the hope of true integration of individuation and attachment. The clinician must attempt to prevent the former and promote the latter. To do this, the therapist must help provide the individual with a wall to protect a boundary made suddenly fragile by the intrusion of an unexpected life event.

The book concludes with chapter 10, which suggests that TILT might be extended to a number of specific areas of life. Brief examples are given of international relations, political economics, and businesses and organizations. The basic concepts of TILT seem quite useful as we enter into a new millennium. As many of the "isms" of the twentieth century have been thrown off, we are searching for a new anchor force for investing our lives and relationships with new meaning, purpose, and spiritual meaning. TILT seems quite promising in this regard.

PART ONE
DEFINITIONS AND MEASUREMENT

Chapter 1

The Problem of Psychological Distance: A Distinction Between Walls and Boundaries

Feeling crowded? Lonely? Searching for commitment? Space? Such words and questions dance continuously through our individual and collective brains. What do people want from themselves and from their closest others? More often than not, people do not seem to really know, instead they seem to be thrashing about in seemingly contradictory ways. Those not in relationships seem to be continuously searching for ways to get into them. Those in relationships often seek to get out of them. Are people as confused as they seem, or is there really some kind of "method to their madness"?

This book attempts to address these issues and summarizes over 15 years of work. Originally the problems were stimulated by largely academic concerns. Now, however, the changing economy may make learning to live together once again an imperative, no longer just one of many possible options. People simply will not have the economic resources to "split" whenever they do not like a situation. To be sure, there have been a number of published works on assertiveness, communication, sexual attraction, and fighting in relationships (e.g., Bach & Wyden, 1968; Falbo & Peplau, 1980; Gottman, 1979; Kaplan & Keys, 1997). However, this book introduces a somewhat unique approach.

A DEFINITION OF INTERPERSONAL DISTANCE

Interpersonal distancing behavior refers to the ways in which individuals approach or withdraw from one another and how they negotiate these tendencies. It has been investigated from a number of different perspectives. One perspective is territoriality. The concept of territoriality has its roots in urban sociology (Park, Burgess, & McKenzie, 1925) and in ethology (Ardrey, 1966). It generally refers to a fixed, relatively permanent physical space used to regulate self-other distance. Reactions to an intruder often involve either "fight" or "flight" responses, each designed to keep a certain interpersonal distance between oneself and another.

A related perspective involves personal space. Sommer (1969) defines personal space as an invisible boundary surrounding the person's body into which intruders may not come. It has been likened to a small shell, a soap bubble, an aura, and "breathing room." Personal space differs from territory in that it is invisible and portable. Nevertheless, it also deals with the regulation of interpersonal distance.

A more sophisticated definition emerges from the work of anthropologist Edward Hall. In *The Hidden Dimension* (1966) Hall proposed a science of "proxemics" or the study of human beings' use of space as a communication vehicle. Hall speaks of four spatial zones used in social interactions: intimate distance (0 to 18 in.), personal distance (1 to 4 ft.), social distance (4 to 12 ft.) and public distance (12 to 25 ft.). Perhaps even more germane is Hall's taxonomy of distancing behaviors beyond the use of physical distance. He suggested, for example, the ways in which visual gaze, smell, touch, and even voice level can be used to signify approach and withdrawal from another.

The concept of interpersonal distance also has emerged in clinical psychology. In *Self-Disclosure*, the late humanistic psychologist Sidney Jourard (1971) focused on intimacy in verbal disclosure as a crucial element in mental health. For Jourard, disclosure intimacy is the primary way in which patient-therapist distance is regulated in the clinical setting. Basically Jourard postulated a "dyadic effect," with therapist disclosure eliciting patient disclosure and vice versa.

TWO DISTANCING PATTERNS

A number of researchers have investigated related antecedents, correlates, and effects of different dimensions or interpersonal distance (e.g., Firestone, Kaplan & Russell, 1973; Kaplan, 1977; Kaplan, Firestone, Klein, & Sodikoff, 1983; Kaplan & Greenberg, 1976). Other studies have revealed complicated interactions with other variables. For example, a recent unpublished study by Daniel Kaplan reported that the effects of self-disclosure were mediated by gender. For women, self-disclosure to close cross-sex others was positively related to positive affect. For both men and women, self-disclosure to all intimates was negatively related to feelings of loneliness.

Generally, a review of the research literature on these four distance dimensions (territoriality, personal space, nonverbal proxemic immediacy, and verbal disclosure) reveals not one, but two dominant theoretical patterns that are in some ways diametrically opposed to each other.

The first pattern, compensation, emerges from the distance equilibrium principal first set forth by Argyle and Dean (1965). They suggested that the expression of intimacy through various behaviors reaches a dynamic equilibrium in an interpersonal interaction. If one person in the interaction increases intimacy in any behavior, the other will decrease it, often on another dimension, to restore the original overall distance. In contrast, if the first person decreases intimacy, the second will increase it. This pattern emerges quite frequently in studies of nonverbal distancing and with verbal factors as well. Certainly compensation also is the principle underlying the concepts of territoriality and personal space. The intruder is either fought off or the defender must flee. In both solutions, the original distance is preserved.

The second pattern, reciprocity, emerges from Jourard's work. For him, verbal exchange follows a norm of reciprocity (Gouldner, 1960) such that increases in verbal intimacy on the part of one person generate pressure on the other to similarly increase intimacy. Likewise, decreases in verbal intimacy on the part of one person generate pressure on the other to similarly decrease intimacy. This pattern receives substantial support in the literature on verbal factors and has received some support in the literature on nonverbal factors as well.

These two patterns are, of course, almost diametrically opposed. In the compensatory pattern a person will block another's distancing moves, whether approach or avoidant (see Figure 1-1). In the reciprocal pattern, a person will match another's distancing moves, again whether approach or avoidant (see Figure 1-2). A number of other theorists have attempted to resolve this controversy by offering a unitary theory of interpersonal distancing (Cappella, 1981; Firestone, 1977; Markus-Kaplan & Kaplan, 1979, 1984; Knowles, 1980; Patterson, 1976, 1982).

We will return to these specific patterns in later chapters. Generally, we can see that this wide array of work has been consistent on one point. Interpersonal distance has been viewed as a unidimensional concept ranging from far or remote distance at one end to near or intimate distance at the other (see Figure 1-3).

The "near" end of the distance dimension offers intimacy but carries the danger of loss of self. The "far" end offers space for oneself but is accompanied by the sensation of loneliness and isolation. These two endpoints, labeled A and C, are mutually exclusive. Intimacy is achieved at the expense of loss of self, and self-definition at the expense of isolation. As such, Position A represents enmeshment and Position C disengagement. No wonder people seem confused, not knowing what they want or, even worse, wanting contradictory things. This book suggests an alternate way of looking at the problem of interpersonal distance, one that does not share this essentially pathological assumption on "mutual exclusivity" with regard to individuation and attachment.[1] We think that this alternate view can be of great therapeutic value for our society.

INDIVIDUATION AND ATTACHMENT

As we begin to consider this problem further, it becomes apparent that the concept of interpersonal distance, in fact, contains two separate dimensions. The first of these can be conceptualized as distance from the other; the second, in contrast denotes distance from oneself.

DISTANCE FROM THE OTHER REFERS TO THE ISSUE OF ATTACHMENT OR DETACHMENT

Attachment is an interpersonal construct and refers to the capacity to bond to another human being. Considerable research has emerged in the last few years around the issue of attachment. The work of John Bowlby (1969, 1973) and of Mary Ainsworth (Ainsworth, 1972, 1973, 1979, 1982, 1989; Ainsworth, Blehar, Waters, & Wall, 1978; Main, 1973; Main, Kaplan, & Cassidy, 1985) and her associates both point to the importance of early attachment history on subsequent development. One way to think of attachment is as the capacity to reach out one's hand to another to give and take help.

DISTANCE FROM ONESELF, IN CONTRAST, REFERS TO THE ISSUE OF INDIVIDUATION OR DEINDIVIDUATION

---

[1] This oppositional view between individuation and attachment is embedded in the ancient Greek legend of Narcissus. Narcissus is portrayed as moving from cold disengagement (detached inviduation) to helpless enmeshment (deindivuated attachment) and finally commits suicide in a state of anomic confusion between the two forces (Ovid, *Metamorphosis III*. 1. 343–511.) A similar oppositional view is portrayed in the Greek story of Prometheus and Pandora, this time with a gender twist. Here the beautiful and all-gifted woman, Pandora, is sent as a trap to man as punishment for Prometheus stealing fire (Hesoid, *Works and Days*, lines 60–86). Woman representing attachment is seen as a trap for man attempting to gain autonomy. Kaplan, Schwartz, and Markus-Kaplan (1984) and Kaplan and Schwartz (1993) discuss both of these stories from an individuation-attachment perspective and suggest that the Biblical stories of Jonah and of Adam and Eve provide a different view. When God asks Jonah to go to warn the people of Nineveh, a place Jonah sees as a center of evil, Jonah is put in a terrible conflict. He does not want to disobey God (detachment) nor does he want to be untrue to himself (deindividuation). Therefore, he does not answer God directly but runs away to Tarshish. Although he is suicidal at various parts in the story, he is protected in his confused state until he can successfully integrate individuation and attachment and go to Nineveh in a way that is true to himself (*Jonah*). Man and woman are also not put in opposition to each other. In the Biblical story of Adam and Eve, man and woman together are portrayed as eating of the tree of knowlege and together being expelled from Eden (*Genesis* 2:21–4:1).

The Problem of Psychological Distance

Figure 1-1 The compensatory distancing pattern.

Individuation is an intrapersonal construct and can be thought of as the capacity to differentiate oneself from others. The work of Margaret Mahler and her associates has stressed the importance of the individuation differentiation in human growth (cf., Mahler, Pine, & Bergman, 1975). Individuation can be thought of as the capacity to stand on one's own two feet.

Figure 1-4 presents a circle. The individual can be portrayed as standing on the circumference of the circle, the self as the center of the circle, and another person as outside the circle. The distance between that circumference point and the center of the circle denotes the individuation dimension. In other words, attachment reflects "nearness to self." The distance between that circumference point and another on

Figure 1-2 The reciprocal distancing pattern.

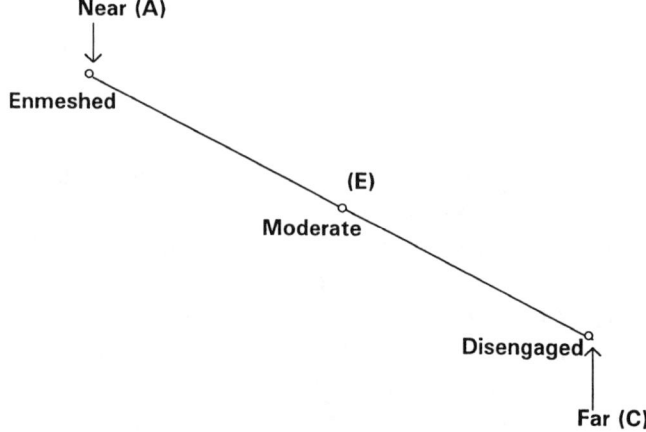

Figure 1-3 A unidimensional view of distance.

The Problem of Psychological Distance

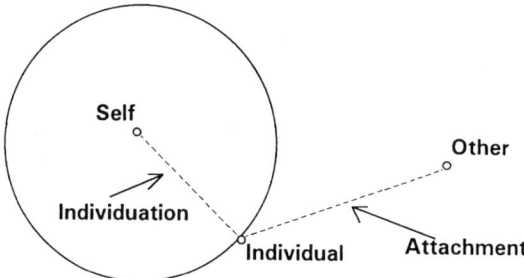

Figure 1-4 Individuation and attachment.

the outside of the circle denotes the attachment dimension. This reflects "nearness to the other."

This bidimensional approach shows us the ambiguity in the unidimensional way of defining interpersonal distance.

"NEARNESS" MAY INDICATE ATTACHMENT; HOWEVER, IT MAY ALSO INDICATE DEINDIVIDUATION

That these two interpretations are very different can be illustrated by the following clinical example.

> Rich, age 28, came to marriage therapy focusing on a lack of direction in his life. His complaint that he did not know "where he was going or who he really was" did not seem in character with his behavior with his wife. On the surface Rich seemed affectionate and eager to spend time with his wife. As therapy progressed, however, it became clear that Rich manifested an "infantile clingingness." Seemingly trivial separations became the occasion for panic responses by Rich. The initial impression that Rich was affectionate (i.e., attached) was replaced by a sense that Rich did not know who he was—a lack of individuation.

Likewise "farness" is open to several interpretations.

"FARNESS" MAY INDICATE INDIVIDUATION; HOWEVER, IT MAY ALSO INDICATE DETACHMENT

Consider another example:

> Barbara, age 23, entered individual treatment complaining that she did not have close friends. This seemed initially to be a strange complaint because she always seemed to be surrounded by people—both male and female—and immersed in activities. However, in the course of therapy it became clear that she organized her schedule so

10   *Definitions and Measurement*

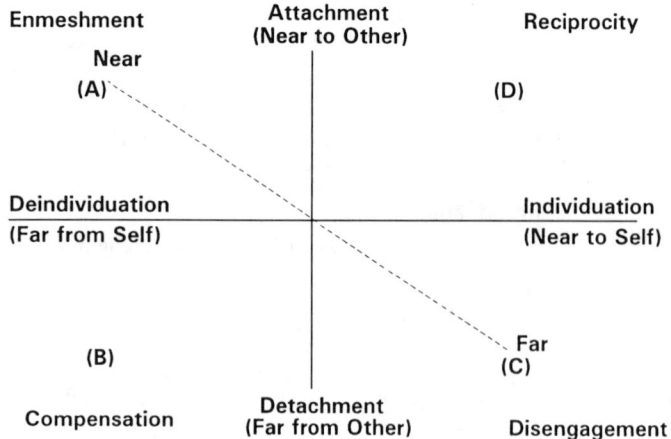

Figure 1-5 A bidimensional view of distance superimposed on a unidimensional one.

as to minimize the possibilities for intimate contacts. In fact, she often went to desperate lengths to avoid one-on-one encounters. A superficial analysis suggested that Barbara was individuated. Closer examination, however, indicated a fundamental fear of attachment.

Figure 1-5 superimposes this bidimensional view of distance on the traditional unidimensional one, thus clarifying the ambiguities in the traditional definitions of "near" and "far." A behavioral tendency toward interpersonal nearness (i.e., an approach response) potentially contains components of both attachment (nearness to other) and deindividuation (farness from self). Likewise, a behavioral tendency toward interpersonal farness (i.e., an avoidant response) potentially contains both an individuation component (nearness to self) and detachment (farness from others).

This reveals a fundamental difference between the unidimensional and bidimensional views of distance.

THE UNIDIMENSIONAL DEFINITION OF DISTANCE ASSUMES AN INVERSE RELATION BETWEEN ATTACHMENT AND INDIVIDUATION

The "near" end of the dimension denotes enmeshment (i.e., high attachment and low individuation). The "far" end of the dimension denotes disengagement (i.e., low attachment and high individuation). Both of these extremes are pathological. Health exists only at the middle points of moderate attachment and moderate individuation.

THE BIDIMENSIONAL VIEW, IN CONTRAST, DOES NOT ASSUME AN INVERSE RELATION BETWEEN ATTACHMENT AND INDIVIDUATION

Four positions emerge in this two-space, labeled, respectively, A, B, C, and D. Positions A and C describe the two endpoints of the unidimensional view as described in Figure 1-3, A representing enmeshment and C, disengagement. Positions B and D represent distance configurations not apparent in the unidimensional presentation. As will become apparent in the unfolding of the TILT model, Position B represents the principle of compensation described previously in Figure 1-1 and Position D, the principle of reciprocity described in Figure 1-2.

Both Cells A and C in Figure 1-5 represent a fundamental imbalance. In Cell A the individual has high regard for others at the expense of the self; in Cell C he or she has high regard for the self at the expense of the other. Although only the C individual is narcissistic in Freud's terms (Freud, 1914, 1957b), both are narcissistic in Kohut's reformulation (Kohut, 1966, 1971): the A individual being an "idealizing narcissist" and the C individual a "mirroring narcissist." Cells B and D, in contrast, are balanced. In Cell B the individual shows low regard both for himself and for others. In Cell D he or she shows high regard both for self and for others. Now we come to an important point. Health is defined as a balance between individuation and attachment rather than in moderation on these dimensions! This leads to an unexpected conclusion. Cell B, although undeniably undeveloped, lies on a fundamentally healthy axis. The implications of this point will become apparent as the TILT model is developed.[2]

---

[2] A rich parallel flows naturally between these concepts and those emerging from transactional analysis. Consider, for example, Ernst's "OK Corral" (Berne, 1961, 1964; Ernst, 1971; Harris, 1969). I'M OK–I'M NOT OK refers to the self and can be mapped into the individuation-deindividuation dimension, with I'M OK indicating individuation and I'M NOT OK indicating deindividuation. Likewise, YOU'RE OK–YOU'RE NOT OK refers to the other and can be mapped into the attachment-detachment dimension, with YOU'RE OK indicating attachment and YOU'RE NOT OK indicating detachment. To put it simply, individuation-deindividuation refers to the degree of self-regard, attachment–detachment to the degree of other-regard.

In initial presentations and discussions of TILT (Gilbert, 1985; Kaplan, 1985; Kaplan, Capace & Clyde, 1984), a one-to-one correspondence was attempted between TILT Cells A, B, C, and D and the cells of the OK Corral. Here Cell A represented an individual who is attached but deindividuated: I'M NOT OK–YOU'RE OK. Cell B represented an individual who is detached and deindividuated: I'M NOT OK–YOU'RE NOT OK. Cell C represented an individual who is individuated but detached: I'M OK–YOU'RE NOT OK. Cell D represented an individual who is individuated and attached: I'M OK–YOU'RE OK. More recently, my colleague John Parr (personal correspondence) has pointed to a potential flaw in this suggested correspondence. For Ernst, the I'm Not OK, You're Not OK position is unhealthy. TILT sees Cell B, deindividuation with detachment, as developmentally necessary. Parr has suggested Cell B corresponds to a neutral rather than a negative point regarding self and other OK-ness. This would place all the positions of TILT into the I'm OK, You're OK, quadrant of Ernst's Corral. Parr is presently developing an integration of TILT and the OK Corral. He superimposes TILT on each quadrant of the Corral and uses the combined models to diagnose and treat clients presenting symptoms of personality disorder. The I'm OK, You're OK TILT positions inform the therapist how to minimize client defense responses while maximizing the potential to build the therapeutic relationship.

WALLS AND BOUNDARIES

Perhaps the most important aspect of the bidimensional approach is the distinction between "walls" and "boundaries." The term "boundary" has been employed by the family therapist Salvatore Minuchin (1974). What is a boundary for Minuchin? It can be thought of as the point of interchange between one member of a family and another. Minuchin (1974, p. 54) describes an enmeshed or overinvolved family as having diffuse boundaries. Such a family has difficulty providing sufficient privacy. A disengaged or underinvolved family, in contrast, is described as having rigid boundaries. This type of family should have difficulty promoting sufficient communication or intimacy. Minuchin sees healthy families as having clear boundaries, lying in the middle between diffuse boundaries and rigid boundaries. This family should allow for both some privacy and also some communication and intimacy.

However, Minuchin's conception of boundaries, although quite popular, implicitly assumes the same pathological unidimensional view of distance described above. Boundary is simply another way of talking about interpersonal distance. Diffuse boundaries denote the "near" pole of the distance dimension. Rigid boundaries denote the "far" pole of the same distance dimension. Finally, clear boundaries represent a balanced or middle distance position, neither too near or too far. This defines health as the absence of pathology rather than anything positive in itself.

Consider an alternate approach to this problem, one in keeping with our bidimensional definition of interpersonal distance.

INDIVIDUATION AND ATTACHMENT ARE NOT OPPOSITE, BUT INDEPENDENT

This approach offers a distinction between walls (denoted by squares) and boundaries (denoted by circles). Walls denote barriers between persons and thus represent an interpersonal construct. They can be conceptualized as ego defense. Boundaries, in contrast, denote the contours of the self and thus represent an intrapersonal construct. They can be conceptualized as ego strength. In a nutshell, walls exist to keep the other out, boundaries to keep the self in. Walls can be thought of as a bandage around the skin and boundaries as the surface of the skin itself.

This distinction between walls and boundaries provides a richer framework than that available in Minuchin's framework. Table 1-1 denotes walls by outer squares and boundaries by inner circles. Walls denote the attachment-detachment dimension (distance from the other) and can take on three levels. Detachment is represented by wall rigidity or impermeability (□), semiattachment by moderate permeability of walls (□), and attachment by wall permeability (▫). Boundaries

Table 1-1
Icons representing levels of individuation and attachment

Attachment/detachment	Individuation/deindividuation
⊡ Full Capacity to Bond	○ Full Capacity to Differentiate
□ Semicapacity to Bond	○ Semicapacity to Differentiate
□ No Capacity to Bond	○ No Capacity to Differentiate

denote the individuation-deindividuation dimension and can also take on three levels. Individuation is represented by boundary articulation (○), semi-individuation by moderate articulation of boundaries (○), and deindividuation by inarticulation or diffuseness of boundaries (○).

Figure 1-6 describes six different wall-boundary combinations. The ordinate refers to the bonding or attachment dimension, and the abscissa refers to the autonomy or individuation dimension. People may fall into different pairings of autonomy and bonding; Figure 1-6 graphically illustrates six possible positions. Three of these—A, C, and E—represent points on Minuchin's dimension. Position A represents a state of low autonomy and high bonding. This enmeshed state is characterized by permeable walls and unarticulated boundaries (▦). Position C represents a state of high autonomy and low bonding. This disengaged state is characterized by impermeable walls and articulated boundaries (▣). Position E represents an in-between state of moderate autonomy and moderate bonding. It is characterized by moderately permeable walls and moderately articulated boundaries (▣).

Three additional positions—B, D, and A/C—emerge from this bidimensional view that cannot be described by Minuchin's system. B represents a state of low bonding and low autonomy, characterized by impermeable walls and unarticulated boundaries (▣). D represents a state of high bonding and high autonomy, characterized by permeable walls and articulated boundaries (▣). A/C represents a position split between enmeshment and disengagement (▣), indicating a conflict on both the autonomy and bonding dimensions. In this Figure, O represents other and P the self and the arrows below as approach and withdrawal. More of this later.

This system treats individuation and attachment as orthogonal dimensions, and likewise walls and boundaries and independent constructs. Health is not defined simply by avoiding extremes but rather by balancing individuation and attachment, ultimately at high levels of both. Before we proceed further with this discussion, it is important at this stage to reiterate clearly the basic manifesto of TILT.

WALLS EXIST TO KEEP THE OTHER OUT; BOUNDARIES EXIST TO KEEP THE SELF IN

14   *Definitions and Measurement*

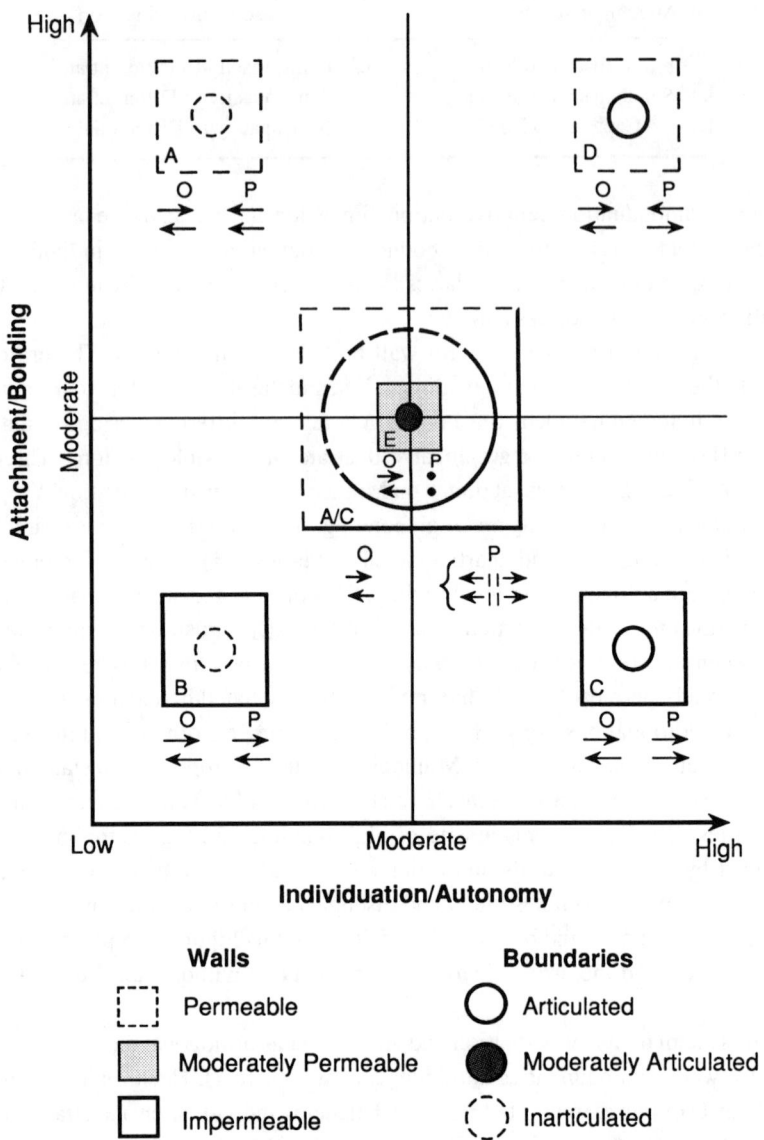

Figure 1-6 A bidimensional view of interpersonal distancing patterns.

A graphic clinical example illustrating the potentially devastating confusion between these two dimensions emerged in a dialogue in a therapy session between a mother and an adolescent daughter hospitalized for a suicide attempt. The background of this case was quite poignant. The mother, now in her 30s, had given birth to the daughter out of wedlock when she herself was a teenager. Her mother, the grandmother, a quite ambivalent figure, raised her grandchild as a daughter while her own daughter completed high school and went on to college and tried to develop her own life. After more than 10 years, the biological mother now felt she was mature enough to return to be a mother to her now teenage daughter.

When the mother attempted to set limits regarding her daughter's sexual behavior with boys, she (the daughter) would rebel stating "You are my sister, not my mother." This blocked the mother in her attempts to express her identity. The mother disagreed but remained on this individuation dimension maintaining, "I am your mother. I must set limits." Thus the mother attempted to individuate herself. The daughter immediately switched dimensions interpreting her mother's action as detachment, "You don't love me." The mother disagreed but again remained on the same attachment dimension, insisting "I do love you." Again the daughter switched dimensions, accusing the mother of deindividuating her, stating, "You are limiting my freedom." Once again the mother disagreed, but remained on the same individuation dimension insisting that her actions were designed to give her daughter freedom. "I want you to have the chance to develop your own life and not get pregnant prematurely the way I did." The daughter responded by running away from home, converting the individuation issue into one of detachment. The mother searched for the daughter and brought her back home telling her that she loved her. Again, the mother stayed on the same attachment dimension while disagreeing with her daughter.

This example is very revealing from a TILT point of view. Whereas the daughter kept confusing the individuation and attachment dimensions, the mother expressed disagreement but always stayed on the same dimension.

This illustrates the importance of two TILT corollaries:

DON'T CONFUSE LOOSENING WALLS (i.e., ATTACHING) WITH LOSING BOUNDARIES (i.e., DEINDIVIDUATING).

DON'T CONFUSE ERECTING WALLS (i.e., DETACHING) WITH ESTABLISHING BOUNDARIES (i.e., INDIVIDUATING).

Untangling such confusion requires a method of independently assessing individuation and attachment. This is the subject matter of chapter 2.

Chapter 2

The Individuation–Attachment Questionnaire: A Bidimensional Measurement Approach

CONCEPTUAL UNDERPINNINGS

The Individuation–Attachment Questionnaire (IAQ) has been designed as an instrument for research and clinical purposes to provide quick and convenient measures of four life forces that have typically been confounded in our traditional measures of interpersonal distance. A behavioral tendency toward interpersonal nearness (i.e., an approach response) potentially contains both a need for attachment and a fear of individuation. Likewise, a behavioral tendency toward interpersonal farness (i.e., an avoidant response) potentially contains both a need for individuation and a fear of attachment.

The IAQ attempts to differentiate boundaries and walls in personality development.

BOUNDARIES REFER TO THE DEGREE OF INDIVIDUATION AND WALLS REFER TO THE DEGREE OF ATTACHMENT

Individuation is defined as the capacity to differentiate one's self from another; deindividuation as the lack of capacity for this differentiation. Attachment is defined as the capacity to connect or bond affectionately to another person; detachment as the absence of this capacity.

Figure 2-1 and 2-2 differentiate two axes: a developmental axis and a clinical axis. The developmental axis contains three positions: B, E, and D. Here individuation and attachment go hand in hand. As one's boundary becomes more articulated (one becomes more individuated), one's wall becomes more permeable (one becomes more attached). The clinical axis contains two basic positions, A and C, and combinations thereof. Here individuation and attachment are in opposition to each other. Position A describes an inarticulate boundary-permeable wall combination (deindividuated attachment or "enmeshment") while Position C

Forward Regression to Next Stage

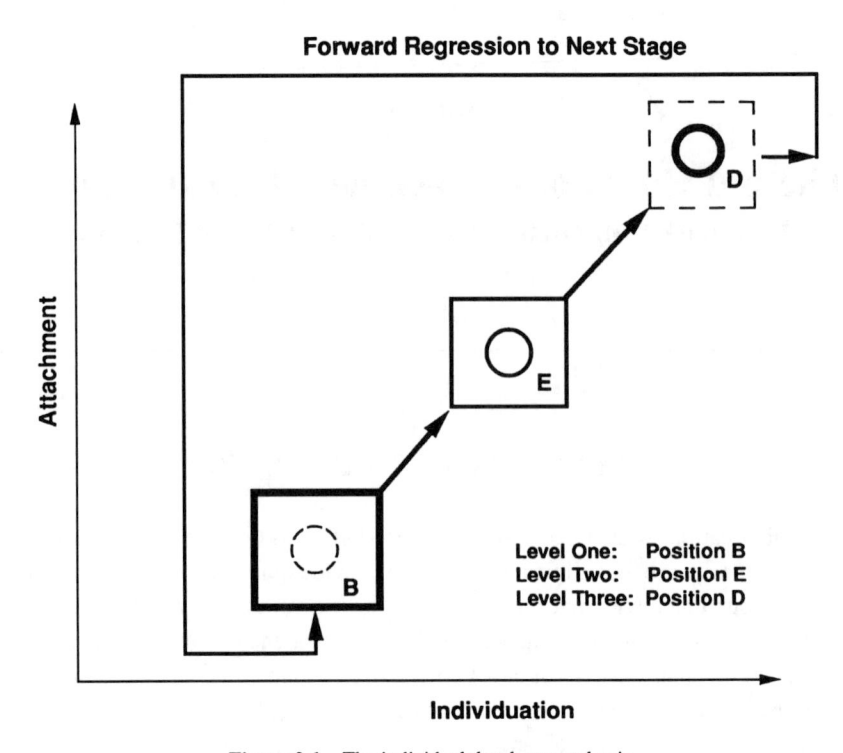

Figure 2-1 The individual developmental axis.

describes an articulate boundary-rigid wall combination (detached individuation or "disengagement"). Position A/C represents a split between Positions A and C, or between enmeshment and disengagement.

The IAQ assumes an inherent ambiguity in our traditional definitions of near and far and attempts to separate out the often fine distinctions found in relation to these dynamics. For example, agreement with the statement, "It is important for me to take other people's needs into account," may indicate a need for attachment. However, agreement with the statement, "It is important for me to meet other people's expectations of me," may indicate a fear of individuation. Likewise, agreement with the statement, "Other people's judgments of me seldom determine how I feel about myself," may indicate a need for individuation. On the other hand, agreement with the statement, "A person does not need involvement with others to be fulfilled." may indicate a fear of attachment.

DIRECTIONS FOR ADMINISTRATION

The IAQ is easy and convenient to administer and can be given individually to couples and families, or to large groups. It is presented in full in Table 2-1. It

The Individuation–Attachment Questionnaire

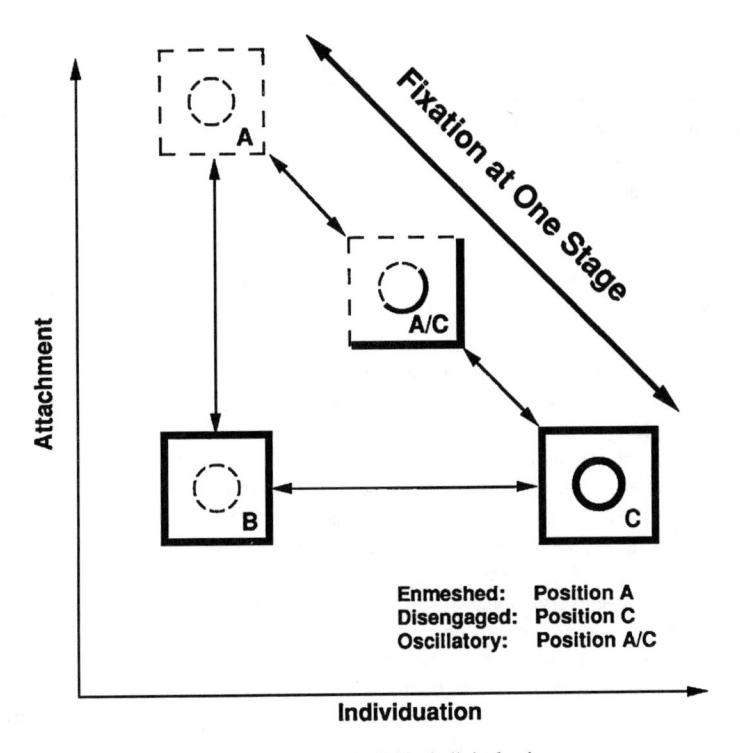

Figure 2-2 The individual clinical axis.

requires approximately 15 to 20 minutes for the average respondent to complete the IAQ. There is no time limit for completing the IAQ (although the time taken in answering the questions may be recorded for interpretive use). Responses to the IAQ allow the scoring of four subscales: need for individuation (NI), fear of individuation (FI), need for attachment (NA), and fear of attachment (FA).

DIRECTIONS FOR SCORING

The IAQ yields four separate scores: (1) NI (for independent thought, feeling, and action), (2) FI (of independent thought, feeling, and action), (3) NA (for cooperation with others in thought, feeling, and action), and (4) FA (of cooperation with others in thought, feeling, and action). The IAQ contains 11 items measuring each of these subscales. Strong agreement with any item is scored 4, agreement 3, indecision 2, disagreement 1, and strong disagreement 0.

Table 2-1
The IAQ

For each statement indicate your attitude or opinion by placing the correct number on the line next to each statement.

4 = strongly agree
3 = agree
2 = undecided
1 = disagree
0 = strongly disagree

FI	1.	I try to avoid being on my own.
NI	2.	I don't hesitate to fight for my own opinions with those I am close to.
FA	3.	One should not be swayed by other people's needs.
NA	4.	I prefer to use my free time talking to other people.
FI	5.	A highly responsible position is too much of a burden.
NI	6.	Other people's judgment of me seldom determines how I feel about myself.
NA	7.	I have a great need for sharing my feelings with other people.
FA	8.	Being in a close relationship often keeps one from doing what he/she wants to do.
NI	9.	I believe everyone has an obligation to find their own way in life.
FA	10.	Love is often more trouble than it is worth.
FI	11.	It is important for me to meet other people's expectations of me.
NA	12.	I feel fulfilled when I'm involved in what is going on with other people.
NI	13.	A contract delineating each person's needs and obligations is an essential part of any love relationship.
FA	14.	If I open myself to others I'll get hurt.
FI	15.	Being with close friends means that you don't need a space of your own.
NA	16.	You are not worth much if you are only occupied with your own concerns.
NI	17.	If I am not for myself I can't expect anyone else to be for me.
NA	18.	One should go out of his/her way to maintain friendships.
FI	19.	Paying attention to your own feelings is typically destructive for a relationship.
FA	20.	A person does not need involvement with others to be fulfilled.
FI	21.	It makes more sense to fit in than to be conspicuous.
FA	22.	I feel that people become less interesting when they form families.
NA	23.	It should be legally negligent not to help an accident victim.
NI	24.	You can never count on support from other people in what you want to do.
FI	25.	I feel inadequate when people disapprove of me.
NI	26.	Ultimately I have to do things my own way.
FA	27.	I think people always try to control others.
NA	28.	Relating to others is essential to coming to know oneself.
FI	29.	I tend to speak softly in public.
NI	30.	My decisions as to what to wear are not determined by what other people say.
NA	31.	I try to help out people with their problems even if it is inconvenient for me.
FA	32.	The most effective way of handling obligations to others is to avoid situations which bring them about.

(Continues)

Table 2-1
(Continued)

NA	33.	The best part of parties is the chance to make new friends.
NI	34.	We should act on our own best judgments even it other people strongly disagree.
FI	35.	You should be friendly with everyone.
FA	36.	I prefer not to get too close to others.
FI	37.	I let people I respect shape my decisions.
NI	38.	I express what I think even if I know my position is extremely unpopular.
FA	39.	There is too much emphasis on connection to others in our culture.
NA	40.	Mealtime is a time when families and friends should be together.
NI	41.	I don't feel guilty when I oppose my friends.
FA	42.	The price of a close relationship is that it keeps you from truly being yourself.
NA	43.	Being responsive to another person is one of the most difficult things there is.
FI	44.	I feel very secure when I have a close friend stronger than myself to rely on.

Answers to the 44 items appearing in the IAQ are recorded in boxes in the left of the question sheet. The IAQ contains 11 items measuring each of the four subscales. NI is assessed by items 2, 6, 9, 13, 17, 24, 26, 30, 34, 38, and 41. FI is assessed by items 1, 5, 11, 15, 19, 21, 25, 29, 35, 37, and 44. NA is assessed by items 4, 7, 12, 16, 18, 23, 28, 31, 33, 40, and 43. FA is assessed by items 3, 8, 10, 14, 20, 22, 27, 32, 36, 39, and 42. The possible range of each of the four subscales goes from 0 to 44.

INTERPRETATION OF SCORES

Scores on each of the four subscales can be classified as high or low on the basis of the means deriving from the normative sample, which will be presented in the next section. Scores above the mean for each subscale are classified as high, and scores below the mean are classified as low. Different combinations of attachment and individuation subscores allow the classification of an individual into a TILT type. Classification of the eight pure TILT types is presented in Table 2-2.

Developmental and clinical axes are distinguished. Developmental maturity is ordered from regressed, to emerging, to advanced; and severity of pathology is ordered from neurotic pathology personality disorder, to borderline, to psychosis.

The TILT types described in Table 2-2 can be seen to fall on one of two axes, a developmental axis or a clinical axis. Each position is illustrated by a "pot-shot" cartoon from the drawings of Ashleigh Brilliant (1979, 1984, 1990, 1992).

Table 2-2
TILT Types and Individuation–Attachment Questionnaire (IAQ) Distribution

Pure TILT types	IAQ distribution NI FI NA FA[a]
1. Developmental axis	
Regressed B (adjustment disorder)	Lo Hi Lo Hi
Emerging E	Lo Lo Lo Lo
Advanced D	Hi Lo Hi Lo
2. Clinical axis	
Neurotic A (dependent personality disorder)	Lo Hi Hi Lo
Neurotic C (avoidant personality disorder)	Hi Lo Lo Hi
Borderline (A/C)$_{\text{INDIVIDUATION}}$ (depressive subtype)	Hi Hi Lo Lo
Borderline (A/C)$_{\text{ATTACHMENT}}$ (paranoid subtype)	Lo Lo Hi Hi
Psychotic (A/C)$_{\text{TOTAL}}$	Hi Hi Hi Hi

[a]NI = need for individuation; FI = fear of individuation; NA = need for attachment; FA = fear of attachment.

A PERSON ON THE DEVELOPMENTAL AXIS EXHIBITS CONGRUENCY BETWEEN INDIVIDUATION AND ATTACHMENT

A person in Position B is dominated by fears with regard to both individuation and attachment. Such a person can be said to be at a regressed or an immature level of development. He or she puts up a rigid wall to defend his fragile boundary. This often is indicative of a temporary adjustment disorder (309.00 to 309.90 on Axis I of the *Diagnostic and Statistical Manual of Mental Disorders* [American Psychiatric Association, 1994; *DSM-IV*]), which he or she will overcome as he or she becomes stronger (see Figure 2-3). A person in Position E has overcome his or her fears but is not yet able to express needs (see Figure 2-4). He or she exhibits a moderate wall surrounding a moderate boundary. Finally, a person in Position D is able to express healthy needs for both individuation and attachment. He or she no longer needs a rigid wall as his boundary has become well-defined (see Figure 2-5).

A PERSON ON THE CLINICAL AXIS EXHIBITS INCONGRUENCY BETWEEN INDIVIDUATION AND ATTACHMENT

A person in Neurotic Positions A or C can be said to have a personality disorder. Position A denotes a dependent personality disorder (301.60 on Axis II of the *DSM-IV*). A person at this position manifests a high need and low fear with regard to attachment but also a high fear and a low need with regard to individuation. He or she displays enmeshed (deindividuated attachment) behavior (see Figure 2-6). Position C typically denotes an avoidant personality disorder (an Axis II diagnosis

Figure 2-3 Position B (From *I feel so much better now that I've given up hope*, 1984, by A. Brilliant, p. 86). Copyright © 1984 by Ashleigh Brilliant.

Figure 2-4 Position E (From *I feel so much better now that I've given up hope*, 1984, by A. Brilliant, p. 47). Copyright © 1984 by Ashleigh Brilliant.

Figure 2-5 Position D (From *We've been through so much together, and most of it was your fault*, 1990, by A. Brilliant, p. 71). Copyright © 1990 by Ashleigh Brilliant.

Figure 2-6 Position A (From *I feel much better now that I've given up hope*, 1984, by A. Brilliant, p. 65). Copyright © 1984 by Ashleigh Brilliant.

of 301.82). A person at this position manifests a high need and a low fear with regard to individuation but also a high fear and a low need with regard to attachment. He or she displays disengaged (detached individuation) behavior (see Figure 2-7).

An individual whose personality is organized at the borderline level (an Axis II diagnosis of 301.83) is at a more severe level of pathology. The borderline exhibits oscillation between dependence and isolation. However, he or she can fall into one of two types, depressed or paranoid (cf., Meissner, 1984), each of which is based on different conflicts. The depressed borderline type, (A/C)$_{IND}$, demonstrates conflict on individuation (exhibiting both a high need and a high fear of need) but not on attachment (exhibiting both a low need and a low fear of need). His or her oscillation should be triggered primarily by individuation issues. In other words, confronting a situation that will give the individual more responsibility should evoke oscillation between dependent and avoidant behaviors. He or she may receive Axis I diagnoses of major depression (296.20) or dysthymic disorder (300.40) in addition to a Axis II diagnosis (see Figure 2-8).

The paranoid borderline type, $(A/C)_{ATT}$, demonstrates conflict on attachment (exhibiting both a high need and a high fear) but not on individuation (exhibiting both a low need and a low fear). This person's oscillation should be triggered primarily by attachment issues. For example, confronting the possibility of a close relationship should evoke in the individual oscillation between dependent and avoidant behaviors. He or she may receive an Axis I diagnosis of 297.10: delusional disorder with jealousy or feelings of persecution (see Figure 2-9).

The most severe level of psychopathology, of course, is that of the psychotic (an Axis 1 diagnosis of 295.10 to 298.90). The psychotic, $(A/C)_{TOT}$, is split between dependent and avoidant behaviors. He or she is conflicted with regard to both individuation (high need and high fear) and attachment (high need and high fear). A psychotic individual should thus be pulled simultaneously in the direction of both dependence–enmeshment and avoidance–disengagement whether the underlying issues involve either individuation or attachment issues (see Figure 2-10).[1]

---

[1] Table 2-2, of course, only presents the eight pure TILT types, involving an even number (0, 2 or 4) of highs and lows. Eight additional mixed TILT types may occur as well, each involving an odd number (1 or 3) of highs and lows distributed across the subscales:

	NI	FI	NA	FA
(9)	Lo	Lo	Lo	Hi
(10)	Lo	Lo	Hi	Lo
(11)	Lo	Hi	Lo	Lo
(12)	Hi	Lo	Lo	Lo
(13)	Lo	Hi	Hi	Hi
(14)	Hi	Lo	Hi	Hi
(15)	Hi	Hi	Lo	Hi
(16)	Hi	Hi	Hi	Lo

Each researcher must examine a particular impure configuration in terms of closeness of fit to the pure types. Thus, for example, the profile of a respondent who falls in Type 9 must be examined in terms of which of his or her subscale scores lies closest to the cutoff norm. Let us say the low NI score falls 2 points below the group mean while the low FI and NA scores fall 4 points below the cutoff mean and the high FA score falls 3 points above the cutoff. This respondent would be reclassified as a pure TILT type: Personality Disorder C (Hi, Lo, Lo, Hi), since this reclassification would involve the least overall disruption to the individual's IAQ structure. In case of ties, my experience suggests classifying the respondent at the lower level of pathology and/or the less mature level of development. I would be interested in coordinating data regarding norms, reliabilities, validities, and item analyses from all users of the IAQ.

Figure 2-7 Position C (From *We've been through so much together and most of it was your fault*, 1990, by A. Brilliant, p. 73). Copyright © 1990 by Ashleigh Brilliant.

Figure 2-8 Position (A/C)$_{IND}$ (From *We've been through so much together and most of it was your fault*, 1990, by A. Brilliant, p. 74). Copyright © 1990 by Ashleigh Brilliant.

Cutoff Norms

In determining whether a particular subscale score, within the range of scores from 0 to 44, for a given variable is high or low, references may be made to the norms developed in Tables 2-3 through 2-7 on each subscale. Initial research has used a mean split defining as "high" all respondents scoring above the means and as "low" all respondents scoring below the mean. Let us begin with Table 2-3, presenting means and standard deviations from a sample of 72 men

The Individuation–Attachment Questionnaire   27

Figure 2-9 Position (A/C)$_{ATT}$ (From *I feel so much better now that I've given up hope*, 1984, by A. Brilliant, p. 47). Copyright © 1984 by Ashleigh Brilliant.

Figure 2-10 Position (A/C)$_{TOT}$ (From *I feel so much better now that I've given up hope*, 1984, by A. Brilliant, p. 98). Copyright © 1984 by Ashleigh Brilliant.

and 150 women ranging in age from 17 to 98. This sample was obtained from volunteers at Wayne State University in Detroit at several adult social organizations and at several religiously affiliated retirement villages in Detroit and Chicago. The means for the four subscales are presented in Table 2-3. Men tend to be slightly more oriented toward individuation (both needs and fears) women need attachment more and fear it less ($p < .05$). The means for both men and women

Table 2-3
IAQ means and standard deviations for an age-free sample (ages 17–98)

	Means		Standard deviations	
Subscale[a]	Males (72)	Females (150)	Males (72)	Females (150)
NI	28.60	28.21	4.53	4.48
FI	18.05	17.13	4.38	4.65
NA	27.68	28.48	4.17	4.08
FA	18.05	16.34	5.69	4.79

[a]NI = need for individuation; FI = fear of individuation; NA = need for attachment; FA = fear of attachment.

Table 2-4
IAQ means and standard deviations for adolescent and young adult sample (ages 17–27)

	Means		Standard deviations	
Subscale[a]	Males (592)	Females (957)	Males (592)	Females (957)
NI	27.88	26.54	5.07	4.98
FI	19.83	20.09	5.48	5.67
NA	26.60	28.05	5.63	5.12
FA	18.35	16.29	6.81	6.63

[a]NI = need for individuation; FI = fear of individuation; NA = need for attachment; FA = fear of attachment.

are significantly higher for the need scores (for both individuation and attachment) than for the fear scores ($p < .01$).

Tables 2-4 through 2-7 break these norms down into four distinct age groups. These samples were obtained with the generous help of Dr. Helen Linkey from samples from university students, adult social clubs, and retirement villages in Michigan, Illinois, and in West Virginia. The largest sample by far, 592 men and 957 women (total $N = 1549$), was obtained in adolescent-young adult age range (ages 17 to 27). These results are presented in Table 2-4. Eighty-seven men and 125 women (total $N = 212$) emerged in the early middle adult sample (ages 28 to 45). These results are presented in Table 2-5.

Table 2-6 presents the means and standard deviations for the late middle-aged sample. This sample contained 91 men and 130 women with ages ranging from 46 to 65 (total $N = 221$). The older adult sample is presented in Table 2-7. This

Table 2-5
IAQ means and standard deviations for early middle adult sample (ages 28–45)

	Means		Standard deviations	
Subscale[a]	Males (87)	Females (125)	Males (87)	Females (125)
NI	27.66	27.45	4.77	4.54
FI	18.03	18.32	5.45	5.82
NA	25.38	26.74	4.44	4.81
FA	17.84	16.11	5.86	5.36

[a] NI = need for individuation; FI = fear of individuation; NA = need for attachment; FA = fear of attachment.

Table 2-6
IAQ means and standard deviations for late middle adult sample (ages 46–65)

	Means		Standard deviations	
Subscale[a]	Males (91)	Females (130)	Males (91)	Females (130)
NI	27.05	27.38	4.28	4.36
FI	18.96	18.91	4.94	5.42
NA	25.78	26.29	4.75	3.92
FA	17.88	16.82	7.36	5.47

[a] NI = need for individuation; FI = fear of individuation; NA = need for attachment; FA = fear of attachment.

Table 2-7
IAQ means and standard deviations for older adult sample (ages 66 and older)

	Means		Standard deviations	
Subscale[a]	Males (48)	Females (52)	Males (48)	Females (52)
NI	27.42	26.79	4.31	3.86
FI	21.48	21.29	6.31	5.24
NA	25.90	27.04	5.21	4.43
FA	18.50	18.00	5.95	6.08

[a] NI = need for individuation; FI = fear of individuation; NA = need for attachment; FA = fear of attachment.

Table 2-8
High-low cutoff point for the Individuation–Attachment Questionnaire (IAQ) subscales[a]

Age-free sample	NI	FI	NA	FA
Men (*N* = 72)				
High	29–44	19–44	28–44	19–44
Low	0–28	0–18	0–27	0–18
Women (*N* = 150)				
High	29–44	18–44	29–44	17–44
Low	0–28	0–17	0–28	0–16
Adolescent–young adults (17–27)				
Men (*N* = 27)				
High	28–44	20–44	27–44	19–44
Low	0–27	0–19	0–26	0–18
Women (*N* = 957)				
High	27–44	21–44	29–44	17–44
Low	0–26	0–20	0–28	0–16
Early middle adults (28–45)				
Men (*N* = 87)				
High	28–44	19–44	26–44	18–44
Low	0–27	0–18	0–25	0–17
Women (*N* = 125)				
High	28–44	19–44	27–44	17–44
Low	0–27	0–17	0–26	0–16
Late middle adults (46–65)				
Men (*N* = 91)				
High	28–44	19–44	26–44	18–44
Low	0–27	0–18	0–25	10–17
Women (*N* = 130)				
High	28–44	19–44	27–44	17–44
Low	0–27	0–18	0–26	0–16
Older adults (66 and older)				
Men (*N* = 48)				
High	28–44	22–44	26–44	19–44
Low	0–27	0–21	0–25	0–18
High	27–44	22–44	27–44	18–44
Low	0–26	0–21	0–27	0–17

[a] NI = need for individuation; FI = fear of individuation; NA = need for attachment; FA = fear of attachment.

sample proved difficult to obtain, only yielding 100 total people over age 65. Of these, 48 were men and 52 women.

Overall, the results reveal remarkable consistency in means and standard deviations for the four subscales across both gender and age. In short, both men and women in all age groups show significantly higher mean scores for the two "need" subscales (NI and NA) than for the two "fear" subscales (FI and FA). The means for the two need scales range roughly between 25 and 28. The means of the two fear scales range between 16 and 21.5. These differences are highly significant ($p < .01$).

Within this overall pattern, there are some slight age patterns, especially for the fear subscales. FI and FA seem to be slightly higher for the adolescent–young adult and the older adult groups than they are for middle-aged adults ($p < .05$). However, these differences are less than two units and should not obscure the pattern of overall consistency. Table 2-8 presents overall cutoff norms for the four subscales using a mean split. These cutoff points are presented separately for men and for women, both calculated across age and within each of the four age groups.

RELIABILITIES

Split-half reliabilities have been calculated for each of the IAQ subscales for the five samples. They are presented in Table 2-9. Over gender and age groupings, reliabilities on the four subscales ranged from .75 (FI) to .84 (FA). Specifically, reliabilities for NI ranged from .79 to .83 and for FI they ranged from .75 to .79. For NA, reliabilities ranged from .80 to .82, and reliabilities for FA ranged from .80 to .84.

DIVERGENT AND CONVERGENT VALIDITIES

Intercorrelations among the four subscales are presented in Table 2-10 for each of the five samples. The validity of the bidimensional approach to distance underlying the IAQ depends on the empirical independence of the attachment and individuation dimensions. Specifically, this approach requires nonsignificant correlations between NI and FA and between NA and FI.

The results of all five samples are remarkably consistent in this regard. No relation even approaching significance emerges between NI and FA (rs range between .08 and .10) or between NA and FI (rs range between $-.02$ and $-.05$). These divergent validities lend empirical support to the bidimensional view of distance underlying the IAQ. Attachment and individuation empirically seem to be independent dimensions.

Table 2-9
Split half reliabilities for IAQ subscales

	NI[a]	FI[b]	NA[c]	FA[d]
Age-free sample				
Men ($N = 72$)	.81***	.75***	.82***	.84***
Women ($N = 150$)	.83***	.77***	.82***	.83***
Adolescents–young adults (17–27)				
Men ($N = 592$)	.80***	.76***	.81***	.84***
Women ($N = 957$)	.82***	.77***	.82***	.82***
Early middle adults (28–45)				
Men ($N = 87$)	.79***	.75***	.82***	.81***
Women ($N = 125$)	.83***	.76***	.83***	.81***
Late middle adults (46–65)				
Men ($N = 91$)	.82***	.76***	.80***	.81***
Women ($N = 130$)	.82***	.78***	.80***	.80***
Older adults (66 and older)				
Men ($N = 48$)	.81***	.79***	.80***	.84***
Women ($N = 52$)	.80***	.79***	.81***	.83***

[a] NI = need for individuation.
[b] FI = fear of individuation.
[c] NA = need for attachment.
[d] FA = fear of attachment.
*** $p < .001$.

The needs and fears within each dimension, however, do tend to be negatively related. For attachment, this inverse relation tends to be significant (rs range from −.23 to −.25, $p < .01$). For individuation, this relationship just fails to meet conventional significance levels (rs range from −.17 to −.19). In short, while individuation and attachment do not seem to be inversely related, attachment and detachment do seem to be inversely related, as do individuation and deindividuation. However, even here the low size of these correlations indicates that even within the individuation and attachment dimensions, needs and fears need not be mutually exclusive. They may be exclusive for some respondent, and not exclusive for others.

Finally, the intercorrelation matrices reveal independence between the two need scores (NI and NA) across samples. The correlations here range between .01 and .04. The two fear scores (FI and FA), however, do tend to be moderately intercorrelated (the rs range between .41 and .46, $p < .01$), indicating that a high fear on one dimension is often accompanied by a high fear on another. However, there is less than 20% common variance.

Table 2-10
Divergent and convergent validities of the IAQ subscales

		NI[a]	FI[b]	NA[c]	FA[d]
Age-free sample	NI	x	−.18	.04	.10
(N = 222)	FI	x	x	−.04	.46**
	NA	x	x	x	−.25**
	FA	x	x	x	x
Adolescents–young					
Adults (17–27)	NI	x	−.19	.02	.09
(N = 1549)	FI	x	x	−.03	.45**
	NA	x	x	x	−.26**
	FA	x	x	x	x
Early middle adults					
(28–45)	NI	x	−.18	.04	.08
(N = 212)	FI	x	x	−.02	.43**
	NA	x	x	x	−.24**
	FA	x	x	x	x
Late middle adults					
(46–65)	NI	x	−.18	.01	.10
(N = 221)	FI	x	x	−.05	.41**
	NA	x	x	x	−.23**
	FA	x	x	x	x
Older adults					
(66 and older)	NI	x	−.17	.02	.09
(N = 100)	FI	x	x	−.04	.46**
	NA	x	x	x	−.25**
	FA	x	x	x	x

[a] NI = need for individuation.
[b] FI = fear of individuation.
[c] NA = need for attachment.
[d] FA = fear of attachment.
*$P < .05$.
**$P < .01$.

Taken as a whole, these intercorrelations support the utility of separate measurements of NI, FI, NA, and FA. First, individuation and attachment seem to be independent dimensions. Two conclusions follow:

NEED FOR INDIVIDUATION IS NOT SYNONYMOUS WITH FEAR OF ATTACHMENT

NEED FOR ATTACHMENT IS NOT SYNONYMOUS WITH FEAR OF INDIVIDUATION

Two more conclusions follow:

NEED FOR ATTACHMENT DOES NOT NECESSARILY RULE OUT FEAR OF ATTACHMENT

NEED FOR INDIVIDUATION DOES NOT NECESSARILY RULE OUT FEAR OF INDIVIDUATION

One point should be made in concluding this section. As is obvious to the reader, the internal validity dates presented above were for the entire sample at each age group and not separated for men and women. This alternate was chosen because the results for men alone and for women alone were practically identical and there seemed to be no point in further complicating this presentation.

EXTERNAL VALIDITY

IAQ Self-Report and Clinician Perception

Three different validity studies have been conducted on the IAQ. The first was administered to a clinical sample ($N = 83$) of 28 males and 55 females ranging in age from 14 to 51 (including 10 single episode or recurrent unipolar depressives, 6 bipolar depressives, 7 generalized anxiety disorders, 14 chronic dysthymics, 4 chronic cyclothymics, 10 conduct disorders, 4 alcohol abuse/dependencies, 3 drug abuse/dependencies, 4 narcissistic personalities, 6 dependent personality disorders, 3 passive-aggressive personality disorders, 6 schizoid disorders, 2 compulsive personalities, and the remaining 11 scattered in different *DSM-IIIR* diagnostic categories). A patient's scores on each of the four subscales were cross-validated against independently derived judgments on these same scales by two clinicians familiar with these same patients. Interclinician reliability was .78 for the male patients and .82 for the female patients. IAQ validity scores between the patients' response and the average of the two clinician judgments are presented in Table 2-11. They likewise are slightly higher for the female than the male patients for each of the four subscores: NA ($r_f = .77, r_m = .72$), FA ($r_f = .69, r_m = .67$), NI ($r_f = .65, r_m = .64$), FI ($r_f = .62, r_m = .58$).

The IAQ and Personality Scales

A second validity study was recently conducted on a sample of 122 college students (54 males and 68 females). It compared IAQ subscale scores (NI, FI, NA, and FA) with comparable scores on the Edwards Personal Preference Schedule (EPPS) and

Table 2-11
Cross-validation of Individuation–Attachment
Questionnaire (IAQ) self-report and ratings by
clinician for four subscales

IAQ subscales[a]	Males ($N = 28$)	Females ($N = 55$)
NI	.64**	.65**
FI	.58**	.62**
NA	.72**	.77**
FA	.67**	.69**

[a] NI = need for individuation.
[b] FI = fear of individuation.
[c] NA = need for attachment.
[d] FA = fear of attachment.
**$p < .01$.

the Interpersonal Style Inventory (ISI). The EPPS (Edwards, 1957) is a standard 225-item forced choice inventory designed in terms of Murray's manifest needs that generates 15 subscales. Internal consistencies range from .60 to .87 and retest correlations from .74 to .88. Furthermore, the subscore intercorrelations are quite low, indicating at least empirical independence. The ISI (Lorr and Youniss, 1973) consists of 300 true-false items empirically broken down into 15 subscales divided over five broad areas of personality: interpersonal involvement, socialization, autonomy, self-control, and stability. Alpha coefficients and norms are given separately for 354 men and 411 women in 12 diverse settings. Of the 30 coefficients (15 for men and 15 for women), only that for approval-seeking (for the female sample) sinks marginally below .70, with most being above .80. Mean alphas are .82 for both men and women. The test-retest stabilities over a 2-week period ranged from .80 to .95, with a mean of .87. Both scales have been validated against other inventories with similar dimensional properties, including the Eysenck Personality Inventory, 16 Personality Factor Questionnaire, the Jackson Personality Inventory, and Comrey's Personality Scale.

The results indicate a good deal of discriminant and convergent validity for the IAQ subscales. NI is correlated at the .01 level to the achievement, autonomy, dominance, and endurance subscales on the EPPS (see Table 2-12) and to the directive, independent, rule free, and deliberate subscales of the ISI (see Table 2-13). NI is correlated at the .05 level to the exhibition, intraception, and change EPPS subscales and to the sensitive, conscientious, and persistent subscales on the ISI. FI is correlated at the .01 level to the deference, succorance, and abasement subscales on the EPPS and to the help-seeking and approval-seeking subscales of the ISI. FI is correlated at the .05 level to the affiliation EPPS subscale

Table 2-12
Cross validation of the Individuation–Attachment Questionnaire (IAQ) and the EPPS

Edwards Personal preference Schedule (EPPS)	NI[a]	FI[b]	NA[c]	FA[d]
Achievement	.52**	−.07	.14	.12
Deference	−.08	.48**	.07	−.03
Order	.16	−.08	.11	.12
Exhibition	.19*	−.13	.17	.34**
Autonomy	.41**	−.04	−.06	.28**
Affiliation	−.03	.18*	.59**	−.13
Intraception	.18*	.16	.13	.17
Succorance	.05	.29**	.43**	−.01
Dominance	.41**	−.13	.04	.21*
Abasement	.03	.37**	.18*	−.04
Nurturance	.16	−.04	.38**	−.08
Change	.20*	−.10	−.03	.11
Endurance	.35**	.03	.18*	−.05
Heterosexuality	.17	.02	.24**	−.03
Aggression	.17	−.15	−.14	.43**

[a] NI = need for individuation.
[b] FI = fear of individuation.
[c] NA = need for attachment.
[d] FA = fear of attachment.
*p < .05 (N = 122).
**p < .01.

and the tolerant (negative correlation) subscale of the ISI. NA is correlated at the .01 level to the affiliation, succorance, nurturance, and heterosexuality subscales on the EPPS and to the sociable, help-seeking, nurturant, and conscientious subscales on the ISI. NA is correlated at the .05 level to the abasement and endurance subscales on the EPPS. FA is positively correlated at the .01 level to the exhibition, autonomy, and aggression subscales on the EPPS and negatively correlated (again at the .01 level) to the trusting and tolerant subscales on the ISI. FA is correlated at the .05 level to the dominance subscale on the EPPS and to the deliberate subscales on the ISI.

What is especially encouraging in these results is the strong pattern of convergent and divergent validity emerging for the IAQ. First, each of the IAQ subscales is correlated with a number of subscales on more traditional long-standing measures

The Individuation–Attachment Questionnaire

Table 2-13
Cross validation of the Individuation–Attachment Questionnaire (IAQ) and the ISI

Interpersonal Style Inventory (ISI)	NI[a]	FI[b]	NA[c]	FA[d]
Interpersonal involvement				
Sociable	−.07	.10	.52**	−.15
Help seeking	−.08	.34**	.29**	−.10
Nurturant	.10	.04	.47**	−.14
Sensitive	.18*	.02	.15	.13
Socialization				
Conscientious	.21*	.03	.27**	.04
Trusting	.12	.04	.14	−.38**
Tolerant	.05	−.22*	.17	−.29**
Autonomy				
Directive	.41**	−.04	.15	−.07
Independent	.57**	−.16	.00	.11
Rule free	.31**	−.03	.04	.12
Self-control				
Deliberate	.31**	−.09	.10	.22*
Orderly	.14	.03	.08	−.05
Persistent	.19*	.06	.13	.07
Stability				
Stable	.05	−.03	.02	.02
Approval seeking	.00	.34**	.15	.03

[a] NI = need for individuation.
[b] FI = fear of individuation.
[c] NA = need for attachment.
[d] FA = fear of attachment.
*$p < .05$ ($N = 122$).
**$p < .01$.

of interpersonal style. Second, each subscale on the IAQ has a unique relational pattern with at least several of the EPPS and ISI subscales. For example, NI is the only subscale that is related to achievement, independence, and directiveness. FI is the only IAQ subscale that is related to deference and approval seeking. NA is the only IAQ subscale that relates to nurturance, heterosexuality, and sociability. Finally, FA is the only IAQ subscale that relates to exhibition, aggression, and trusting (the last being a negative correlation).

The IAQ, Self-Consciousness, and Interpersonal Reactivity

The third validity study (Figurski & Kaplan, 1989) was conducted on a college sample of 42 undergraduate students. In addition to the IAQ, subjects responded to the Self-Consciousness Scale (SCS) and to the Interpersonal Reactivity Index (IRI). The SCS (Fenigstein, Scheier, & Buss, 1975; Burnkrant & Page, 1984) consists of 23 five-point items designed to tap self-awareness. Four factors emerged from this scale. The first of these factors has been termed self-reflection (the tendency to try to understand oneself in general) and the second, internal state awareness (or the tendency to focus more specifically on one's emotional states and bodily sensations). The third factor in the SCS is public self-consciousness and refers to the tendency to attend to one's status as a social object to others. The fourth subscale, social anxiety, refers to the tendency to feel uncomfortable when self-aware in the presence of others.

The IRI (Davis, 1983) consist of 28 five-point items designed to differentiate cognitive empathy, or the ability to understand someone else's experience, from emotional empathy as an effective response to another's emotional situation whether that experience is understood or not. Cognitive empathy itself is broken up into fantasy (the tendency to imagine the feelings and actions of fictitious characters in books or movies) and perspective taking (the tendency to spontaneously adopt the psychological point of view of others). Emotional empathy likewise is broken up into empathic concern (the tendency to feel sympathy and concern for unfortunate others) and personal distress (the tendency to feel personal anxiety and unease in tense interpersonal settings).

The results further support the convergent and divergent validity of the IAQ (see Table 2-14). NI is correlated at the .01 level to internal state awareness (SCS) and at the .10 level to public self-consciousness (SCS), to fantasy (IRI), and to the absence of personal distress (IRI). FI is correlated at the .01 level to social anxiety (SCS) and at the .05 level to personal distress. NA is correlated at the .10 level to self-reflection (SCS). FA is correlated at the .10 level to personal distress (IRI).

Attachment Styles, Self-Confidence, and Sociability

In an independent research project, Bartholomew and Horowitz (1991) also propose a four-category model of attachment styles combining an individual's self-image (positive or negative) and his image of the other (positive or negative). They base their model on the work on attachment by Bowlby (1977) and on Ainsworth's (Ainsworth, Blehar, Waters, & Wall, 1978) distinction of three distinct patterns of infant attachments: secure, anxious–resistant, and avoidant. Bartholomew and Horowitz delineate *secure* (positive self-regard, positive other-regard), *preoccupied*

Table 2-14
Cross validation of the IAQ, SCS, and IRI

	IAQ subscales			
	NI[a]	FI[b]	NA[c]	FA[d]
Self-consciousness Scale (SCS)				
Self-reflection	.19	.07	.28*	.15
Internal state Awareness	.56***	−.03	.12	.16
Public self Consciousness	.29*	.11	.17	.04
Social anxiety	.08	.44**	.09	.24
Interpersonal Reactivity Index (IRI)				
Cognitive empathy				
Fantasy scale	.27*	.05	.06	.03
Perspective-taking	.22	−.09	−.17	.02
Emotional empathy				
Empathic concern	.02	−.16	.00	−.19
Personal distress	−.27*	.35**	−.12	.27*

[a] NI = need for individuation.
[b] FI = fear of individuation.
[c] NA = need for attachment.
[d] FA = fear of attachment.
*$p < .10$.
**$p < .05$ ($N = 42$).
***$p < .01$.

(negative self-regard, positive other-regard), *dismissing* (positive self-regard, negative other-regard), and *fearful* (negative self-regard, negative other-regard) prototypes.

A developmental application of TILT will be discussed at length in chapter 5. For present purposes, a direct correspondence can be seen between the Bartholomew and Horowitz types and TILT positions. Their *fearful* position corresponds to TILT Position B, *secure* corresponds to D, *preoccupied* to A, and *dismissing* to C. As such, their findings have direct relevance to the question of external validity of the TILT model.

Bartholomew and Horowitz classified 77 subjects (40 female and 37 male) into four attachment styles by means of a semistructured attachment interview regarding the subjects' friendship patterns. On the basis of audio recordings of the interviews, three raters independently rated each subject on four 9-point scales describing the subject's degree of correspondence with each of the four attachment prototypes discussed previously and described below.

The *secure* prototype is characterized by a valuing of intimate friendships, the capacity to maintain close relationships without losing personal autonomy, and a coherence and thoughtfulness in discussing relationships and related issues. The *dismissing* prototype is characterized by the downplaying of the importance of close relationships, restricted emotionality, an emphasis on independence and self-reliance, and a lack of clarity or credibility in discussing relationships. The *preoccupied* prototype is characterized by an overinvolvement in close relationships, a dependence on other people's acceptance for a sense of personal well-being, a tendency to idealize other people, and incoherence and exaggerated emotionality in discussing relationships. The *fearful* prototype is characterized by an avoidance of close relationships because of a fear of rejection, a sense of personal insecurity, and a distrust of others. Alpha coefficients were computed to assess the reliability of the prototype ratings. The reliabilities ranged from .87 to .95. The ratings were averaged, and the highest of the four average ratings was considered to be the best-fitting category for that subject. From this procedure, 47% of the sample was classified as *secure*, 18% as *dismissing*, 14% as *preoccupied*, and 21% as *fearful*. In addition, all subjects completed demographics and friendship questionnaires, two self-concept measures, and a sociability measure.

The Demographics Questionnaire included family information (e.g., marital status of parents, number of siblings) and personal activities (e.g., exercise, religious observance). Seven-point items expressed the degree of experienced depression, anxiety, and happiness (with reversed scoring). These three items were combined into a composite measure of subjective distress ($\alpha = .68$).

The Friendship Questionnaire contained equivalent demographic, factual, and personal questions about the friend. One item assessed the duration of the friendship (e.g., "Compared with close friendships you've had in the past, how close is your friendship with F?"). The latter five items were combined into a friendship closeness scale (target sample $\alpha = .80$; friend sample $\alpha = .86$).

The Rosenberg Self-Esteem Inventory (Rosenberg, 1965) is a 10-item scale that measures global self-esteem. A sample item is, "I certainly feel useless at times" (reverse scored; coefficient $\alpha = .85$).

The Fey Self-Acceptance Scale (Fey, 1955) is a 20-item measure of self-acceptance. A representative item is, "I'm pretty satisfied with the way I am" (coefficient $\alpha = .86$).

The Sociability Scale (Cheek & Buss, 1981) is a 5-item measure that assesses the degree to which people like to socialize with other. A sample item is "I like to be with people" (self-report coefficient $\alpha = .74$; friend report coefficient $= .78$).

Table 2-15
Mean interview ratings across attachment groups[a]

Model	Secure	Dismissing	Preoccupied	Fearful	$F(3, 76)$
Self	Positive	Positive	Negative	Negative	
Other	Positive	Negative	Positive	Negative	
n	36	14	11	16	
			Measure		
General					
Elaboration	6.84	5.74	7.95	6.23	6.90*
Coherence	6.08	5.45	4.76	5.00	16.54*
Friendships					
Self-disclosure	4.00	3.33	5.12	3.05	19.40*
Intimacy	5.09	4.10	4.54	3.79	23.12*
Balance and control	2.94	3.10	2.62	2.60	7.94*
Romantic relationships					
Highest level involvement	3.61	2.60	5.20	3.39	12.32*
Balance of control	3.29	3.73	2.91	2.72	8.50*
Personal characteristics					
Self-confidence	3.54	3.93	2.86	2.24	27.77*
Emotional expressiveness	3.76	2.60	5.20	3.39	12.32*
Crying frequency	2.52	1.45	3.32	2.17	5.75*
Interpersonal characteristics					
Warmth	3.13	2.21	2.94	2.70	11.77*
Reliance on others	4.25	3.26	5.15	3.46	14.65*
Others as secure base	3.34	2.43	4.12	2.61	21.09*
Nonsocial vs. social crying	2.50	2.17	3.70	1.75	7.60*
Caregiving	4.25	3.79	4.80	4.25	6.51*

[a] Adapted from Bartholomew and Horowitz, 1991, Table 1, p. 230.
*$p < .01$.

As shown in Table 2-15, the *secure* group obtained uniquely high ratings on the coherence of their interviews and the degree of intimacy with their friendships. They also received high ratings of warmth, balance of control in friendships, and level of involvement in romantic relationships.

The *dismissing* group scored uniquely high on self-confidence and uniquely low on emotional expressiveness, frequency of crying, and warmth. They scored lower than the *secure* and *preoccupied* groups on all scales reflecting closeness in personal relationships: self-disclosure, intimacy, level of romantic involvements, capacity to rely on others, and use of others as a secure base. They were also rated as being low on elaboration and caregiving and as being more in control than their partners in both friendships and romantic relationships.

The profile shown by the *preoccupied* group was opposite to that of the *dismissing* group in almost every respect; the mean of the two groups differed significantly on each of the rating scales. The *preoccupied* group scored uniquely high on elaboration, self-disclosure (showing a tendency to disclose inappropriately), emotional expressiveness, frequency of crying, reliance on others, use of others as a secure base, crying in the presence of others, and caregiving. They were also rated high on level of romantic involvement and low on coherence and balance of control in friendships.

Finally, the *fearful* group was rated significantly lower than the *secure* and *preoccupied* groups on self-disclosure, intimacy, level of romantic involvement, reliance on others, and use of others as a secure base when upset. They were also rated as uniquely low in self-confidence and as low on both balance-of-control scales.

A discriminant analysis was performed to assess the degree to which the various interview ratings accounted for the overall discrimination among the four attachment groups. The analysis (using a stepwise method with immunization of Wilks' lambda as the selection criterion) resulted in three significant discriminant functions, which correctly classified 92% of the sample, including 86% of the *secure* group, 94% of the *fearful* group, and 100% of both the *preoccupied* and *dismissing* groups.

Finally, female subjects received higher ratings than male subjects on the interview-based *preoccupied* rating (women's $M = 3.10$, men's $M = 2.00$), $t(75) = 2.88$, $p < .01$; male subjects received significantly higher ratings than female subjects on the interview-based *dismissing* rating (women's $M = 3.10$, men's $M = 4.01$), $t(75) = 2.70$, $p < .01$. Although Bartholomew and Horowitz's results do not deal with the IAQ scores per se, they do provide genuine support for a bidimensional approach to interpersonal distance embodied in the TILT conceptualization and in the TILT delineation of personality types.[2]

SUMMARY

Taken as a whole, the psychometric data presented on the IAQ in this section provides increasing support for both the reliability and the validity of the IAQ. The four subscales are largely independent of each other. Furthermore, there is a good deal of internal consistency among the 11 items within each subscale. Finally, there is a good deal of both convergent and divergent validity with (1) independently

---

[2] The reader is also referred to the very creative work of Hansburg (1980) who employed ink drawing of mild and severe separation experience to measure separate individuation and attachment scores among adolescents.

obtained clinical ratings, (2) subscales of the EPPS and the ISI, (3) subscales of the SCS and the IRI, and (4) similar results conducted by an independent research team with regard to a four-category model of attachment styles.

Part II gives a fuller articulation of the model itself, as applied to individuals. Chapter 3 begins with the basic model distinguishing the developmental and clinical axes. Chapter 4 will provide clinical illustration of this model. Chapter 5 will extend this model to a multistage conception across the life span.

PART TWO
TILT FOR INDIVIDUALS

Chapter 3

Developing a Model: Distinguishing Developmental and Clinical Axes

NEED AND FEAR ENERGY

Western culture has erroneously come to stigmatize the individual with needs as "needy." Such an individual is seen as childish and dependent. Yet, an equally plausible stance is to see needs as the mark of a mature person. It has been said that great people have great needs, lesser people, lesser needs.

A unique aspect of the Individuation–Attachment Questionnaire described in chapter 2 is the independent measurement of four subscales: NI, FI, NA, and FA. An individual can be described as either high or low on each of four subscales. These different combinations can then be portrayed schematically. They can be divided into two axes: the developmental (BED) axis and the clinical (AC) axis.

The Developmental Axis

Consider first the developmental axis. Position B is portrayed in Figure 3-1. The B individual is regressed and defended. His or her energy is concentrated in fears, both of attachment and of individuation. Fear of attachment results in rigid walls, fear of individuation results in amorphous boundaries. The B person is heavily defended because he or she is so fragile. B's energy is invested exclusively in fears.

As the individual develops on the BED axis, he or she moves into the E position (Figure 3-2). The E individual has resolved his fears of individuation and of attachment and is different from the B individual in that his or her energy is no longer invested in fear. However, this individual has not yet been able to convert the energy into genuine needs. The E individual can be described as having moderate walls and moderate boundaries. As the person becomes more defined, his or her defenses are relaxed.

Now consider the D individual (Figure 3-3). He or she has matured to the point of having genuine needs, both for attachment and for individuation. D's energy

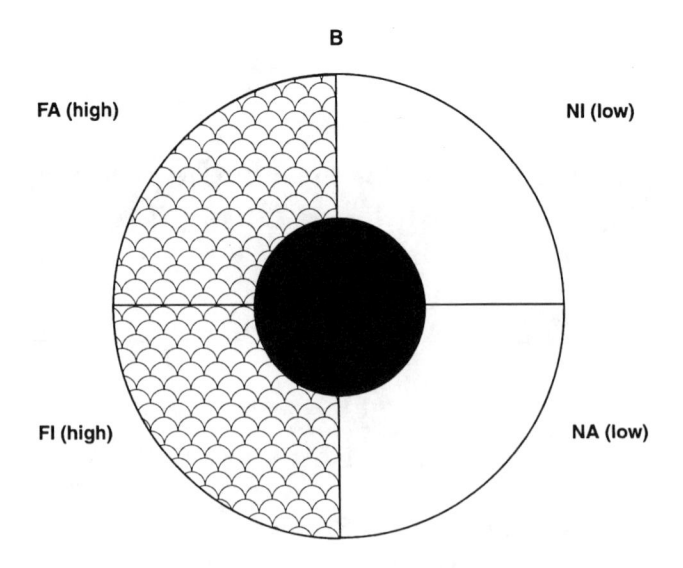

48   *TILT for Individuals*

FI = Fear of Individuation   NI = Need for Individuation
NA = Need for Attachment   FA = Fear of Attachment

Figure 3-1   Position B on the developmental axis.

FI = Fear of Individuation   NI = Need for Individuation
NA = Need for Attachment   FA = Fear of Attachment

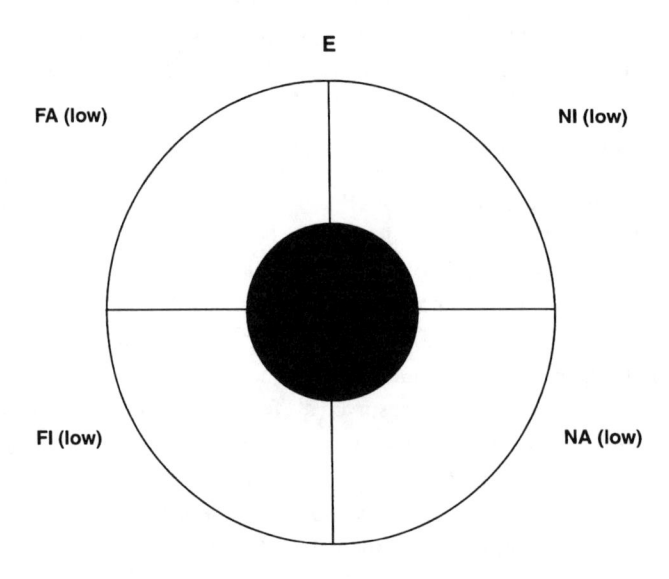

Figure 3-2   Position E on the developmental axis.

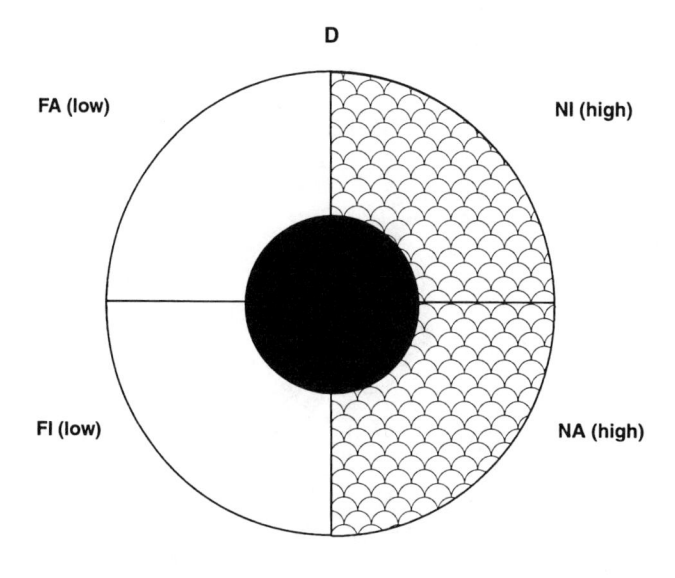

Developing a Model: Distinguishing Developmental and Clinical Axes 49

FA (low) **D** **NI (high)**

FI (low) **NA (high)**

FI = Fear of Individuation   NI = Need for Individuation

NA = Need for Attachment   FA = Fear of Attachment

Figure 3-3   Position D on the developmental axis.

can be described as exclusively invested in needs. His or her need for attachment results in permeable walls and the need for individuation in articulated boundaries.

Taken as a whole, development on the BED axis involves the conversion of fear–energy into need–energy. As the individual matures, fears become resolved and energy can thus be withdrawn from them. As the individual matures further, needs develop and can be expressed and energy can be invested in them. At each level of development, investment of energy is balanced between individuation and attachment, first in fears, later in needs. This suggests yet another TILT axiom.

AS AN INDIVIDUAL MATURES, WALLS ARE REPLACED BY BOUNDARIES

Consider a young girl who falls in the school yard and scrapes her knee. Her mother cleans the wound and bandages it. The bleeding skin can be thought of as a shattered boundary, the bandage as a protective wall. In a few days the girl's mother sees the wound is healing, and she removes the bandage. The restored boundary has replaced the need for a wall that is now superfluous. What is critical here is that wall application and boundary development are coordinated.

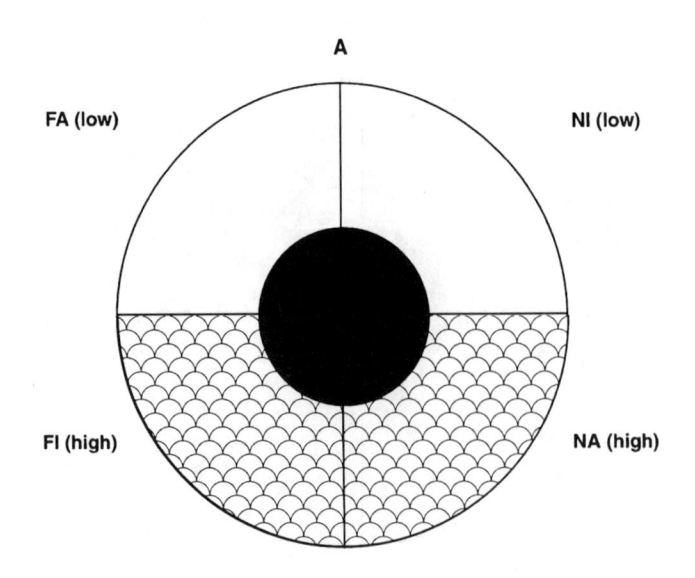

50 TILT *for Individuals*

A

FA (low) NI (low)

FI (high) NA (high)

FI = Fear of Individuation   NI = Need for Individuation
NA = Need for Attachment   FA = Fear of Attachment

Figure 3-4 Position A on the clinical axis.

The Clinical Axis

The clinical axis is very different. Here the application of walls is not coordinated with the establishing or restoration of boundaries. Consider first the A individual (Figure 3-4), whose energy is invested in fear of individuation and in need for attachment. He or she is enmeshed (has a dependent personality disorder) and all his or her energy is directed toward avoiding abandonment. This is clearly an imbalanced and neurotic position. The enmeshed neurosis can be summarized as follows:

WALLS ARE LOOSENED PREMATURELY, BEFORE BOUNDARIES HAVE BEEN ESTABLISHED

The flip side of this position is the equally imbalanced C individual (Figure 3-5), whose energy is invested in fear of attachment and in need for individuation. He or she is disengaged or has an avoidant personality disorder. All his or her energy is directed toward avoiding absorption. This also is an imbalanced neurotic position. This disengaged neurosis can be expressed as follows:

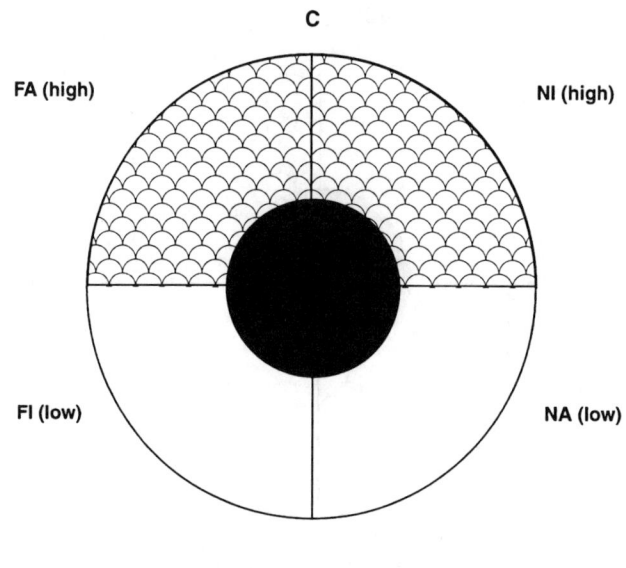

Developing a Model: Distinguishing Developmental and Clinical Axes 51

FA (high) NI (high)

FI (low) NA (low)

FI = Fear of Individuation   NI = Need for Individuation
NA = Need for Attachment   FA = Fear of Attachment

Figure 3-5 Position C on the clinical axis.

WALLS ARE MAINTAINED UNNECCESARILY, AFTER BOUNDARIES HAVE BEEN ESTABLISHED

Both the A and C positions show confusion between individuation and attachment.

Now let us consider more severe clinical pathologies. First consider Position $(A/C)_{IND}$ based not on confusion alone but on conflict. This represents a borderline configuration–depressive subtype (Figure 3-6). This individual's energy is invested totally in the individuation dimension. However, it is equally distributed between needs and fears. Such a person is ambivalent about individuation, both needing it and fearing it. However, he or she is indifferent about attachment, neither needing it nor fearing it. This depressive subtype can be defined as having boundaries that vacillate between articulateness and amorphousness. His or her walls, in contrast, are moderate.

Consider now position $(A/C)_{ATT}$, the borderline configuration–paranoid subtype (Figure 3-7). The energy of this individual is invested in the attachment dimension, equally distributed between needs and fears. This person is ambivalent about attachment, both needing it and fearing it. However, he or she is indifferent toward individuation. This paranoid subtype has moderate boundaries but walls

(A/C)_{INDIVIDUATION}

FA (low) NI (high)

FI (high) NA (low)

FI = Fear of Individuation   NI = Need for Individuation
NA = Need for Attachment   FA = Fear of Attachment

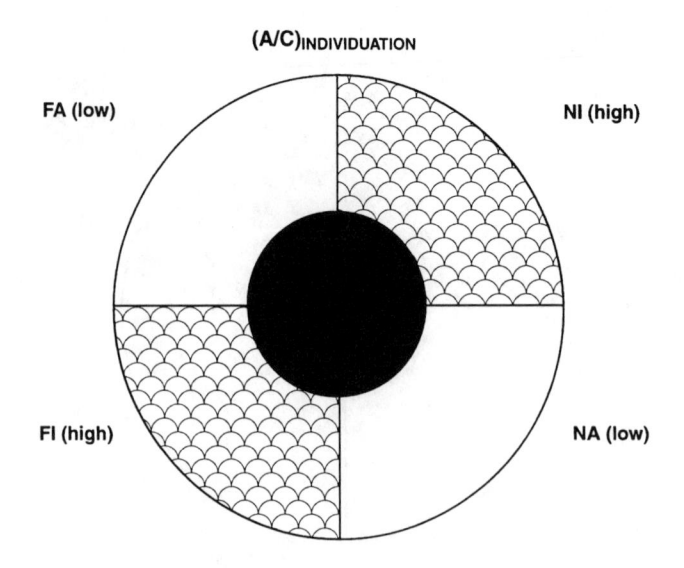

Figure 3-6 Position (A/C)_{INDIVIDUATION} on the clinical axis.

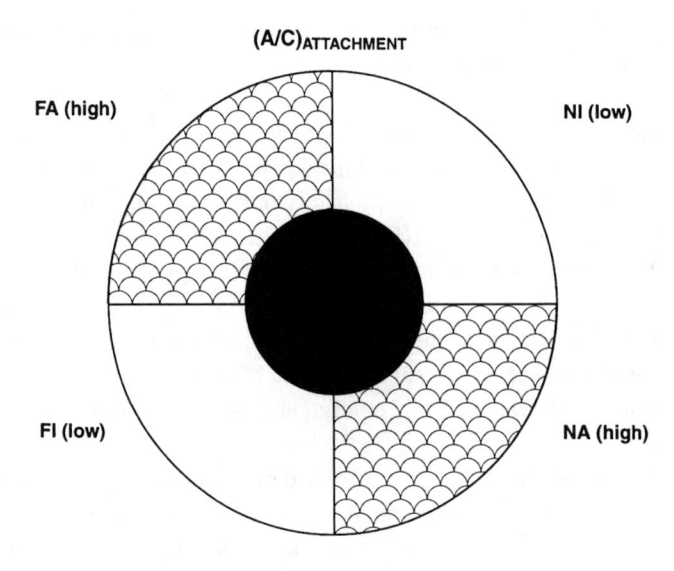

(A/C)_{ATTACHMENT}

FA (high) NI (low)

FI (low) NA (high)

FI = Fear of Individuation   NI = Need for Individuation
NA = Need for Attachment   FA = Fear of Attachment

Figure 3-7 Position (A/C)_{ATTACHMENT} on the clinical axis.

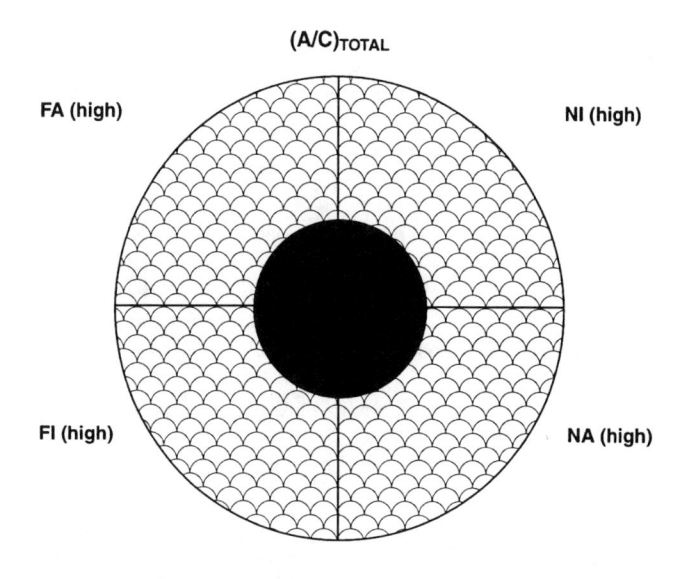

Developing a Model: Distinguishing Developmental and Clinical Axes 53

(A/C)_{TOTAL}

FA (high)   NI (high)

FI (high)   NA (high)

FI = Fear of Individuation   NI = Need for Individuation
NA = Need for Attachment   FA = Fear of Attachment

Figure 3-8 Position $(A/C)_{TOT}$ on the clinical axis.

that vacillate between rigidity and permeability. Both of these positions show genuine conflict between needs and fears.

Consider, finally, position $(A/C)_{TOT}$ (see Figure 3-8). This represents a psychotic configuration. This individual has both need and fear energy invested in both individuation and attachment. He or she is ambivalent about both forces. His or her walls vacillate between rigidity and permeability and his or her boundaries between articulateness and amorphousness. This position shows both confusion between individuation and attachment and conflict between needs and fears.

NEUROTICS CONFUSE INDIVIDUATION AND ATTACHMENT; BORDERLINES ARE CONFLICTED BETWEEN NEEDS AND FEARS; PSYCHOTICS ARE CONFUSED AND CONFLICTED

All these clinical positions represent states of confusion, conflict or both. In the neurotic positions, energy-investment is imbalanced between individuation and attachment. In the borderline positions energy is invested in only one of the two issues and equally balanced between fears and needs. In the psychotic position energy is totally conflictual, invested equally in needs and fears for both individuation and attachment.

Table 3-1
Individual Distancing Patterns

IAQ type	P's boundary	P's wall	O's probe	P's response	P's distancing pattern
B (regressed)	Amorphous	Rigid	Approach Withdrawal	Withdrawal Approach	Compensation Compensation
E (emerging)	Moderate	Moderate	Approach Withdrawal	Inertia Inertia	Indifference Indifference
D (advanced)	Articulated	Permeable	Approach Withdrawal	Approach Withdrawal	Reciprocity Reciprocity
A (neurotic–enmeshed)	Amorphous	Permeable	Approach Withdrawal	Approach Approach	Approach Approach
C (neurotic–disengaged)	Articulated	Rigid	Approach Withdrawal	Withdrawal Withdrawal	Withdrawal Withdrawal
(A/C)$_{IND}$ (borderline, depressed)	Mixed	Moderate	Approach Withdrawal	Inertia Conflict	Indifference Ambivalence
(A/C)$_{ATT}$ (borderline, paranoid)	Moderate	Mixed	Approach Withdrawal	Conflict Inertia	Ambivalence Indifference
(A/C)$_{TOT}$ (psychotic)	Mixed	Mixed	Approach Withdrawal	Conflict Conflict	Ambivalence Ambivalence

PATTERNS OF INTERPERSONAL DISTANCING

Consider yet another comparison of the positions emerging on the two axes, now not simply in terms of investment of energy, but extended to patterns of interpersonal distancing. Interpersonal distancing here refers to the combination of approach and avoidant/withdrawal moves occurring between two or more people. Table 3-1 displays the need–fear position of an individual (P) and the pattern of interpersonal distancing in relation to a programmed other (O) who initiates approach and avoidance probes. It is important to remember that:

WALL STATES DETERMINE RESPONSES TO APPROACH; BOUNDARY STATES DETERMINE RESPONSES TO WITHDRAWAL

First consider the developmental BED axis. Position B represents a fear-dominated patient (P), afraid of both individuation and attachment (i.e., rigid walls

Developing a Model: Distinguishing Developmental and Clinical Axes 55

Figure 3-9 Position B: developmental regressed.

with amorphous boundaries). Such an individual compensates for both approach and avoidance probes from the other (O), meeting approach with avoidance (rigid walls) and avoidance with approach (amorphous boundaries). This is illustrated in Figure 3-9.

Position E represents an in-between state of a person who has overcome his or her fears but has not yet developed needs. A—P in this position neither fears nor needs individuation or attachment (i.e., moderate walls with moderate boundaries). He or she thus remains stationary in response to O's probes, whether they are approach (moderate walls) or avoidance (moderate boundaries). This is illustrated in Figure 3-10.

Position D is need-dominated. Here P needs both individuation and attachment (i.e., boundaries with no walls). This kind of person reciprocates both approach and avoidance probes from O, meeting approach with approach (permeable

Figure 3-10 Position E: developmental emerging.

walls) and avoidance with avoidance (articulated boundaries). This is illustrated in Figure 3-11.

The clinical AC axis is very different. In Position A, P neurotically fears individuation and craves togetherness (i.e., permeable walls with amorphous boundaries). He or she thus responds invariably with an approach to O's probes, whether they are approach (permeable walls) or avoidance (amorphous boundaries). This position is illustrated in Figure 3-12.

In Position C, P neurotically fears attachment and craves aloneness (i.e., rigid walls with articulated boundaries). Such a person thus responds invariably with avoidance to O's probes, whether they are approach (rigid walls) or avoidance (articulated boundaries). This is illustrated in Figure 3-13.

Now let us consider more severe clinical pathologies. First consider Position $(A/C)_{IND}$. This represents a borderline configuration–depressive subtype (Figure 3-6). This individual's (P's) energy is invested totally in the individuation

Developing a Model: Distinguishing Developmental and Clinical Axes 57

Figure 3-11 Position D: developmental advanced.

dimension. However, it is equally distributed between needs and fears. Such a person is totally ambivalent about individuation, both needing it and fearing it. However, he or she is indifferent about attachment, neither needing it nor fearing it. This P will show an indifferent response to approach (mixed walls) but a conflictual response to O's withdrawal (mixed boundaries). This is illustrated in Figure 3-14.

Consider now Position $(A/C)_{ATT}$. This represents the borderline configuration–paranoid subtype (Figure 3-7). This individual (P) has invested all his or her energy in the attachment dimension, equally distributed between needs and fears. P is ambivalent about attachment, both needing it and fearing it, but is totally indifferent toward individuation. P will show a conflictual response to approach (mixed walls) on the part of the other but an indifferent response to O's withdrawal (moderate boundaries). This is illustrated in Figure 3-15.

Finally, consider Position $(A/C)_{TOT}$, a psychotic individual who is split between noncontingent approach and noncontingent withdrawal (i.e., mixed walls

58 *TILT for Individuals*

Figure 3-12 Position A: neurotic enmeshed.

and boundaries). Such a P is likely to respond in a conflicted way (both approach and avoidance) to any probe on the part of O, whether it be approach (conflicted walls) or avoidance (conflicted boundaries) (see Figure 3-16). A person may withdraw through psychosis or thought disorder to avoid this conflict.

THE TILT THERAPY

TILT is a therapy program that has been developed in an attempt to *tilt* narcissistic oscillation between individuation and attachment into healthy, integrated, individual growth. Figures 2-1 and 2-2 represent the logic of TILT in schematic form. Figure 2-1 depicts the developmental BED axis at a particular stage of development. Position B is seen as the first level, representing neither the capacity for

Developing a Model: Distinguishing Developmental and Clinical Axes 59

Figure 3-13 Position C: neurotic disengaged.

individuation (i.e., defining one's boundaries) nor attachment (i.e., taking down one's walls). Position E represents semiattachment and semiindividuation (i.e., moderate walls and moderate boundaries). Position D is seen as the third level of development, representing the full capacity for both individuation and attachment. Figure 2-2 depicts the clinical AC axis. Positions A and C are seen as polarized pathological second-level stops. A represents enmeshment (i.e., neither walls nor boundaries). C represents disengagement (i.e., both walls and boundaries). Position (A/C) represents a full split between A and C (mixed walls and boundaries) whereas $(A/C)_{IND}$ (mixed boundaries) and $(A/C)_{ATT}$ (mixed walls) represent partial splits. These last two positions are not portrayed in Figure 2-2.

Three assumptions of this model should be emphasized. First, there is no direct route between Position A or Position C and Position D. The only way off of the AC axis involves a "TILT" back to Cell B. The first part of this assumption views A and

Figure 3-14 Position (A/C)$_{IND}$: borderline depressed.

C as neurotic dead ends.[1] The second part of this assumption advocates regression back to a less advanced Position B as the only way off of the AC axis. This is controversial because regression has often been viewed as a marker of psychosis. However, the idea of a positive regression to Position B emerges from three diverse lines of thinking: first, that of Laing and Esterson (1970) with regard to coping with unliveable families; second, that of Schiff and her associates with regard to

---

[1] This may reflect stereotyped feminine and masculine socializations (Sangiuliano, 1978), each narcissistically polarized and incomplete. Two well-known examples of oscillation between A and C in the psychological literature include Jung's postulation of a yin and yang between the anima and the animus (Jung, 1928) and Gutmann's funding of a midlife crossover in personality for both males and females, males moving from an active to a nurturant mastery style and females moving in the opposite direction (Gutmann, 1980; Gutmann, Griffin, & Grunes, 1982; Neugarten & Gutmann, 1958). It has been suggested previously that both of these phenomena may represent an exchange of symptoms rather than any true developmental integration and completion of personality (Kaplan, 1985).

Developing a Model: Distinguishing Developmental and Clinical Axes 61

Figure 3-15 Position (A/C)$_{ATT}$: borderline paranoid.

her transactional analysis approach to the reparenting of psychotics (Schiff et al., 1975; Schiff & Day, 1970), and third, that of Kaplan and his associates with regard to discovering the suicide-preventive element in Biblical narratives (Kaplan, 1987; Kaplan, Schwartz, & Markus-Kaplan, 1984). Each of these approaches suggests that regression to an earlier level of development, if protected, allows for the working through of pathologies in a manner unavailable at a more advanced stage. In other words, protected regression to B provides the opportunity for resolving A-C pathologies.

The second assumption of TILT is that healthy growth involves the graduated and integrated replacement of an interpersonal wall by a self–other boundary. Such a progression seems to occur naturally in healthy individuals across the life span beginning at our earliest stage of development. Prior to birth, the fetus is dependent on the mother for nourishment. Simultaneously, the walls of the uterus

Figure 3-16 Position (A/C)$_{TOT}$: psychotic.

protect him or her from the outside environment (Position B). The newborn infant is somewhat less dependent, attached to the breast rather than by the umbilical cord. The infant is also protected somewhat less, by the mother's arms rather than by the walls of her uterus (Position E). Finally, the infant feeds from a bottle without the direct bodily protection of the mother—her surveillance may be sufficient. The infant then has a strong enough boundary to allow for more relaxed walls (Position D).

However, taking one's wall down prematurely (i.e., before one's boundary is strong enough) as in Position A or leaving it up too long (i.e., after one's boundary has already formed) as in Position C leads to a narcissistic imbalance between self and other. In the example described earlier, a C position might involve nursing an infant after it was no longer appropriate to do so (walling it off from the environment); an A position would be leaving it prematurely to feed alone without surveillance (leaving it prematurely exposed to the environment).

On the practical level, what is required is the selection by the individual of behaviors that are simultaneously individuating and attaching. As a person advances from B to E to D, he or she must learn to find a repertoire of giving actions that are self-expressing. This involves personalizing the manner of giving rather than viewing a gift as an object that is disconnected from the creative self. This theme will recur throughout this book.

The third assumption of TILT is that advance in stage (Erikson, 1950) is accomplished through temporary regression in level. In other words, the attainment of Position D (Level 3) at one stage opens up the possibility of growth to the next advanced stage. However, this more advanced stage must be entered at Position B (Level I) and the process undergone again (Kegan, 1982). This assumption is a refinement of the first assumption discussed earlier. Regression is viewed as necessary in normal BED development as well as in resolving AC axis pathologies. However, there is a difference. Normal regression in level is coordinated with advance in stage. Pathology-resolving regression occurs within a stage. Pathology-resolving regression is exemplified by a teenager who is unable to master individuation–attachment conflicts emerging at the beginning of dating. He or she may need to withdraw from dating temporarily to work through these issues.[2] Normal regression, in contrast, is exemplified by a 5-year-old child, who may have reached level D in his parental home, but now must adjust to school—a new and more advanced stage. The child will regress to level B (i.e., become defensive) in that more advanced stage. This is part of the normal adjustment process in moving on to more challenging activities. We must give up the familiar, which, although perhaps stagnating, is secure.

TILT is aimed at developing a therapeutic program designed to accomplish goals corresponding to each of these ends respectively: (1) TILT regression off the AC axis back to B; (2) integrated progression through E to D; and (3) advance to a more complicated stage with the regression back to B that such growth entails. It is the therapist's job to encourage patients to pay attention to the "itch" that signals they have outgrown their now restrictive stage, even though they have reached a healthy level—boundaries and no walls. The therapist must then help provide them with walls to protect boundaries made suddenly fragile by their advance.

And this, perhaps, is the basic notion of TILT:

WALLS IN THEMSELVES ARE NEITHER GOOD NOR BAD. IT IS THEIR JUXTAPOSITION WITH BOUNDARIES THAT GIVES THEM THEIR VALUE.

WITH BOUNDARIES, WALLS ARE UNNECESSARY; IN THE ABSENCE OF BOUNDARIES, HOWEVER, WALLS ARE NECESSARY, AT LEAST TEMPORARILY.

---

[2] This idea parallels that of Schiff and her co-workers except that TILT does not advocate regression back to infancy, but rather to the first level at that stage of development.

Chapter 4
Psychotherapy Illustrations for Individuals

This chapter presents case summaries of patients fitting into the different TILT positions described in Chapter 3. Let us first consider three young adults whose scores fall on the developmental BED axis. All of these cases show balance between individuation and attachment issues, though with different mixtures of needs and fears. Case 1 indicates a regressed level, Case 2 an emerging level, and Case 3 an advanced level.

DEVELOPMENTAL CASES

Regressed Position B—Edwin

Regressed Position B is characterized by high fears and low needs of both individuation and attachment. Consider the case of Edwin. At the time he first entered treatment, Edwin was 13 years old and quite big for his age. He lived with his mother and his younger brother in Michigan. His parents were separated, and his father lived in Kentucky, though he moved back to Michigan a few months after the beginning of Edwin's treatment. Edwin's parents' divorce was pending at the time Edwin entered treatment. Edwin was diagnosed with adjustment disorder with mixed disturbance of emotions and conduct (309.4) according to *DSM-IV* diagnosis.

Edwin's mother reported that although Edwin was very intelligent and imaginative (something confirmed by intelligence testing), he continuously performed poorly in his freshman year in high school. Edwin's mother pointed to his lack of organization in receiving and doing his homework assignments. This problem was exacerbated by a hectic schedule resulting from Edwin being on his high school football team. The patient also displayed a good deal of rebellious behavior toward his mother at home and occasionally was aggressive toward his younger brother as well.

Examination of Edwin's responses to the IAQ provides some insight into Edwin's situation. To begin with, Edwin's overall subscale scores placed him in a B position. He showed high fears of both individuation and attachment and low needs for both. Edwin's overall configuration puts him in TILT Position B, a regressed position.

His failure to perform up to his capabilities at school is reflected in his high FI score. For example, Edwin strongly agreed (4) with the statement "It makes more sense to fit in then to be conspicuous" (high FI). The etiology of this outlook can be seen in Edwin's attitude toward his father who, although highly intelligent, was essentially a 60's dropout. He had left Michigan with Edwin's mother in the mid-1970s and moved to Tennessee to live off the land, working odd jobs, and smoking marijuana. He never went to college nor pursued any serious profession. Edwin's strong attachment to his father may well have prevented him from developing his own abilities to the fullest.

At the same time, Edwin's rebelliousness toward his mother is reflected in his high FA score. For example, Edwin agreed (3) with the statement, "I think people try to control others" (high FA). This pattern is consistent with Edwin's tendency to blame his mother for his parents' break up. His identification with his father seemed to imply a distrust of his mother, women in general, and any attachments. Edwin felt that his mother left his father because he was not successful.

Edwin simultaneously showed little need for either individuation or attachment. He disagreed (0) both with the statement, "I express what I think even if I know my position is extremely unpopular" (low NI) and the statement, "I have a great need for sharing my feelings with other people" (low NA). Therapy proceeded with Edwin in an attempt to show him he could remain loyal to his father and at the same time achieve better grades in school. Several approaches were employed in this regard. Edwin's father was brought into one session and gave Edwin his blessing to succeed. In another session the therapist stressed that Edwin's father chose to drop out but that Edwin was setting it up so he would not have that choice.

Another facet of therapy was to disentangle Edwin from his parents' relationship and to show him a way of being loyal to his father without being antagonistic toward his mother. Edwin's father told him that he wanted him to obey his mother. Edwin's mother insisted she still thought a lot of Edwin's father and that she was glad Edwin resembled him. Treatment was quite successful in both arenas. Edwin's FA and FI both decreased with treatment. He started doing better at school and also fought less with his mother. At the end of treatment, Edwin had not yet fully developed a healthy NA and NI but he had largely overcome his fears of both life issues, putting him in Position E. The process of TILT therapy advanced Edwin from Position B to Position E as diagnosed by a later IAQ (Figure 4-1). For example, Edwin was more uncertain (2) regarding the statements "I think people try to control others"

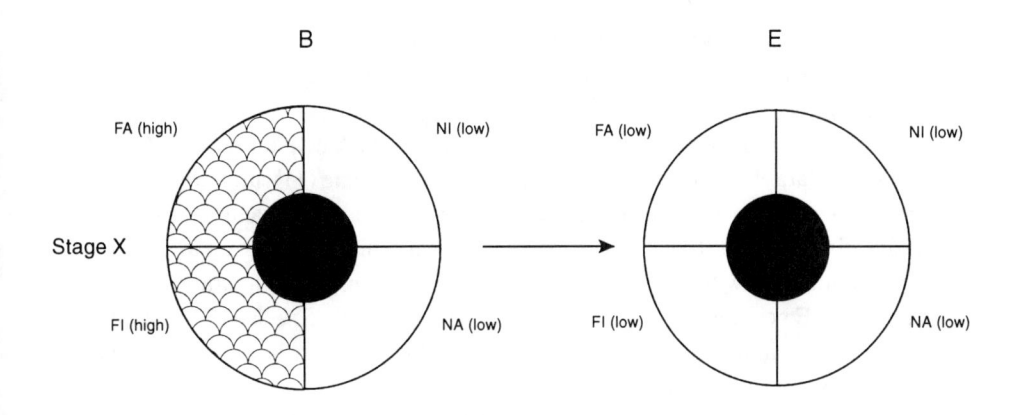

Psychotherapy Illustrations for Individuals 67

FI = Fear of Individuation   NI = Need for Individuation
NA = Need for Attachment   FA = Fear of Attachment

Figure 4-1   Edwin.

(uncertain FA) and "It makes more sense to fit in than be conspicuous" (uncertain FI) (see Figure 4-1).

Emerging Position E—Tara

The Emerging Position E is characterized by both low fears and low needs of both individuation and attachment. Tara provides an excellent example. Tara was a highly intelligent and attractive single woman, who entered therapy in her midtwenties. She had completed 2 years of college and was living alone in an apartment in downtown Detroit. Tara's parents were both highly intelligent professionals. Her mother was a retired school teacher and a graduate student, her father an engineer. Tara was working as a closer at a savings and loan.

Tara's presenting symptoms were adjustment disorder with a depressed mood (309.0) manifested by a general aimlessness, low self-esteem, and an up-and-down dead-end relationship with her boyfriend, who she felt was abusing her. At the time of admittance to treatment, Tara reported that she was getting over an abortion. Underlying all her symptoms was a sense of being unable to control her own life. Examination of Tara's initial IAQ score provides some insight into her condition. She shows low fears of individuation and attachment but also low needs with regard to these same issues.

For example, with regard to individuation Tara disagreed (0) with the statement "I try to avoid being on my own," indicating she is not afraid of individuation (low FI). However, Tara also disagreed (1) with the statement, "I believe everyone has an obligation to find their own way in life," indicating very little need for individuation (low NI).

The same apathy manifested itself regarding the attachment dimension. On the one hand, Tara showed low fear of attachment, disagreeing (1) with the statement, "If I open myself to others I will get hurt" (low FA). On the other hand, Tara showed strong disagreement (0) with the statement, "I feel fulfilled when I am involved in what is going on with other people" (low NA). This initial configuration placed Tara in the E position, halfway up the developmental axis. She had overcome her fears (of both individuation and attachment) but had not yet begun to assert her own needs in either realm.

As therapy proceeded, the patient began to assert her needs in both areas. She ended her relationship, which was going nowhere, and at the same time decided to return to school to pursue a career as an artist. At the end of treatment the patient showed a strong drop in depression and an increase in self-esteem. She ended her dead-end relationship and was moving ahead in both her work and her social life. In TILT terms, therapy advanced Tara from Position E to Position D. A later IAQ indicated that Tara had began to develop healthy needs for both individuation and attachment (see Figure 4-2). For example, Tara now showed mild agreement (3) with the statement "I believe that everyone has an obligation to find their own way in life" (high NI) and "I feel fulfilled when I am involved in what is going on with other people" (high NA).

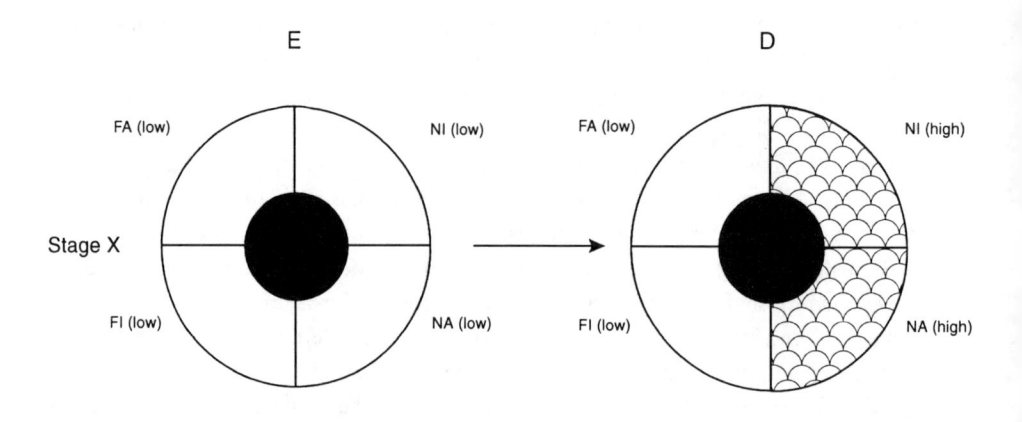

FI = Fear of Individuation   NI = Need for Individuation
NA = Need for Attachment   FA = Fear of Attachment

Figure 4-2   Tara.

Advanced Position D—Monisha

The Developed Position D is characterized by high needs and low fears of both individuation and attachment. Consider Monisha, a highly intelligent young Hindu girl in her midtwenties, who comes from a family with two professional parents. In many ways Monisha presented as a well-adjusted young woman who enjoys swimming, tennis, reading, writing, music, and movies. On the other hand, Monisha still lived with her parents and had been unsuccessful in fixing on a career and a relationship, although she was taking graduate courses in psychology as a special student and had a number of fairly successful relationships. None of these relationships were with Hindu men, however, which presented a problem as she stated she wanted a strong sense of Hindu tradition in her home. Monisha's presenting symptoms at the time of treatment were difficulty in separating herself from her mother, concern as to how to express her Hindu identity in a relationship, and how to find a career that was meaningful for her. Monisha was diagnosed at intake as having an adjustment disorder with anxiety regarding separation from her family of origin (309.24). This seemed to involve not so much dependency as an unwillingness to leave what she saw as a source of Hindu culture.

Monisha's IAQ profile at intake indicated she was a very evolved young woman. She had overcome fears of both individuation and attachment and was now capable of expressing healthy needs in both domains. For example, she strongly disagreed (0) with the statements "I try to avoid being on my own" (low FI) and "Love is often more trouble than its worth" (low FA). She strongly agreed (4) with the statements, "You are not worth much if you are only occupied with your own concerns," (high NA) and, "I believe everyone has an obligation to find their own way in life" (high NI). This pattern indicated Monisha's initial position was a D on the developmental axis.

Therapy revealed that many of Monisha's problems seemed to come from her attempts to meet her needs in a social structure that was too limited to comprehend her. She was encouraged to expand her horizons, to become more involved with people, both men and women, who had the same interest in Hindu culture as she did and generally to mix with people who were interested in developing an active professional life. She also was encouraged to travel more internationally to attempt to find a more cosmopolitan setting where she did not have to compromise her identity.

As the result of treatment, Monisha changed to a considerable degree her friendship and activity circle, and was able to move out of her parental home to graduate school in Boston without compromising herself, although at the beginning she moved into a more defended position in this new exciting environment. A subsequent IAQ indicated that Monisha forwardly regressed from Position D at one

70   *TILT for Individuals*

Figure 4-3 Monisha.

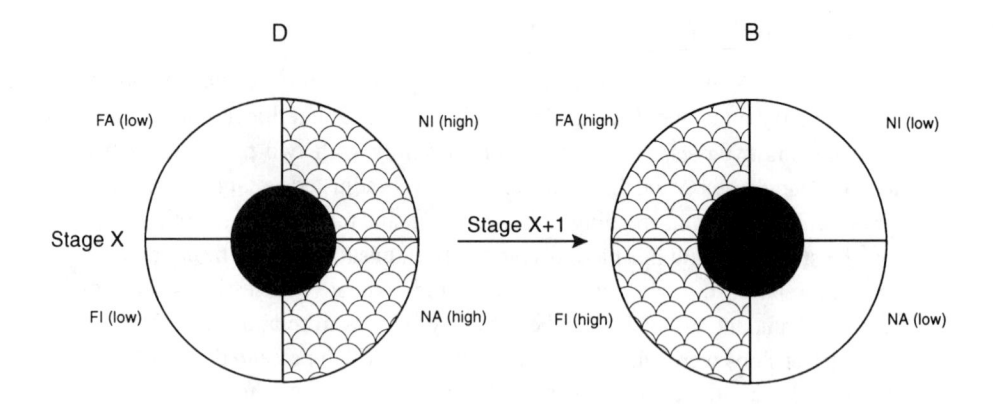

FI = Fear of Individuation   NI = Need for Individuation
NA = Need for Attachment   FA = Fear of Attachment

life stage to Position B at a potentially more fulfilling stage (see Figure 4-3). For example, she now agreed (3) with the statement "Love is often more trouble than it's worth" (high FA) and was uncertain (2) regarding "I believe everyone has an obligation to find their own way in life" (uncertain NI). This regression, however, should be seen as only temporary as she shows every sign of growing into her expanded environment in which she is far more likely to find expression for her needs (of both individuation and attachment).

CLINICAL CASES

Let us now consider five additional cases that fall on the AC clinical axis. Unlike the previous three cases, all of these clinical cases represent imbalance between individuation and attachment and/or conflict within these dimensions. Cases 1 and 2 represent a neurotic level of pathology, Cases 3 and 4 a borderline level of pathology, and Cases 5 and 6, a psychotic level of pathology.

Neurotic Enmeshed Position A—Ken

Enmeshed Position A is characterized by high needs for attachment and fears of individuation. Ken, a divorced male, was 39 years old when he entered therapy. His presenting symptom was an inability to get along with others at his job at a prestigious interior design firm in Lansing, Michigan. Although he was very talented, trainees typically shied away from him. Ken's initial diagnosis was a dysthymic disorder on Axis I (300.4) mixed with some paranoid ideation and an overall dependent personality diagnosis on Axis II (301.6). He tended to develop enmeshed dual relationships with many of his assistants. He mixed socially with them and was oversensitive to their actions. He was quite afraid of being abandoned by his assistants at work, yet typically set these situations up through being obsessively perfectionist, demanding, and controlling. As therapy progressed, it became clear that Ken felt undervalued and unappreciated at his firm. Ken felt that other people who had much less ability than he were being promoted ahead of him, and one such colleague, Alex, was even offered a junior partnership. Yet at the same time, Ken felt inferior to many of the "big names" in the firm who had contacts in the community. So Ken stayed on the job and remained discontented, afraid to go to another firm or to strike out on his own.

Examination of Ken's responses to the IAQ at intake clarified his initial psychological problem. Ken was an A in TILT terms. He was an enmeshed or dependent personality type with an imbalance toward attachment at the expense of individuation. He displayed high scores on FI as well as NA and low scores for NI and FA. For example, Ken agreed with the statements "It is important for me to meet other people's expectations of me" (high FI) and "I have a great need for sharing my feelings with other people" (high NA). At the same time, Ken disagreed (1) with the statements "I express what I think even if I know my position is extremely unpopular" (low NI) and "Love is often more trouble than it is worth" (low FA).

Over the course of therapy, the source of Ken's insecurity became clear. His father, an architect, had never supported Ken's artistic abilities as he was growing up. Instead, he had berated Ken for not being more sports-minded and masculine like his brother. Ken's mother supported him, but made him feel infantilized and girlish. Ken had felt inadequate in his marriage and had serious questions about his masculinity. On the one hand, he scoffed at the macho male image; on the other, he did not have full confidence in his own more artistic temperament. His resolution was to stay in a perpetual state of adolescence, never really using his own talents, but being continuously frustrated by his lack of recognition.

Therapy focused on overcoming Ken's fear of individuation even if it meant sacrificing temporarily his need for attachment. Ken was encouraged to end his dual relationship with his assistants, removing himself emotionally from them. This initially seemed to regress Ken back into a B position, where he was afraid of both attachment and individuation. However, there was a positive side to this. Although Ken was less close to his subordinates, he also became less critical toward them and easier to get along with.

Over the next few months Ken was encouraged to develop more healthy relationships with peers and at the same time explore the possibility of starting his own firm. He began discreetly to feel out many of his clients and was elated to learn that most of them would come with him if he left the firm. They were more attached to Ken's talent than to the prestigious name of the firm.

Ken came gradually to know a peer in his firm whom he felt he could work with and they began to discuss plans to open up a small office together. At the present time Ken and his partner have resigned their jobs in the firm and set up an office in Ken's house. Ken and his partner have closed several contracts and seem on their way. Ken, for example, has sold his two-seater sports car and bought a larger car in which he can carry samples. This seemed to him to represent giving up his adolescence and becoming serious about succeeding. At the same time, Ken has worked in depth in therapy on his relationship with his parents regarding his feelings of self-worth. He is now beginning to think about confronting his parents on many of these issues and is beginning to confront his own sense of masculinity as well.

In TILT terms, Ken has regressed from Position A to Position B and is now slowly moving ahead to Position E. A subsequent IAQ indicated that while he had not developed fully healthy needs for individuation and attachment, he had achieved a balance between these two forces. At the present time, Ken is beginning to overcome these fears and is uncertain (2) about the statements "It is important for me to meet other people's expectations of me" (uncertain FI), "I have a great need for sharing my feelings with other people" (uncertain NA), "I express what I think even if I know my position is extremely unpopular" (uncertain NI), and "Love is often more trouble than it's worth" (uncertain FA). In TILT terms Ken has taken one step backwards to go two steps forward (see Figure 4-4).

Neurotic Disengaged Position C—Stacey

Disengaged Position C is characterized by high need for individuation and fear of attachment. Consider Stacey, a 16-year-old girl who presented herself as rather anxious and complained about feeling depressed. She reported that she had been drinking since she was 13 to relieve stress, largely caused by her parents' quarreling and their subsequent separation and divorce.

Stacey had moved often and was forced to adjust to a number of schools. Her academic performance was below average even though intelligence testing revealed that Stacey's overall IQ score fell in the average range. Stacey appeared to be having a difficult time coping with general adolescent concerns, especially regarding dating, her academic achievement, and her relationship with her mother. She seemed to have resorted to drinking to "escape." Stacey was depressed

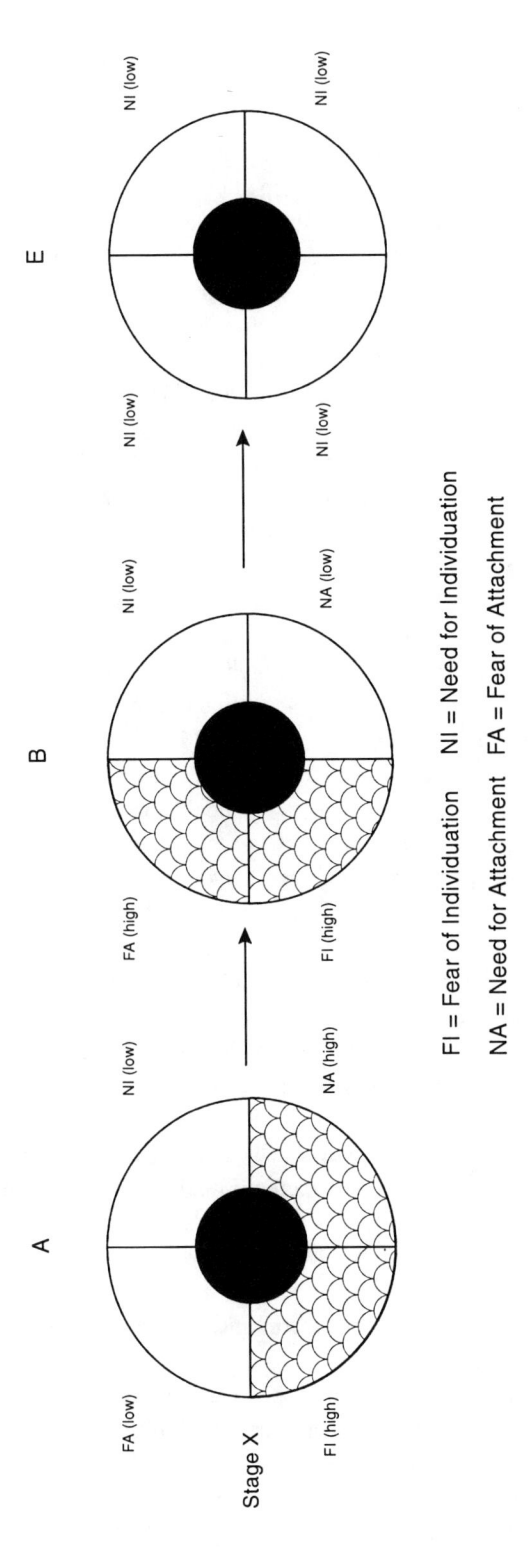

Figure 4-4 Ken.

FI = Fear of Individuation   NI = Need for Individuation
NA = Need for Attachment   FA = Fear of Attachment

and confused and seemed to lack insight into her drinking. Her initial diagnosis was an adjustment disorder with disturbance of conduct on Axis I (309.3) with an Axis II diagnosis of schizotypal personality disorder (301.22).

Stacey's responses on the IAQ placed her initially in the C position. She was disengaged and imbalanced toward individuation at the expense of attachment. Her scores indicated high need for individuation and fear of attachment, and low need for attachment and fear of individuation.

For example, Stacey strongly agreed (4) with the statement "I don't feel guilty when I oppose my friends" (high NI) and agreed (3) with the statements "There is too much emphasis on connection to others in our culture" and "The most effective way of handling obligations to others is to avoid situations which bring them about" (both high FA). In contrast, Stacey expressed disagreement (1) with the statements "I feel fulfilled when I'm involved in what is going on with other people" (low NA) and "A highly responsible position is too much of a burden" (low FI).

Therapy revealed that much of Stacey's high fear of attachment was rooted in her perception of her father as an alcoholic. Although she seemed to be mimicking his use of alcohol as an escape, Stacey blamed her father for the break-up of her parents' marriage and for leaving her mother financially compromised. Stacey tended to see relationships with men as undependable and became obsessed with the idea of becoming totally self-reliant, thus accounting for her high NI scores. Yet, ironically, Stacey's drinking mimicked her father's withdrawal from reality and left her in a dependent position. Therapy focused on overcoming Stacey's fear of attachment even at the expense of diminishing her need for individuation. Stacey was encouraged to be temporarily less self-reliant, as this self-reliance was seen in opposition to others. This was especially difficult, given Stacey's perception of her mother as having been left in a vulnerable position. This at first regressed Stacey back to a B position where she was afraid of both individuation and attachment.

During the course of therapy Stacey slowly began to develop a more balanced view of her parents' relationship. She came to realize her father was not totally at fault and that he had tried to look after Stacey's mother as well as he could, given the degree of his drinking problem. Stacey slowly became more relaxed, became more friendly to classmates at school, and even began to date several young men. At the same time, Stacey's drinking decreased and her performance at school became better.

Although Stacey had yet to develop healthy needs for individuation and attachment, she seemed to be overcoming her fears on both dimensions. For example, she now disagreed (1) with the statement "The most effective way of handling obligations is to avoid situations which bring them about" (low FA). In TILT terms

Stacey regressed from Position C to Position B and was moving slowly ahead to Position E (see Figure 4-5).

Borderline-Depressed Position (A/C)$_{IND}$—Julie

Borderline depressed position A/C is conflicted with regard to individuation. Consider Julie, a 35-year-old school teacher who displayed both a high need and high fear of individuation. She entered therapy with a *DSM-IV* diagnosis of borderline personality disorder (301.83) on Axis II with an Axis I diagnosis of 297.1, delusional disorder with persecutory beliefs. Therapy revealed that depression underlay Julie's explosive temperament. For example, during several couples therapy sessions, Julie threw something from her purse at her husband's head immediately after becoming depressed over an issue. In other words, she seemed to externalize her depression. Thus, the Axis I diagnosis was changed to that of dysthymic depressive disorder (300.4).

Julie displayed unresolved conflicts surrounding her mother's death as well as her own marital problems and disappointments, including the birth of a daughter after a traumatic 15 months of trying to conceive. The birth was made more painful by Julie's medical history of Mediterranean fever.

Julie came into therapy with three major complaints. First, she was unhappy because she was unable to spend more time with her daughter because of her full-time teaching job. Second, Julie felt unable to express her own needs within the marriage because she felt her husband had too many needs. She did not feel that he behaved like the man in the house. Finally, Julie reported problems in adjusting to her husband's two children from his first marriage.

Examination of Julie's IAQ profile at intake sheds light upon her conflicts. While Julie was highly ambivalent regarding individuation issues, she was relatively indifferent to those of attachment. Julie was a borderline personality (depressed position) in TILT terms, (A/C)$_{IND}$. She was highly invested in individuation, showing high needs and high fears, although the issue was clearly unresolved for her. Julie was not so invested in attachment, the issue seemingly a matter of indifference to her.

For example, Julie agreed (3) with the statements, "I express what I think even if I know my position is extremely unpopular," "I don't hesitate to fight for my own opinions with those I am close to," and "I believe everyone has an obligation to find their own way in life" (all high NI). However, she also agreed (3) with the statements "A highly responsible position is too much of a burden" and "It makes more sense to fit in than be conspicuous" (both high FI). Julie showed no such involvement in the attachment issue, strongly disagreeing (1) with the statements "If I open myself to others, I'll get hurt" and "The price of a close relationship

Figure 4-5 Stacey.

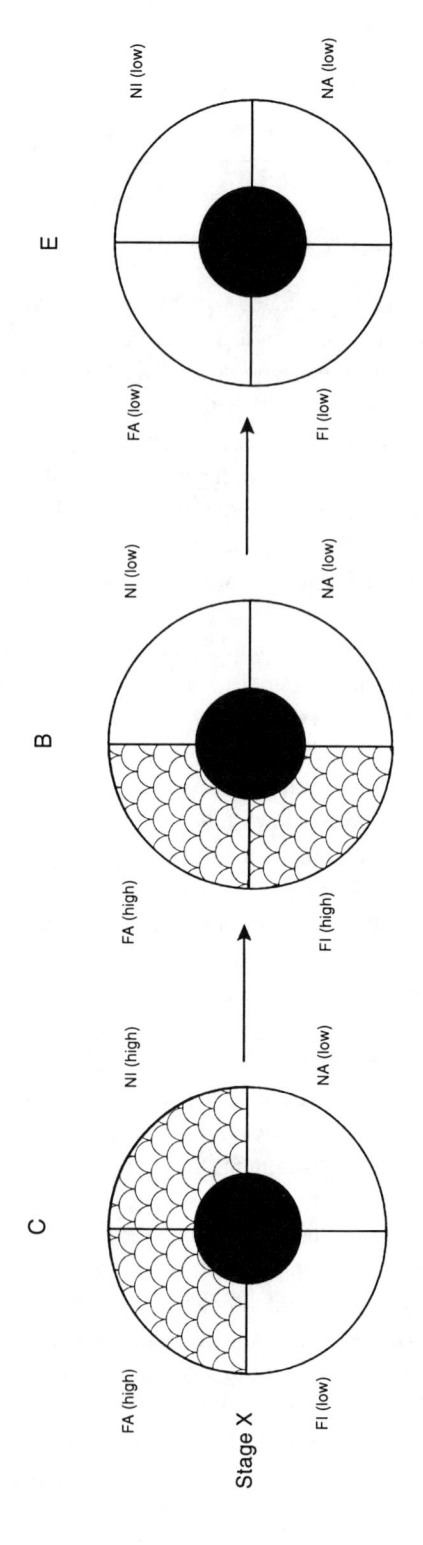

FI = Fear of Individuation   NI = Need for Individuation
NA = Need for Attachment   FA = Fear of Attachment

is that it keeps you from truly being yourself" (both low FA). However, she also disagreed (1) with the statements "I feel fulfilled when I am involved in what is going on with other people" and "The best part of parties is the chance to make friends" (both low NA).

Therapy revealed much of the underlying dynamic for Julie's conflict. As a young girl, Julie developed Mediterranean fever, a debilitating illness that afflicts people of Mediterranean origin. It manifested itself in Julie with severe flu-like symptoms, leaving her exhausted. Having Mediterranean fever kept Julie from being involved in many of the activities that others her age were involved in. She became racked with sobs when she recalled how she had to lay in bed for several summers as a young girl and was unable to play with her friends.

These deprivations filled Julie with an intense desire to live, to plunge fully into life, to taste it to its fullest. She developed a tremendous need to be strong, to be her own person. At the same time, Julie also developed a fear of being on her own. What if she became sick again? Who would take care of her? With all this concern regarding individuation issues, Julie simply did not have much energy left over to devote to the question of attachment.

These early experiences were intensified in Julie's efforts to have a baby, which she pursued despite her doctor's warnings. She was sick with Mediterranean fever throughout her pregnancy. She became afraid she would lose her baby. In the culminating expression of her individuality (motherhood) she was brought down once again.

Julie's husband, an intelligent but emotionally distant accountant, was put in an impossible position. Julie demanded autonomy and space to be herself. On the other hand, she was afraid to be left alone, making it very difficult for him to have any life of his own aside from her. Their emotional and sexual life was quite unfulfilling at the beginning of therapy.

Therapy proceeded in the following manner. The counterphobic nature of Julie's intense individuation drives were explored. Initially, Julie tended to become more passive, still showing fears of individuation and developing a fear of attachment as well. At least her individuation and attachment drives were in balance.

Slowly over the course of therapy Julie recovered her need for individuation. However, now her fear of individuation became replaced by a genuine need for attachment toward her husband. Rather than resent her husband's needs to have his own activities, she became much more interested in doing creative enjoyable joint activities. As a result, Julie's husband slowly became weaned away from his preoccupation with all-male activities (e.g., hunting with his male friends) and began to look forward to going on family activities and couple weekends with his wife.

In TILT terms, Julie regressed from Position (A/C)$_{IND}$ back to Position B and then began to move ahead to Position E, with the possibility of achieving Position

D (high needs and low FI and FA). This movement was indicated in subsequent IAQs and is diagrammed in Figure 4-6. For example, Julie now disagreed (1) with the statement "I express what I think even if I know my position is extremely unpopular" (low NI) and "It makes more sense to fit in than be conspicuous" (low FI).

Borderline-Paranoid Position (A/C)$_{ATT}$—Doug

Borderline-paranoid position A/C is characterized by conflict on attachment. Doug is a 41-year-old husband and father with a borderline personality diagnosis (301.83) on Axis II who displayed both a high need and high fear of attachment. He entered therapy severely depressed (296.2 on Axis I) over his suspicions that his wife was being unfaithful. Although Doug insisted that his marital problems largely stemmed from his desire to have greater intimacy with his wife, it became clear that he also blocked intimacy with an uncompromising moralistic stance reflecting an underlying anger toward women. Doug was quite a bit overweight and seemed to spend most of his time at home with his two daughters, rather than with his wife.

Doug also displayed a paranoid tendency, being obsessively suspicious of his wife's femininity and her displays of sexuality. He continuously expressed distrust of her motives, bringing up former relationships that she had had and claiming she lost interest in him when his business ventures (health care) failed. Given this, Doug's Axis I diagnosis was changed to delusional disorder with jealousy (297.1). It should also be added that Doug had invested much of the couple's savings in his business and was living solely off of the salary and benefits accumulated by his wife, a middle school teacher. Doug's wife resented him very much for this and felt he was not behaving like a "responsible adult man" should.

Doug's initial IAQ profile sheds a good deal of light on the situation. He was not very invested in the question of individuation, showing neither high needs nor high fears in this regard. The attachment issue, however, was highly charged. Doug simultaneously needed it and feared it at the same time. In TILT terms, Doug's initial diagnosis was a borderline personality (paranoid position), (A/C)$_{ATT}$.

For example, Doug agreed (3) with the statements "I have a great need for sharing my feelings with other people," "I feel fulfilled when I'm involved in what is going on with other people," and "Meal-time is a time when families and friends should be together" (all high NA). However, Doug also agreed (3) with the statements "Being in a close relationship often keeps one from doing what he/she wants to do" and "I think people always try to control others" and strongly agreed (4) with the statement "Love is often more trouble than it is worth" (all high FA). Doug showed indifference with regard to individuation items. For example, he

Figure 4-6 Julie.

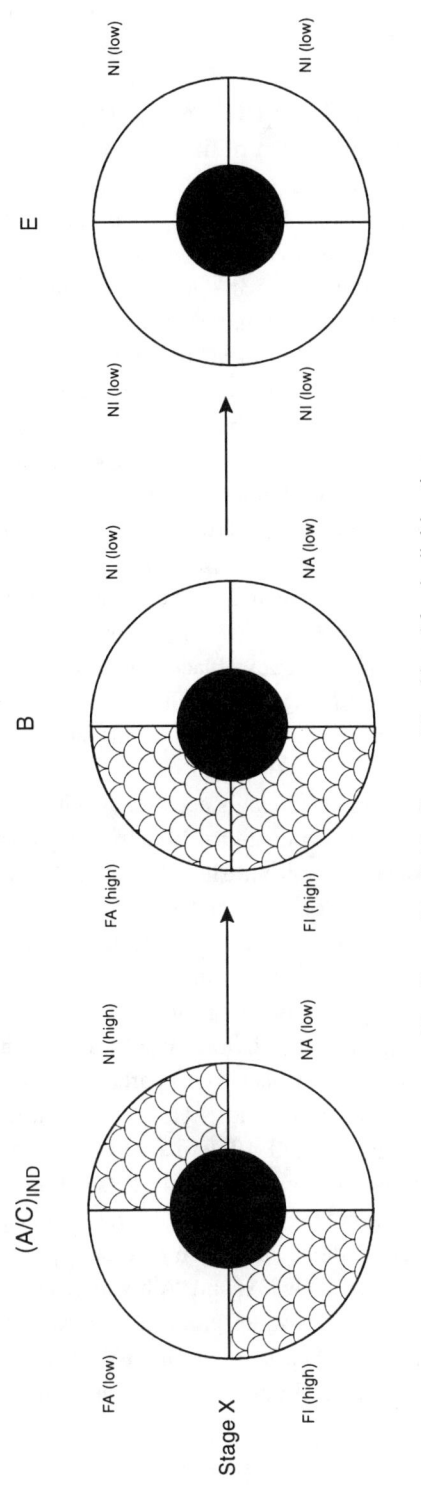

FI = Fear of Individuation   NI = Need for Individuation
NA = Need for Attachment   FA = Fear of Attachment

disagreed (1) with the statements "I don't feel guilty when I oppose my friends" (low NI) and "A highly responsible position is too much of a burden" (low FI).

Therapy revealed much of the history beneath Doug's problem. Doug was one of four children from a lawyer's family. His father was off at work much of the time and was generally uncommunicative. His mother, who ran the household, was quite domineering and manipulative. Doug reported generally being seen as a failure by his family because he did not follow his father in becoming an attorney. The patient reported being highly ambivalent toward his mother, who he felt gave him a good deal of attention, but did not give him much support. He felt she always unfavorably compared him to two of his brothers, who had become lawyers. When Doug first met his wife, he felt he finally found a woman who supported him. She moved with him away from her hometown but then seemed to resent it very much, especially when his business ventures failed. However, it became clear that while on the one hand, Doug craved support from her, on the other he did not trust her or women in general. He continuously blamed her for having affairs, even going so far as to check whether she had taken her sexy black panties out of her dresser in the morning. Finally it seemed that Doug's suspicions about his wife's infidelity were justified but the question remained as to whether his suspiciousness drove her to it.

Therapy attempted initially to reduce Doug's need for attachment as it seemed to mask dependency (i.e., a fear of individuation). Initially Doug regressed to a B position with both a high fear of attachment and a high fear of individuation. Slowly Doug was encouraged to begin to explore new relationships and to simultaneously concentrate on more limited and realistic success in his health care business. He was also encouraged to repair the relationship with his parents.

At the time of this writing, Doug was going through a divorce. He was beginning to mix socially, joining singles activities at a local church. He was in the process of deciding whether to move back to his parents' home town and become administrator for the family law practice. He was also in the process of fighting for custody of his daughters. In TILT terms, Doug had regressed from $(A/C)_{ATT}$ to B, with the potential of moving ahead to E (see Figure 4-7). However, as the IAQ indicated, he was not there (Position E) yet. Although Doug now disagreed (1) with the statements "Being in a close relationship often keeps one from doing what he/she wants to do" (low FA) and "A highly responsible position is too much of a burden" (low FI). He was uncertain (2) regarding statements "I feel fulfilled when I'm involved in what is going on with other people" (uncertain NA) and "I don't feel guilty when I oppose my friends" (uncertain NI) (see Figure 4-7).

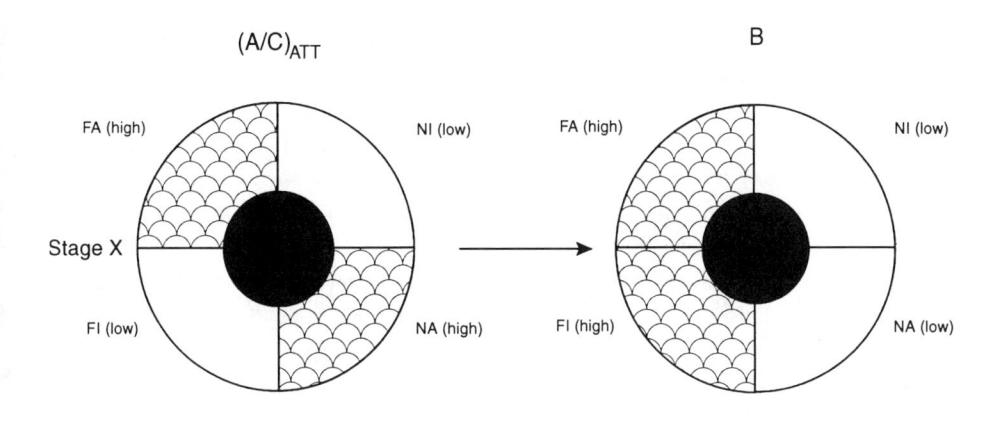

Psychotherapy Illustrations for Individuals 81

FI = Fear of Individuation   NI = Need for Individuation
NA = Need for Attachment   FA = Fear of Attachment

Figure 4-7 Doug.

Psychotic Position (A/C)$_{TOT}$—Roberta

Consider finally, psychotic position A/C$_{TOT}$, which is characterized by conflict on both individuation and attachment. A prime example is Roberta, a nurse in her midforties, who entered therapy with serious difficulties in her marriage with Harry, a physician-businessman who was 20 years older and had been her employer. Throughout the marriage she had turned to Harry for support and guidance and simultaneously rebelled against it when it was offered, often to the point of breaking communication with him temporarily.

Roberta showed similar inconsistency with regard to her needs for affection and physical intimacy. At times Roberta complained that her husband did not respond to her as a woman. Other times her complaint seemed to be the opposite, that Harry was "all over her," and, "wouldn't get out of her face."

At the time she entered therapy, Harry was going through a bankruptcy and the marriage was falling apart. Harry felt abandoned by Roberta, writing her an accusing letter in which he threatened suicide. Roberta generally responded to events with a pessimistic orientation. For example, she spoke of her marriage as, "emotionally bankrupt," and she described herself as "depressed economically." Closer scrutiny revealed some thought disorder on Roberta's part. It was not always clear whether she was speaking about emotional or financial issues. She would refer to herself as the "wife of depression," and comment that her husband grew up in the 1930s and was a "child of depression." Roberta's diagnosis at intake was a schizoaffective disorder (295.70).

Examination of Roberta's initial IAQ profile indicated that she was highly invested and conflicted in both the domains of individuation and attachment. In other words, Roberta displayed high needs and high fears with regard to both individuation and attachment. In TILT terms Roberta's profile reflected psychotic conflict throughout her personality, $(A/C)_{TOT}$.

Here are some examples from responses to individual IAQ items. With regard to individuation, Roberta strongly agreed (4) with the statement "we should act on our best judgments even if other people strongly disagree" (high NI). At the same time, she agreed (3) with the contradictory statement, "It makes more sense to fit in than to be conspicuous" (high FI). Again, Roberta agreed (3) with the statement "I don't feel guilty when I oppose my friends" (high NI). At the same time, she agreed (3) with the opposite statement "I let people I respect shape my decisions" (high FI).

Roberta's responses were equally conflicted with regard to attachment. On the one hand Roberta strongly agreed (4) with the statement "Relating to others is essential to coming to know oneself" (high NA). On the other hand, Roberta agreed (3) that "I think people always try to control others" (high FA). Likewise, Roberta agreed (3) that "Meal-time is a time when families and friends should be together" (high NA). Simultaneously, Roberta felt (3) that "people become less interesting when they form families" (high FA).

The course of therapy revealed the tragic implications of Roberta's conflict for her marriage. Roberta blamed Harry for having undergone a vasectomy while they were dating. This was done without her knowledge and against her wishes; she wanted to have children. Yet, she married Harry anyway, and then punished him by spending more time with her sister and her sister's children than with Harry. Harry continuously complained that Roberta was married to her sister rather than to him. Harry and Roberta's separation was also marked by severe conflict. They would separate after a fight and then convulsively call each other on the phone in an attempt to reconcile. Also, Roberta would send out job applications and letters, and then not respond to replies which indicated interest.

A final attempt to patch up the marriage resulted in a conflict-ridden driving trip to New Mexico. On the one hand Roberta complained that Harry was imposing an itinerary for the trip. On the other, Roberta had showed no sign of taking any initiative in developing plans for the trip. The trip ended with Roberta flying back alone, leaving Harry to drive their car back on his own. When Harry returned to Michigan, he discovered that Roberta had filed for divorce and said she wanted no further contact, although she continued to call him. Shortly thereafter Harry attempted

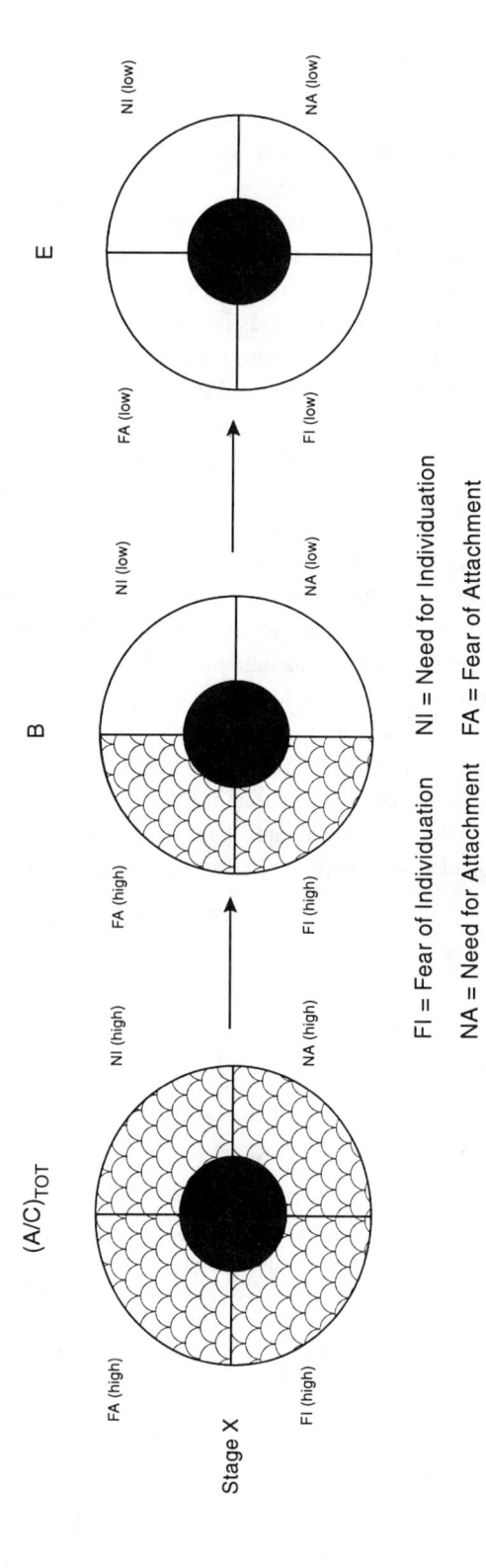

Figure 4-8 Roberta.

suicide through overdosing. Harry survived and Roberta interpreted his act as a manipulative attempt "to get his own way."

During the course of therapy, treatment attempted to reduce Roberta's conflict on both individuation and attachment. The process of separation first lowered her need for attachment. Although she was afraid to live alone, Roberta was able to stop calling Harry. The next thing to change was her need for individuation. Roberta stopped sending out job applications because she realized she was too blocked to pursue them. In TILT terms, Roberta regressed from Position $(A/C)_{TOT}$ to B.

At the time of this writing she was slowly overcoming her fears of individuation and attachment. By dealing with issues of early childhood, the depression began to lift somewhat. Her thoughts became clearer with the help of psychotropic medication. However, she was still not ready to move ahead to form a new relationship, or find a serious job. In TILT terms, Roberta first regressed from position $(A/C)_{TOT}$ to B and now is slowly moving ahead to E (see Figure 4-8). IAQ responses indicated that fears were reduced but she had not yet developed healthy needs. For example, Roberta now disagreed (1) with the statements "I think people always try to control others" (low FA) and "I let people I respect shape my decisions" (low FI). However, Roberta remained uncertain (2) in response to the statements "I don't feel guilty when I oppose my friends" (uncertain NI) and "Relating to others is essential to coming to know oneself" (uncertain NA).

Chapter 5 extends TILT into a multistage, multilevel model of interpersonal development. An expanded version of the Eriksonian life stages will be examined from this perspective.

Chapter 5

TILT Across the Lifespan: From Mistrust to Trust[1]

This chapter applies TILT to the Eriksonian life stages, expanded from 8 to 11 stages to describe life from womb to tomb. TILT defines healthy development as integrated increases in the capacity for both individuation and attachment, and clinical pathology as nonintegration between these two life needs. In healthy development, nonpermeable walls (ego defenses) are seen as necessary to protect inarticulated boundaries (ego strength), the walls becoming more permeable as the boundaries become more articulated.

TILT views Erikson's negative or dystonic ego qualities (such as mistrust, shame, and guilt) as positions necessarily evoked by the directly previous life events or stressors (such as weaning, toilet training, and restraint of sexual impulses) rather than as qualities that can be avoided. These dystonic qualities must be worked through to achieve satisfactorily the positive or syntonic ego equilibrium states (such as trust, autonomy, and initiative). Central to this "verticalized" view of the Eriksonian life stages is the conception of *forward regression* (i.e., regression in level in the service of advance from one stage to another).

ERIKSON'S EIGHT STAGES

In his seminal work, Erik Erikson (1951, 1968, 1980, 1982) has described stages in ego development at eight different stages of life. Each stage presents its own psychosocial crisis. If the crisis is satisfactorily resolved, a positive quality is added to the ego. If it is unsatisfactorily resolved, a negative factor is added. For

---

[1] An earlier version of this chapter appeared as Kaplan, K. J. & O'Connor, N. (1993), "From Mistrust to Trust: Through a Stage Vertically." In G. H. Pollock and S. I. Greenspan, *The Course of Life*, Vol. VI, pp. 153–198, Madison, Conn.: International University Press.

example, the crisis at infancy is between the infant's physiological needs such as hunger, need for contact, and alleviation of discomfort and how caregivers respond to such needs. Satisfactory resolution of this crisis leads to the acquisition of the positive ego quality of *basic trust*. Unsatisfactory resolution of this crisis leads to the negative quality of *basic mistrust*. A similar analysis can be made at the next stage, toddlerhood, starting at 24 months and going on to 48 months. Improved neuromuscular coordination facilitates the potential for many new areas of conflict with the environment. The toddler may soil himself, eat in a messy fashion, or destroy the property of others. He or she may thus encounter societal prohibitions or discipline to keep his or her behavior in line. Satisfactory resolution of these crises will add the positive ego trait of *autonomy*, whereas unsatisfactory resolution will lead to *shame*.

Consider next Erikson's play age (ages 4 years to 6 years). Here the crisis is between the heightened awareness of the play-age child with his sexual organs and adult embarrassment with regard to the frank exposure of body parts. Satisfactory resolution of this crisis will lead to the positive ego trait of *initiative*, while unsatisfactory resolution will lead to the negative trait of *guilt*. A comparable analysis can be made for each of the other five stages of Erikson. Satisfactory resolution of the psychosocial crisis at school age leads to addition of the positive ego quality of *industry*; unsatisfactory resolution leads to addition of the negative ego quality of *inferiority*. Satisfactory resolution of the psychosocial crisis at adolescence leads to the positive ego quality *identity*; unsatisfactory resolution leads to the negative ego quality *identity confusion*. At young adulthood for Erikson, the issue becomes intimacy versus isolation. Satisfactory resolution of this life stage leads to acquisition of *intimacy*; unsatisfactory resolution leads to *isolation*. Satisfactory navigation of the age of middle adulthood leads to the positive ego quality of *generativity*; unsatisfactory resolution leads to *stagnation*. Finally, old age must be satisfactorily navigated to add the final positive ego quality of *integrity*; unsatisfactory resolution leads to the negative quality of *despair*.

Although progression through these stages represents the very dynamic of human development, it is often seen in a somewhat flattened horizontal manner that does not reflect ontogenetic within-stage development. Typical interpretations of Erikson suggest healthy development is achieved by resolving each stage crisis in favor of the syntonic as opposed to the dystonic ego quality. Thus, for example, the psychosocial crisis of infancy is resolved by achieving a balance between trust and mistrust in the direction of trust. The underlying developmental process seems to be one of horizontal oscillation on a continuum where both aspects of trust and mistrust are necessary for successful navigation of the infant stage.

TILT, in contrast, suggests an often obscured ontogenetic view of the developmental process within a stage. By this is meant that the precursors of processes at later stages are already visible at earlier stages. Further, it suggests a between-stage conception of "forward regression," or what Anna Freud (1936) referred to as regression in the service of development. A life event forwardly regresses an organism into the negative or dystonic quality at the beginning of the next life stage. Successful vertical navigation through this stage involves passing from the negative to the positive quality and the attaining of a stage-specific syntonic equilibrium. However, that very syntonic quality interacts with the subsequent life event or stressor to promote dystonicity with regard to the now broader social radius (i.e., to upset that now inadequate equilibrium). For example, the life event of weaning invariably forwardly regresses the infant into the dystonic position of mistrust toward the mother and the self. It must be worked through vertically to attain the syntonic position of trust.

Trust toward the mother (and self) then interacts with the next life event, fecal embarrassment, to forwardly regress the infant into shame, a negative ego quality—albeit at the next advanced stage and with the broader social radius, parental persons—and the within-stage process must be worked through once again. Thus, the trusting infant now experiences toilet training, which plunges the now-toddler into the dystonic position of shame with regard to parental persons. This in turn must be worked through vertically to attain the syntonic quality of autonomy. In other words, what we are suggesting is that successful development involves not the avoidance of the negative or dystonic ego qualities at each stage but plunging into each of them as the natural sequel of the preceding life event. Successful development involves working through a stage vertically to attain the respective stage-specific positive or syntonic ego position.

TILT ACROSS LIFE STAGES

This section specifically explores the TILT model across life stages. We have already differentiated two axes in Figures 2-1 and 2-2, a developmental BED axis (Figure 2-1), and a clinical AC axis (Figure 2-2). Consider the developmental BED axis first. Cell B represents an immature individual who is deindividuated but detached. Deindividuation (◌) represents a low state of individual organization and definition, and detachment (□) can be thought of as defensive in structure. An impermeable wall is necessary to shield the inarticulately defined individual from external engulfment (▣). In Cell E the individual is slowly maturing. He or she is semiindividuated and semiattached. He has achieved a modicum of self-definition, a semiarticulated boundary (○). Some defensive structure is necessary, a semipermeable wall (▭). The E individual can be described as semiindividuated and semiattached (▣). In Cell D the individual is individuated and attached

(⊙) and has matured to the point where he or she has achieved a high degree of self-definition, an articulated boundary (O). Here the defensive structure can be quite minimal, a permeable wall (⊡), as there is little danger of external engulfment. The logic of this developmental axis is simply that the loosening of one's defenses (i.e., greater permeability of walls) should occur in conjunction with the strengthening of one's ego (i.e., greater definition of boundaries). It is this ongoing congruency between individuation and attachment that describes healthy development in this model and differentiates it from the spiraling, alternating, or oscillating view of expression of these two forces outlined by Kegan (1982, p. 108).

The present model, in contrast, views continuous oscillation or fixation between individuation and attachment as pathological. Specifically, it is seen as reflecting incongruent resolution of the individuation–attachment dilemma (i.e., imbalanced movement from B to either A or C). What makes this AC axis clinical (Figure 2-2) is the bad fit and lack of coordination between walls and boundaries. The A individual attempts to become attached to the external world before he or she is individuated (⊡). In other words, defenses are loosened (permeable walls: ⊡) while the ego is still ill-defined (inarticulated boundaries: ◌). The C individual, in contrast, remains detached even after becoming sufficiently individuated (⊡). In other words, he or she holds onto defenses (impermeable walls: ☐) even after the ego has become sharply defined (articulated boundaries: O). The A/C individual oscillates between these two styles (⊡), first favoring enmeshment and then disengagement. A and C individuals thus represent polarities on this clinical axis, the A individual manifesting a tendency toward enmeshment (deindividuated attachment) and the C individual a tendency toward disengagement (detached individuation). These pathologies, it is suggested, may have long-term effects in the absence of corrective intervention by which the individual may reenter (through the initial B position) the developmental BED axis. Further, life demands might prompt an individual to attempt to pseudoresolve imbalances on the AC axis through rapid oscillation between enmeshment and disengagement (A/C). Such a pseudoresolution may serve to mask pathology, both to self and to others. However, it does not represent any true integration between individuation and attachment and may even deepen and disguise the disintegrative process.[2]

It should be emphasized at this point that this model is stage-specific. In other words, the developmental progression from Level One (B) to Level Two (E) to Level Three (D) occurs within a specific stage. Each successive stage must be

---

[2] For the purposes of simplicity, this chapter will not specifically discuss the two borderline positions, (A/C)$_{IND}$ and (A/C)$_{ATT}$. Position (A/C) always refers to the psychotic position (A/C)$_{TOT}$.

entered at Level One (B). In other words, "progression in stage" is achieved through "regression in level" and is precipitated by the specific life event initiating that respective stage. This between-stage process is called forward regression.[3] On the other hand, unfinished business at any stage (i.e., fixation on the clinical AC axis) will be carried over to each succeeding stage, reducing the probability of healthy development along the BED axis within that new stage. The demands of life event $i + 1$, for example, may actually prompt an AC individual at Stage i to achieve an A/C pseudoresolution. Such a pseudoresolution may mask the pathology of the individual and allow him to proceed to Stage $i + 1$. However, the unresolved imbalance between individuation and attachment at Stage i will reemerge and push the individual once again to the AC axis, albeit through the forms expressive of Stage $i + 1$.[4]

We concentrate here on the conception of *forward regression*, which is long overdue in developmental psychology. It reflects both the traditional psychoanalytic view that regression represents a return under stress to an earlier stage of development (Noam, O'Connell, Higgins, & Goethals, 1982) and the specific insight of Anna Freud (1936) that in some circumstances regression is the way by which, paradoxically, the individual moves forward in development. In my view, a new life event $(i + 1)$ represents the stressor precipitating movement to the next stage whether the individual is on the developmental or clinical axis. A person at the D level of Stage i on the developmental BED axis forwardly regresses to B_{i+1} at the next stage, $i + 1$. A person on the AC axis at Stage i may be prompted to achieve an A/C pseudoresolution to enter stage $i + 1$. However, such a pseudoresolution represents a dangerous, disguised, and disintegrated oscillation between the pathological polarities of enmeshment and disengagement and does not offer any hope of true integration of individuation and attachment.

*TILT*ING ERIKSON: THROUGH A STAGE VERTICALLY

We are now ready to apply TILT to an expansion and reconceptualization of the Eriksonian life stages. The template presented previously is applied sequentially

---

[3] The reader is referred to Dabrowski's distinction between "negative integration" and "positive disintegration" (Dabrowski, 1973, pp. 37–47).

[4] Indeed, the very life issues of Stage $i + 1$ will be experienced through the filters of these previous unresolved imbalances. Nevertheless, life events are imbued with hopeful and growth-promoting potential, even for those who confront them while on the AC axis. They present the opportunity for within-stage backward regression from A_i or C_i back to B_i as a prelude for healthy development on the BED axis. However, a healthy resolution at stage i becomes more difficult given a history of A or C resolutions at previous stages.

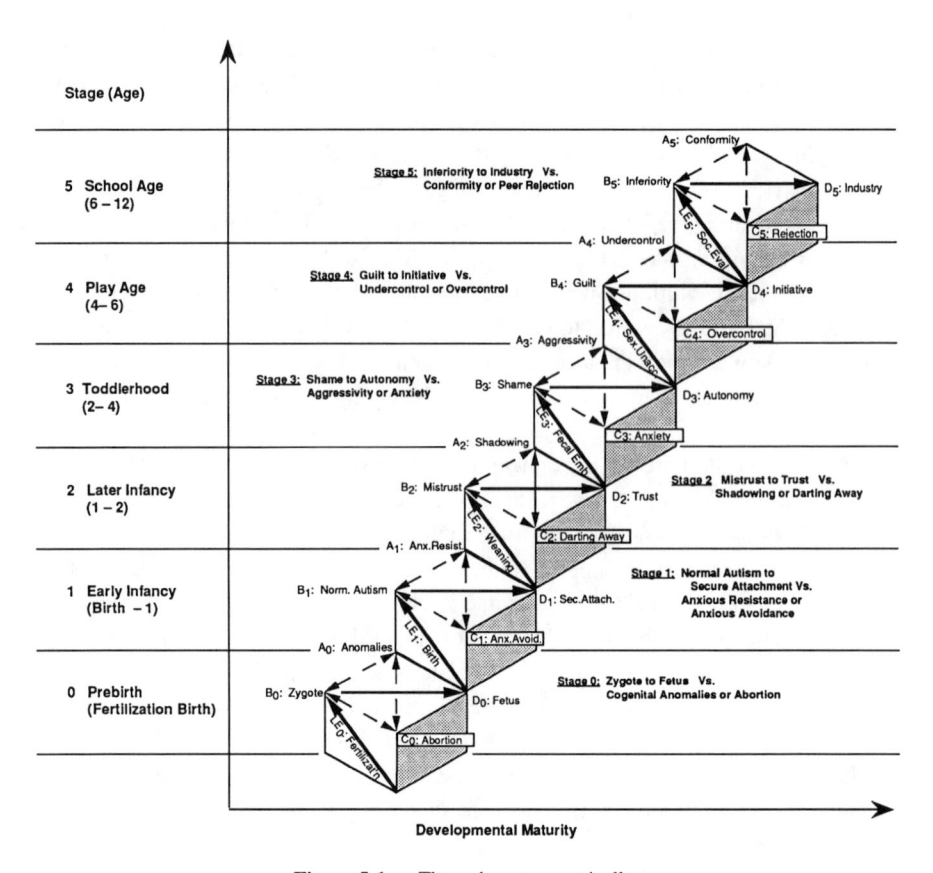

Figure 5-1a Through a stage vertically.

in Figures 5-1a and 5-1b to an expanded version of Eriksonian life stages.[5] A stage in this model is initiated by a life event (LE) that forwardly regresses the individual into Level B, a dystonic position. The core strength propels the individual forward to a syntonic D level. The core pathology veers the individual off of this developmental BED axis and onto the clinical AC axis.

A person is confronted with a particular life event that thrusts the individual into Level B at that life stage. Healthy navigation of the issues paramount at that life stage represents successful developmental change along the BED axis. This can be seen as corresponding to Erikson's concept of the basic strength at that life stage. Unhealthy navigation of these life issues represents a veering onto the clinical AC axis. This fixation and oscillation between polarities corresponds, in

---

[5] Three additional stages are added to Erikson's eight stages to complete the journey from "womb to tomb."

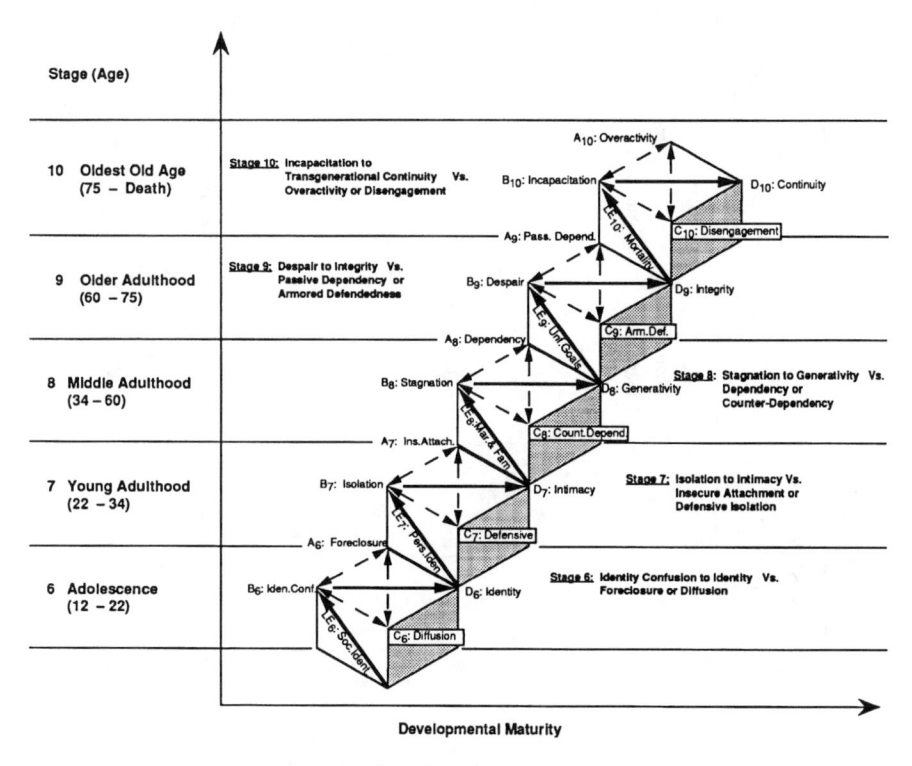

TILT Across the Lifespan: From Mistrust to Trust 91

Figure 5-1b Through a stage vertically.

my mind, to Erikson's conception of core pathology. In either case the person confronts the next advanced life event, which regresses the individual forward into Level B at the next advanced stage.[6] Once again, the individual must work his or her way forward to Level D and once again will be confronted with another life event, perhaps the continuous refrain of the entire life journey. Table 5-1 summarizes all of Erikson's negative or dystonic ego qualities as Level B structures at each respective stage; all of his positive or syntonic ego resolutions are described as Level D structures. Incongruous and unhealthy solutions are described as A and C structures. Let us now apply TILT to each consecutive life stage.[7]

---

[6] It should be noted, however, that individuals who enter B from the developmental axis are probably more prone to continue on this axis than those who enter from the A or C positions. This is because the unresolved incongruencies between individuation and attachment from the previous stage leave an individual with insufficiently developed ego strength (boundaries) or inappropriate defenses (walls) with which to cope with this new life event.

[7] Note that TILT verticalizes Erikson's conception of ego strength and bidimensionalizes his understanding of core pathology.

Table 5-1
Developmental versus Clinical Axes at Each Life Stage.

Stage Number	Precipitating Life event	Stage	Social Radius	Core Strength	Developmental Axis B Level	Developmental Axis D Level	Core Pathology	Clinician Axis A Expression	Clinician Axis C Expression
0	Fertilization	Prenatal (Fertilization–Birth)	Mother's Uterus	Survival	Zygote	Fetus	Genetic-Environmental Inadequacy	Birth Defects/Some Congenital Anomalies	Ectopic Pregnancies/Some Spontaneous Abortions
1	Birth	Early Infancy (Birth–1)	Physical Presence of mother	Reciprocity	Normal Autism	Secure Attachment	Noncontingency	Anxious Resistance	Anxious Avoidance
2	Weaning	Later Infancy (1–2)	Psychological Presence of Mother	Hope	Mistrust	Trust	Withdrawal	Shadowing	Darting Away
3	Fecal Embarrassment	Toddlerhood (2–4)	Parental Persons	Will	Shame	Autonomy	Compulsion	Anxiety	Aggressivity
4	Sexual Impulse Unacceptability	Play-age Childhood (4–6)	Nuclear Family	Purpose	Guilt	Initiative	Inhibition	Under-Control	Over-Control
5	Social Evaluation	School-Age Childhood (6–12)	School/Neighborhood Peers	Competence	Inferiority	Industry	Interia	Conformity	Peer Rejection
6	Social Identity Demands	Adolescence (12–22)	Peer Group/Outgroups	Fidelity	Identity Confusion	Identity	Repudiation	Foreclosure	Diffussion

(*Continues*)

7	Personal Identity Demands	Young Adulthood (22–34)	Intimate Partners	Love	Isolation	Intimacy	Exclusivity	Insecure Attachment	Defensive Isolation
8	Marriage and Family Demands	Middle Adulthood (34–60)	Household and Children	Care	Stagnation	Generativity	Rejectivity	Dependency	Counter-Dependency
9	Unfulfilled and Fulfilled Goals	Older Adulthood (60–75)	Mankind/ My Kind	Wisdom	Despair	Integrity	Disdain	Passive-Dependency	Armored-Defendedness
10	Mortality Physical Decline (Life Cycle Shock)	Oldest Old (75–Death)	Present/ Future	Faith	Incapacitation	Trans-Generational Continuity	Doubt	Overactivity	Disengagement

(Continued)

94 *TILT for Individuals*

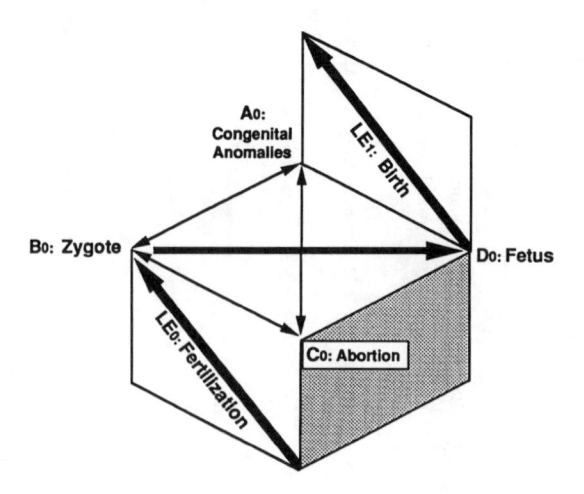

Figure 5-2 Stage 0: Zygote *to* fetus versus congenital anomalies *or* abortion.

Stage 0–Prebirth: From Zygote to Fetus

Stage 0 (see Figure 5-2) represents an extension of Erikson's model to the prebirth period (see Figure 5-2). The social radius of the fetus in the prebirth period (SR_0) is the mother's uterus.[8] The prebirth period is initiated by the very first stressor or life event, fertilization (LE_0), which results in the dystonic position of an undifferentiated cell mass (B_0) known as a zygote or blastocyst. This zygote is neither individuated nor attached. The core strength is survival, which is manifested physiologically in this primal stage. Critical life processes of differentiation (individuation) are crucial during the first 2 weeks of zygote life, known as the

---

[8] The logic for extending TILT into prebirth is threefold. First, the model proposes that the integration of individuation and attachment represents a basic ontogenetic process. Thus, it posits the beginnings of this process to be visible at all stages of life, including "life in utero," albeit in concrete physiological terms. Perhaps it is the very early kinesthetic imprinting of the individuation-attachment process that enables its further recognition, development, and refinement across the life span. Second, the prebirth period is one of increasing importance in preventive health care, from both a physiological and psychosocial viewpoint. Thus, it must be included in any complete life stage theory in the 1990s. Third, the area of object relations so critical to a verticalized individuation-attachment view of Erikson has its roots in mother-child interaction. It can only deepen the understanding to extend it to the prenatal period. Nontheless, my treatment of the prebirth period differs from the tradition of psychological research during this periods which focuses on maternal-fetal attachment from the maternal perspective. Leifer (1977) and Cranley (1981) have studied the phenomonon extensively and seem to be continuing the line of inquiry into the psychological processes of pregnancy as experienced by the mother. This body of knowledge focuses on maternal incorporation of the fetus (Deutch, 1948), the developmental tasks of pregnancy (Clark, 1976), maternal tasks of pregnancy (Rubin, 1975), maternal affect behaviors during pregnancy (Leifer, 1977), the extent of maternal affiliation and interaction with the fetus (Cranley, 1981) and the importance of these events to postbirth mother–child interaction. My emphasis here, in contrast, is on the developmental position of the developing fetus as a precursor to later development of the organism.

germinal stage (Papalia & Olds, 1982). Yet, the zygote is also preparing for implantation into the uterus (attachment). Early in development the blastocyst separates its cells into outer and inner layers. The outer trophoblastic layer (a wall, in TILT terms) is mainly concerned with the process of attachment to the uterine lining via chorionic villi, whereas the inner layer (a boundary) individuates into the fetus.

Once implantation has occurred, the zygote becomes known as the embryo (E_0) and undergoes further processes of differentiation and attachment (further progression along the developmental BED axis). Major organ systems are formed (or individuated, creating more articulated boundaries), and the placenta grows to become the organ of attachment between the embryo and the mother. By the end of the embryonic stage (8 weeks) all major structures and organs that will be found in the full-term infant are present (Olds, London, & Ladewig, 1988). A gradually increasing social radius accompanies the early fetal period as the fetus begins to respond to mild stimulation and then becomes increasingly more responsive (is attached and has a more permeable wall) to extrauterine sensations such as touch and light (Newman & Newman, 1987). Given healthy development via the core strength of survival, the fetus further individuates and becomes more securely attached. The fetal period (8 weeks till full-term) then ensues with continuing refinement of fetal structures and physiological function. For example, the development of fingerprints occurs by 24 weeks (Moore, 1982), and signs of fetal temperament such as feeding, sleeping, and activity patterns occur after 5 months (Olds et al., 1988). This process culminates in a firmly individuated full-term fetusy (articulated boundary) that is temporally associated with a degenerating placenta and a thinning-out cervix (loosening of wall). Thus, the fully developed fetus in the ninth month (D_0) displays the familiar syntonic TILT template of a more articulated intrapersonal boundary enabling a more permeable interpersonal wall.

The core pathology within this prenatal period can be viewed as genetic and/or environmental inadequacy. It can be expressed either in A or C forms, both positions on this clinical AC axis reflecting incongruencies between individuation and attachment. The prenatal A_0 structure (deindividuated attachment) is expressed in congenital anomalies that are carried to term. These fetuses display pathological inadequacy in differentiation but remain firmly attached. Conversely, the prenatal C_0 expression (detached individuation) can be seen in ectopic pregnancies, some spontaneous abortions, in placenta previa, and abruptio placentae. In all these latter conditions, the problem is primarily one of inadequate attachment rather than individuation–differentiation. At the same time, 50% of commonly occurring spontaneous abortions are thought to result from extreme congenital inadequacy (Carr & Gedeon, 1977). Thus, survival and healthy development from zygote (B_0) to full-term fetus (D_0) depend upon an integrated and synchronous dovetailing of the processes of individuation and attachment (i.e., the loosening of

Stage 1–Early Infancy: From Normal Autism to Secure Attachment

The division of infancy into its earlier and later stages is necessitated by distinct life events, an expanding social radius, and an enlarging developmental capacity of the human infant. The great preponderance of research has concentrated on attachment in the period of early infancy and its ability to predict later developmental outcomes (Ainsworth, 1973; Bowlby, 1969; Sroufe & Waters, 1977). One of the few researchers into later infancy is Sroufe (cf., Joffe & Vaughn, 1982), and he has focused primarily on individuation within this later infancy phase (Sroufe, 1979). Both Mahler (1968, Mahler, Pine, & Bergman, 1975) and Stern (1977), in contrast, reflect the present model's rejection of an oscillatory view of individuation and attachment and a call for the recognition of their reciprocal intertwining at each stage. With this in mind, I now turn to a description of these stages.

Stage 1 (see Figure 5-3) in the present model refers to the earliest infancy stage (birth to approximately age 1). It corresponds to the first part of Erikson's infancy stage and Freud's oral stage (Freud, 1905/1953). The activating stressor is Life Event 1 (LE_1), the birth process itself, which forwardly regresses the syntonically secure fetus (D_0) out of its now restrictive social radius, the uterus, into the more expanded radius (SR_1) of the mother's arms and body and into a position of

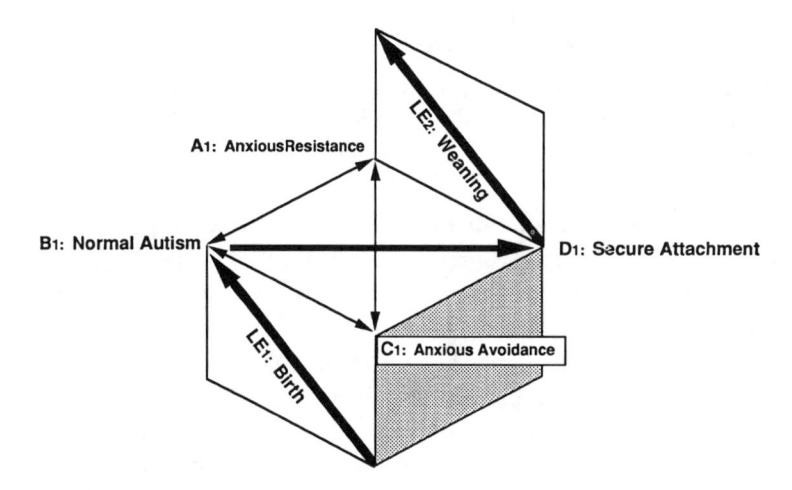

Figure 5-3 Stage 1: Normal autism *to* secure attachment versus anxious resistance *or* anxious avoidance.

normal antism (B_1). This new radius is a prime example of what Winnicott (1965) calls the "holding environment." According to Mahler (1968), the stage of early infancy is characterized by the development of a "social symbiosis" analogous to the physiological symbiosis of intrauterine life. This continuing physiological and now social–emotional dependency of the early infant on the mothering agency is absolutely necessary for the infant's ego development.

Normal development along the BED axis at this stage is promoted by the core strength of reciprocity between mothering agency and infant. Ainsworth (1973) has described this process as an "attachment-exploration" balance proceeding from a "secure base"; Mahler (1968, 1975) describes it as "mutual cueing"; whereas Stern (1977) and Brazelton, Koslowski, and Main (1974) describe it as a reciprocal dance or cycle that occurs simultaneously between mother and infant. Various metaphors have been used to describe the B_1 (deindividuated and detached) infant. Khan (1964) describes the "protective shield" of the mother while Mahler refers to the mother serving as an auxiliary ego for the infant. The mother acts as an impermeable wall protecting the infant's still inarticulated boundary. Mahler further describes this stage as one of absolute primary narcissism and of normal autism in which the infant does not distinguish between his own tension-reduction efforts and those of his mother. By the end of the second month, this normal autistic period gives way to the "symbiotic stage proper," an E_1 structure in the TILT model. Here the infant "behaves and functions as though he and his mother were an omnipotent system—a dual unity within one common boundary" (Mahler, 1968, p. 8). The infant begins to perceive that need satisfaction comes from a "part object" (i.e., breast or bottle) which is still within the dual unity system. Given optimal symbiosis or "good enough mothering" (Winnicott, 1971), the infant is ready to "hatch" (Mahler) from the symbiotic orbit. The caretaker may also gradually "de-adapt," a process that allows the beginning of differentiation between self representations and the heretofore fixed self-plus-object representations (D_1). At this syntonic level, termed the "practicing period" by Mahler, the infant has achieved the beginning sense of "I" as distinct from "not I" and can sustain this sense given the presence and emotional availability of the mothering agency. This syntonic D_1 structure can also be recognized in the behavior of the securely attached infants described by Ainsworth (1979). These infants can actively explore their environment in the presence of the mother. Furthermore, upon reunion with the mother after brief periods of separation, they are comforted by her and then return to their environmental explorations.

Without optimal symbiosis (Mahler) or given any missteps in the dance (Stern), safe developmental passage along the BED axis is blocked, primarily by the core pathology that I label noncontingency of mother or caregiver response. Prototypical A and C expressions can be discerned in Ainsworth's (1972) anxious–resistant (A_1)

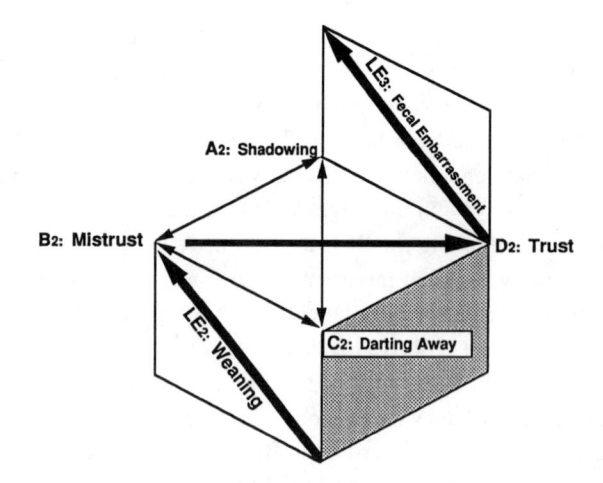

Figure 5-4 Stage 2: Mistrust *to* trust versus shadowing *or* darting away.

and anxious–avoidant (C_1) behaviors upon reunion after a mother's absence. In subsequent data Main (1973) reported that mothers of avoidant (C_1) infants differed from those of resistant infants (A_1) in that they expressed dislike of establishing physical contact with their infants. The former A_1 (deindividuated attachment) infants display anger at the mother and also resist her efforts to comfort them, while ambivalently wanting to be held. The latter C_1 (detached individuation) infants avoid or ignore the mother upon her return, displaying a high tolerance for being alone. Significantly, mothers of infants changing from an insecure (A_1 and C_1 structures) to a secure (D_1) attachment relationship reported a significantly greater reduction in stressful life events than did mothers of infants changing in the opposite direction (Vaughn, Egeland, Sroufe, & Waters, 1979). Longitudinal studies demonstrate that mental representations of attachment are shown by the end of the first year of life (Main et al., 1985).[9]

Stage 2–Later Infancy: From Mistrust to Trust

Stage 2 (approximately ages 1 to 2) denotes the period of later infancy (see Figure 5-4) corresponding to the latter part of Erikson's infancy stage and Freud's oral stage (Freud, 1905/1953). The precipitating stressor is the life event of weaning (LE_2), which forwardly regresses the previous securely attached D_1 infant into a dystonic state of profound mistrust (B_2). The infant is shockingly reminded once again of his or her separateness from the mother, albeit at a more representational stage than that experienced through birth trauma. The social radius thus expands

---

[9] The A and C designations employed here refer to TILT terminology and not to Ainsworth's original letter designation: A denotes anxious resistance and C, anxious avoidance.

from the physical to the representational presence of the mother (SR_2) and begins to include the father as well (Mahler, Pine & Bergman, 1975). Mahler (1968) puts it this way: "at the very height of mastery, toward the end of the practicing period, it already had begun to dawn on the junior toddler that the world is not his oyster, that he must cope with it more or less on his own, very often as a relatively helpless [deindividuated] small and separate [detached] individual unable to command relief or assistance merely by feeling the need for it or even giving voice to that need." (bracketed inserts added). This sense of separateness is only enhanced by the infant's increasing locomotor ability to move physically away from the mother (further individuate). The accompanying increments in cognition and language make possible a more representational (rather than primarily physical) sense of attachment.

This new process is reflected in Erikson's core strength of hope, which Mahler has described as "confident expectation." At about 15 months, the weaned infant becomes more aware of his or her physical separateness yet seems to have an increased need to share with the mother each new skill experienced (Mahler, 1975). The source of the child's pleasure shifts from independent locomotion to social interaction such as peek-a-boo games (Kleeman, 1967). The father, too, is becoming included into the infant's psychological world (Abelin, 1971; Greenacre, 1966; Mahler, 1968). From 16 to 17 months on, Mahler (1975) and Feldman and Ingham (1975) observe that early toddlers like to spend increasing amounts of time away from their mothers (individuation) and begin to form close attachments to substitute adults. They often engage in symbolic play (Galenson, 1971). For most children, this period of early rapprochement culminates at age 17 to 18 months in a seeming acknowledgment and acceptance of separateness. However, the fragility of this equilibrium is indicated by the high occurrence of temper tantrums for young toddlers at this age. By 18 months, the late infants seem quite willing to express their rapidly emerging autonomy, and conflicts emerge between their desire to push their mothers away (individuate) and to cling to them (attach). During the 18–21 month period, the infant develops the capacity to realize that his or her physically absent mother has not permanently disappeared. The attainment of "object permanence" (Piaget, 1954) in conjunction with increased verbal skills makes possible increasingly representational forms of attachment that enable ever further environmental exploration (individuation). Indeed by the age of 2 years some (in my mind D_2) infants can attach to photographs of their mothers in the mothers' absence (Passman and Longeway, 1982). This representational attachment demonstrates both the infants' trust (D_2) in the mothers' return and in their own capacity to function in her absence.

The syntonic D_2 state of trust also involves an overcoming of the pathological splitting of the object world into "good" and "bad" objects (Kernberg, 1967) and the beginning of libidinal "object constancy" (Hartmann, 1964), through which a constant relationship with the mother can be maintained throughout normal ambivalences. Mahler (1968), however, has pointed to the time lag between the attainment of object permanence and that of object constancy that may, given inconsistent mothering, lead to oscillation on the clinical AC axis. This is reflected in Erikson's core pathology of withdrawal from navigating the life issue of representational attachment. Stability has been demonstrated in both Ainsworth's secure (D) and insecure (A or C) attachment styles in the period of 12 to 20 months and beyond (Main et al., 1985). Bowlby (1969, 1973a, 1973b, 1977) has suggested that in the absence of security, infants may become anxious or insecure (A), whereas Parkes (1972) has pointed to the opposite (C) pole of compulsive self-reliance. Though there is a paucity of empirical research at this later stage of infancy (Joffe & Vaughn, 1982), Mahler (1975) has pointed to two patterns of infant–mother attachment that, in exaggerated form, may represent stage-specific forms of these A-C pathologies. The first (A_2) pattern can be discerned in a pretoddler's prolonged and excessive shadowing of his mother whereby the child does not want to let her out of his or her sight. The opposite (C_2) pattern is displayed by a pretoddler who incessantly darts away from the mother, perhaps in an attempt to induce her to chase. Both of these patterns, unresolved, may represent a failure to attain object permanence and/or constancy and inadequacies in the achievement of individuation and attachment.

Stage 3–Toddlerhood: From Shame to Autonomy

Stage 3 (approximately ages 2 to 4) denotes Erikson's toddlerhood and Freud's anal stage (Freud, 1905/1953) (see Figure 5-5). The initiating life event is fecal

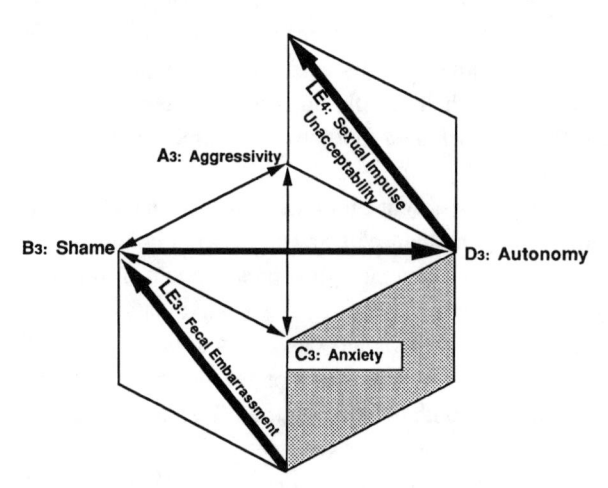

Figure 5-5 Stage 3: Shame *to* autonomy versus aggressivity *or* anxiety.

embarrassment (LE_3), which is brought on by the necessary stressor of toilet training—the toddler learns to his dismay that "his feces are not golden." This shock forwardly regresses the syntonically trusting later infant (D_2) into a profoundly dystonic state of shame (B_3) that he or she has done something wrong. The social radius has expanded, too, from a warm maternal figure with whom the later infant has painfully achieved rapprochement to impassive parental persons (SR_3) who insist that the toddler deposit his or her feces in a toilet (White, 1960). Classic psychoanalytic thinking (Freud, 1905/1953, 1913/1958) has considered this anal stage to lie at the source of many obsessive–compulsive characteristics. This is perfectly understandable from the point of view of the present model. Obsessions are persistent ritualized thoughts; compulsions, repetitive ritualized actions. Both serve a protective function: to bind the anxiety the suddenly vulnerable toddler must feel. Toddlers seem to assert a pseudoindependence (setting up impermeable walls to protect inarticulated boundaries) through bed, dress, and other well-ordered rituals (Albert, Amgott, Krakow, & Marcus, 1977) and a general unreasonable negativity (Erikson, 1951/1963). Alternatively, shameful toddlers may attempt to shield a lack of confidence (deindividuation) through refraining from all kinds of new activities (detachment). If the child does not try new things, he or she will not be further embarrassed for violating social norms. Shame is the signal that prompts the 2-year-old toddler to withdraw.

Although the B_3 level may be effective temporarily in protecting the toddler, it will not suffice in this period of rapidly expanding environments. The toddler is becoming proficient in walking and is rapidly developing in thought and language (Anglin, 1977; Molfese, Malfese, & Carrell, 1982). Erikson's core strength at this stage is will, which works to propel the toddler ahead on the BED developmental axis toward the new syntonic equilibrium of autonomy (D_3). This D_3 structure is reflected in the toddler's sense that his or her impulses can be controlled (Freud, 1905/1953) and thus the toddler can safely reengage with the environment in a more masterful (White, 1960) and less defensive way. Erikson (1951/1963) describes the journey of toddlerhood as proceeding from "naysaying" and ritualization (B_3) to independence and persistence (D_3). Newman and Newman (1987) characterize it as proceeding from doing things "one's own way" to doing them "on one's own." Murphy and Moriarty (1976) have noted that between the ages of 2 and 4, children come both to experience less frustration than they did previously and to manage better whatever frustration they still feal. Toddlers may learn to control their environment through symbolic imagery and fantasy play (Singer, 1973, 1975) and through imitation (Bandura, 1977; Grusec & Abramovitch, 1982; Parton, 1976). Learning through imitation has the advantage of bypassing the child's anxiety regarding the violation of social norms (the shame signal) and allowing the attainment of autonomy and efficacy (D_3).

Hoffman (1977) has discovered that parental discipline techniques based on "inductions" (i.e., explanations to the toddler as to why behavior was wrong and appeals to the toddler's sense of mastery and fairness) may be more effective in producing a D_3 "autonomously concerned" child (Baumrind, 1971; Leizer & Rogers, 1974; Odom, Seeman, & Newbrough, 1971) than are two other discipline techniques, "power assertion" and "love withdrawal," each of which seem to trigger Erikson's core pathology compulsion, albeit in opposite forms. Power assertion involves physical punishment, shouting, and inhibitions of the child's behavior (an intrusive A parenting style), whereas love withdrawal reflects parental disapproval, refusal to communicate, and a general turning away (a disengaged C parenting style). It is not surprising that research has shown that the power assertion style tends to produce aggressive (C_3) children (Anthony, 1970; Chwast, 1972) who lose control of their anger and moral prohibitions in interactions with others (deindividuated attachment). Love withdrawal, in contrast, tends to produce anxious (A_3) toddlers who remain overly controlled in their emotions and interact in a compliant (Forehand, Roberts, Doleus, Hobbs, & Resick, 1976) or conformist (Hoffman, 1980) way with adult authorities (detached individuation). Both of these toddler types fall on the clinical AC axis and must be distinguished from autonomous (D_3) children who, in Bandura's (1977) terms, can express anger while not losing control (individuated attachment). Significantly, this autonomous toddler may represent a developmental bridge between the securely attached (D_1) infant (Matas, Arend, & Sroufs 1978) and the confident, skilled, and initiating (D_4) preschooler (Arend, Gove, & Sroufe, 1979; Sroufe, 1979).

Stage 4–Play-Age Childhood: From Guilt to Initiative

Stage 4 (approximately ages 4 to 6) denotes Erikson's play age and Freud's classic Oedipal period (Freud, 1933/1964) (see Figure 5-6). The environmental stressor is Life Event 4, sexual impulse unacceptability, which interacts with the previous social radius, parental persons, to forwardly regress a syntonically autonomous toddler (D_3) into a dystonic position of guilt (B_4) with regard to the expanded social radius, the nuclear family (SR_4). From an orthodox psychoanalytic point of view, the phallic stage is the period in which the *Oedipal conflict* emerges. For the less orthodox psychoanalysts, girls experience an *Electra conflict*. Both of these conflicts (Oedipal for the son, Electra for the daughter) involve the giving up of the opposite-sex parent as a sexual object and the identification with the same-sex parent. A result of this outcome is the emergence of a well-differentiated superego (thus, the psychoanalytic axiom "the superego is heir to the Oedipus complex"), guilt, and a repression of the sexual and aggressive tendencies on the part of the

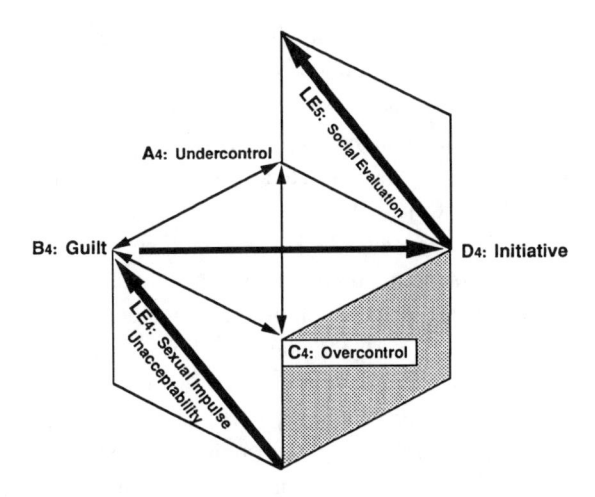

TILT Across the Lifespan: From Mistrust to Trust 103

Figure 5-6 Stage 4: Guilt *to* initative versus undercontrol *or* overcontrol.

child toward his or her parents (see the review by Greenspan & Pollock, 1980, on current psychoanalytic thinking in this period).

The Eriksonian view of this stage is somewhat looser but the outcome is the same. The play-age child is faced with a heightened awareness of the sexual organs and often becomes involved with exploration of his or her own body and that of friends. Embarrassment on the part of adults as to the sexual implications of this frank exposure of body parts may create guilt and withdrawal in the child. This guilt may extend beyond sexual issues per se to all areas of open conflict between the social norms of the culture as represented by adults and the child's age-appropriate tendencies to actively question and investigate his or her universe. Newman and Newman (1982) suggest that "guilt is the internal psychological mechanism that signals when a violation of a forbidden area is about to occur," for example, the incest taboo (Gagnon, 1977; McCary, 1978). I suggest that guilt becomes the signal for social withdrawal (detachment) to protect the particularly vulnerable (deindividuated) school-age child from adult criticism and resultant fluctuation in self-esteem (Cicirelli, 1976; Kegan, 1982; Long, Henderson, & Ziller, 1967; Wells & Marwell, 1976). Thus, we have the guilty (B_4) child who erects impermeable walls around himself (detachment) to protect his suddenly inarticulated boundaries (deindividuation).

The core strength for Erikson at this stage is purpose, which nudges the B_4 guilty child ahead on the developmental BED axis. Psychoanalytic thinkers suggest that the process of moral development (i.e., the internalization of values that sustain impulse control under conditions of temptation) is achieved through identification with the parents (Bronfenbrenner, 1960). They view the superego emerging from the resolution of the Oedipus complex as the structure for internalization of parental and societal standards. Jacobson (1964) has viewed identification more broadly as the process by which children gain independence from parents (i.e., individuation) and at the same time internalize many of their (and society's) values (i.e., attachment). This process is facilitated by a warm and democratic parenting style (Baumrind, 1975; Hoffman, 1979). This syntonic (individuated attachment) state of initiative (D_4) has been described as "ego resilient" by Arend et al. (1979) and allows for a healthy blend of control and spontaneity.

The core pathology at this stage is inhibition, which tends to fixate a play-age child on the clinical AC axis. Harsh parental discipline techniques tend to produce children who are physically aggressive and who do not control their behavior well when they are away from home (Anthony, 1970; Chwast, 1972). Other children develop strong phobias toward surrounding objects (whether school, the dark, strangers, or certain animals), sharply curtailing their ability to explore their environment. For example, Davison and Neale (1982) estimate 17 per 1000 school children experience school phobia each year. This polarized structure is indicative of an inability to integrate successfully the child's need for individuation and attachment. Arend et al. (1979) define this axis by the endpoints of overcontrol (C_4) and undercontrol (A_4). Overcontrol leads to rigidity and lack of spontaneity (detached individuation), whereas undercontrol relates to the inability to delay gratification (deindividuated attachment). This research also demonstrates striking continuity in distancing positions across the life span. Using Blocks' Q-sort measure (Block & Block, 1980), Arend et al. demonstrated that children who had been classified as securely attached (Ainsworth, 1979) at 18 months of age (D_1) were independently described by their teachers at ages 4 and 5 as highly ego-resilient (D_4). They were also described as being moderate on control, neither over- nor undercontrolled. Similar results have been reported by Vaughn et al. (1979), showing that securely attached infants display increased resiliency, self-control, and curiosity as preschoolers. In contrast, infants classified at 18 months as anxiously attached (either A_1 or C_1) were found by Arend et al. to be significantly lower on resiliency. Furthermore, those in the anxious–avoidant infant group (C_1) were described as overcontrolled (C_4) at ages 4 and 5 and those in the anxious–resistant infant group (A_1), undercontrolled (A_4) at 4 and 5. Unresolved A–C pathology at one stage seems then to bias an individual in that same direction at later stages, whereas healthy BED development seems to further subsequent healthy development.

Stage 5–School Age Childhood: From Inferiority to Industry

Stage 5 (see Figure 5-7) denotes Erikson's school age (approximately ages 6 to 12). It is initiated by Life Event 5, social evaluation, with the new social radius of

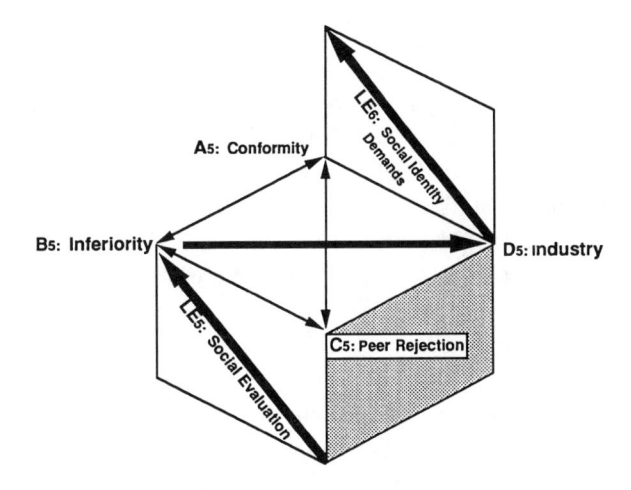

TILT Across the Lifespan: From Mistrust to Trust 105

Figure 5-7 Stage 5: Inferiority *to* industry versus conformity *or* peer rejection.

the school-age child being school and neighborhood peers (SR$_5$) rather than the nuclear family. According to Barker and Wright (1955) about 50 of the school-age child's interactions are with other children as opposed to only 10% in this regard for 2 year olds. Social evaluation forwardly regresses the syntonically initiating (D$_4$) play-age child into a dystonic state of inferiority (B$_5$). The B$_5$ child has been studied by Dweck and Licht (1980), Ruble (1983), and Phillips (1984) among others. Criticism from peers and negative social comparison can lead to a pessimistic self-definition with regard to future success and even a sense of "learned helplessness" and depression (cf., Seligman, 1975). Withdrawal from social interaction (detachment) accompanies the self-doubt (deindividuation) for the B$_5$ child and may well provide a protective shield until the child begins to feel better about exposing (permeable wall) his or her abilities (articulated boundary).

The core strength behind this BED journey is Erikson's competence, and the major process is education (cf., Newman & Newman, 1987). Children are exposed to a range of disciplines and to the language of concepts that allow them both to organize experiences and acquire new skills (Cole & D'Andrade, 1982; Rubin, 1980). Children can be helped to set realistic goals for themselves so they can experience success. Each child is different in response to critical evaluation. For some it may be devastating, for others it may be quite helpful in this developmental journey (Crandall, 1963). When tasks are difficult, a child's concentration and persistence may be adversely affected by external evaluation (Maehr and Stallings, 1972). Under more relaxed conditions, however, outside evaluation can improve the child's performance (Hill & Sarason, 1966). In any case, individuation and attachment are inextricably linked in healthy development. Pellegrini (1985), for example, has shown that children who display maturity in their social reasoning (individuation) are likely to be more positively evaluated by their peers (attachment). The strength of a healthy child's (D_5) need for success is well established by the end of the school-age stage (Atkinson & Birch, 1978). These are also the years when children can have "best friends" (Berndt, 1981), a process Sullivan (1949) argued is crucial for later heterosexual relations.

There are many pitfalls along this developmental journey, however. Calhoun and Morse (1977), for example, have shown that failure in school and the experience of public ridicule can interact with an initially negative self-concept to cause long-lasting damage to a child's self esteem. The core pathology for Erikson at this stage is inertia, which can be expressed either in A or C pathologies. One type of A5 pathology may be labeled hyperactivity (Sainz, 1966; Werry, 1968). The hyperactive child is unable to control his or her impulses (insufficiently articulated boundaries). Stewart (1967) estimated that hyperactive children represented some 4% of the grade school population in the United States. Another form of the A_5 (deindividuated attachment) structure can be labeled conformity (Pepitone, Leob, & Murdock, 1977). Children learn to dress, talk, and joke in ways that gain peer approval, in extreme cases showing willingness to go along with antisocial peer behavior. Indeed Costanzo (1970) has shown that late childhood–early adolescence represents a peak period of conformity. The A_5 child is quite simply afraid to be different lest he or she receive negative social evaluation. Thus, the child blends in (deindividuates) to avoid the evaluation process.

The child may accomplish the same goal through going to the opposite polarity, a C_5 (detached individuation) structure. This can be labeled peer rejection with associated feelings of loneliness. The direction of this process is not always clear. Sometimes the C_5 child may reject (detach) to avoid being rejected. However, the result is the same: loneliness and feelings of social dissatisfaction (Asher, Hymmel, & Renshaw, 1984). A significant proportion of children in this study felt left out, had trouble making friends, and felt that they were alone. Furthermore, children who are rejected tend to be disruptive and aggressive with peers and often require psychiatric treatment in adolescence or adulthood (Coie & Krehbiel, 1984; Robins, 1966; Sroufe & Rutter, 1984). Though Robins (1978, p. 611) cautions that "most antisocial children do not become antisocial adults," there is no question that the clinical conformity–peer rejection axis is more problematic for the school-age child than is the developmental inferiority–competence one.

Stage 6–Adolescence: From Identity Confusion to Identity

Stage 6 (see Figure 5-8) in the TILT model describes Erikson's very important adolescent stage (approximately ages 12 to 22). It is initiated by the life event of social

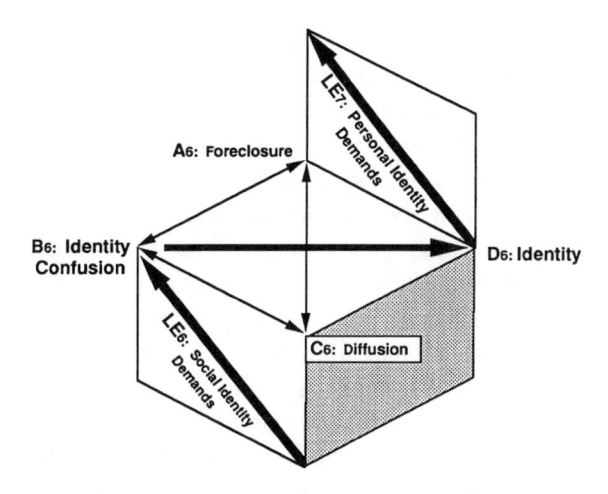

TILT Across the Lifespan: From Mistrust to Trust 107

Figure 5-8 Stage 6: Identity confusion *to* identity versus foreclosure *or* diffusion.

identity demands (LE$_6$), which forwardly regresses the syntonically industrious (D$_5$) school-age child into an initial dystonic position of identity confusion (B$_6$). The social radius at this stage is peer groups and outgroups (SR$_6$). The life task is to find what groups one belongs to and what groups to avoid. The adolescent may experience a sense of omnipotentiality with the resultant lack of ability to commit to any particular group. This stage has been studied at length by Marcia (1966, 1980) and by Bourne (1978a, 1978b) among others and refers to the process by which adolescents mature to the point of achieving a social identity that allows them to make a realistic social commitment. According to Marcia, this journey involves the process of both exploration (what is meant by individuation) and commitment (what is meant by attachment). This dystonic first level (B$_6$) represents neither individuation nor attachment and seems to correspond quite well to what Marcia has labeled moratorium. Individuals in this moratorium or identity-confusion state have not proceeded very far into exploration (deindividuation) nor have they made any commitment (detachment).

Erikson has labeled the core strength at Stage 6 as fidelity, which is realized through the integrated achievement of both individuation (Marcia's exploration) and attachment (Marcia's commitment). A successful integrated progression along the developmental BED axis with regard to both of these life issues leads to a syntonic position of identity achievement (D$_6$), which for Marcia involves an individual who has both undergone exploration and made commitments. A number of studies have shown that such individuals do well on a number of achievement and interpersonal indicators (Cross & Allen, 1970; Donovan, 1975; cf., Jordan, 1971; Josselson, 1973; Marcia & Friedman, 1970; Orlovsky, 1978).

The core pathology at this stage has been described by Erikson as repudiation, which can lead to fixation and oscillation on the clinical AC axis expressed either in what Stierlin (1974) has called "expelling" (adolescents pushed by their families into premature autonomy) or "binding" (adolescents infantilized by their families). Marcia has labeled these polarities diffusion (an adolescent who engages in pseudoexploration without social commitment) and foreclosure (an adolescent who prematurely commits to a group without sufficient exploration). Diffusion represents the C_6 (detached individuation) structure and foreclosure the A_6 (deindividuated attachment) position.[10]

Bourne (1978b) has described the diffusion state as one of withdrawal, whereas Donovan (1975) has described individuals in this state as feeling out of place and socially isolated from the world. Maccoby and Jacklin (1974) evaluated the results of over 1600 studies comparing individuation (agency) and attachment (communion) responses between males and females. Lerner and Shea (1982) conclude that most of these reviewed studies show no sex differences, but when they do occur, females score higher on attachment–communion (foreclosure) behaviors such as dependency, social desirability, compliance, general anxiety, and staying in the proximity of friends. Males tend to score higher on individuation–agency (diffusion) behaviors such as aggression, confidence in task performance, dominance, and activity level (Block, 1976). Other studies have documented a strong relationship for both males and females between foreclosure status and authoritarianism (Marcia, 1966; Marcia & Friedman, 1970; Schenkel & Marcia, 1972) and conformity (Podd, 1972). Significantly, still other studies have shown that both foreclosures and diffusions have tended to score at lower moral stages (Podd, 1972; Poppen, 1974; Rowe, 1978) and are less ethical, empathic, or socialized (Hayes, 1977) than are identity achievers or moratoriums. In other words, adolescents on the developmental moratorium–identity achievement axis tend to do better in a variety of personal, social, and moral indicators than do individuals on the clinical diffusion–foresclosure axis.

Stage 7–Early Adulthood: From Isolation to Intimacy

Stage 7 (see Figure 5-9) in the TILT model describes Erikson's younger adulthood (approximately ages 22 to 34) with a social radius of partners in friendship and sex (SR_7). It is initiated by Life Event 7, personal identity demands, which forwardly regresses a previously syntonic identity-achieving adolescent (D_6) into a dystonic

---

[10]The placement of Marcia's moratorium and diffusion categories requires a brief comment. Moratorium might be rigidly labeled as a C structure (exploration without commitment) and diffusion as a B (neither exploration nor commitment). Fuller consideration of Marcia's intent led me to reverse the above placement.

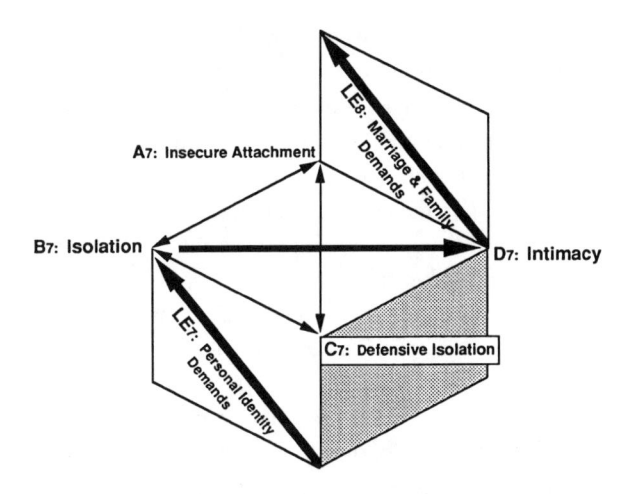

TILT Across the Lifespan: From Mistrust to Trust

Figure 5-9 Stage 7: Isolation *to* intimacy versus insecure attachment *or* defensive isolation.

state of isolation (B_7). The hard-won social identity emerging from group commitment and membership is no longer enough. The young adult requires a more developed personal identity but must first be free of the intense peer pressures emerging from the preceding social radius (deindividuation). This confusion in personal identity (deindividuation) leads to a sense of loneliness and isolation (detachment). Marcia's previously discussed moratorium position also applies here. Young adults in this moratorium or isolation level have only begun the personal exploration (individuation) necessary for any intimate interpersonal commitment (attachment).

Erikson has labeled the core strength at this stage love, which in Buber's (1970) sense allows the formation of one's own identity and respect for that of the other (in other words, an I-thou relationship) essential to any genuine syntonic intimacy (D_7). Central to this journey is the establishment of a self separate from one's parents on which one can base one's own life. Peers have served the adolescent well in facilitating this separation process. But now the young adult must turn to more intimate dyadic encounters to further develop this separation. This process has been studied by a number of researchers, some (Offer & Offer, 1975; Silber et al., 1961) focusing on the movement from high school to college, others looking at the development from childhood to adulthood (MacFarlane, 1964; Kagan & Moss, 1962). With regard to healthy development on the BED axis, Katz (1968) discovered that healthy young adults learned to make decisions without seeking permission from their parents and moved toward closer relationships and assumption of the marital role. Vaillant (1977) found that the "best outcome" younger adults tended to be well-integrated and practical in late adolescence and early adulthood, whereas the "worst outcome" young adults were asocial. Vaillant argues that the "best outcome" individuals shifted to more mature defenses and adaptation modes (in my terms, more permeable walls with more articulated boundaries). In a cross-sectional study of young adult clinic outpatients, Gould (1972) found two distinct periods: 18 to 22 (in my model, late adolescence) and 22 to 28. In the former period, the individuals were in the process of taking steps to implement separation from parents. In the latter, the subjects felt established and secure in this separation. They were engaged in the work of being adults.

Exclusivity is the core pathology in Stage 7 for Erikson that blocks this healthy developmental journey. It can be expressed either in what Minuchin (1974) calls enmeshment (A_7) or disengagement (C_7). Enmeshment refers to a diffuse set of self-other boundaries (in my sense, a premature removal of walls); disengagement refers to rigid self-other boundaries (a delayed removal of walls). Marcia has called these same structures foreclosure (A_7) and diffusion (C_7), and Stierlin has described them in family terms: either as bound (infantilized) by the family (A_7) or expelled by it (C_7). Work by Bellington and Becker (1986) points to longitudinal consistency across the life span in these positions. Ainsworth's pathological early infant attachment styles (A_1 and C_1) are reflected in high insecure attachment (A_7) and defensive isolation (C_7) scores on the Bell Object Relations Inventory as administered to young adults. Hawkins, Weisberg, and Ray (1980) contrast different interaction styles for these young adults, the pathological polarities represented by speculation (exploring the other's point of view without revealing one's own), an A_7 structure, and control (expressing one's own view without taking the other's into account), a C_7 structure. These AC polarities are clearly not as healthy as is their D_7 "contactful" communication style, which reflects openness to the other while expressing one's own opinion. This contactful style must be achieved developmentally and is essential to the attainment of syntonic intimacy at Stage 7.

Stage 8–Middle Adulthood: From Stagnation to Generativity

Stage 8 in the TILT model (see Figure 5-10) corresponds to Erikson's middle adulthood (approximately ages 34 to 65), with a social radius of household and children (SR_8). It is initiated by Life Event 8, marital and family demands, which forwardly regresses a syntonic intimacy-achieving younger adult (D_7) into the dystonic stage of stagnation (B_8). Here a middle adult feels overwhelmed by the demands of marriage and family (deindividuated) and finds himself in a state of confused withdrawal. Indeed the very intimacy he has achieved with a particular partner in Stage 7 must make room for the expanded social radius of household and children in Stage 8. Neugarten (1973) has focused on middle adults' increased preoccupation with inner life, or "interiority" which enables them to look backward

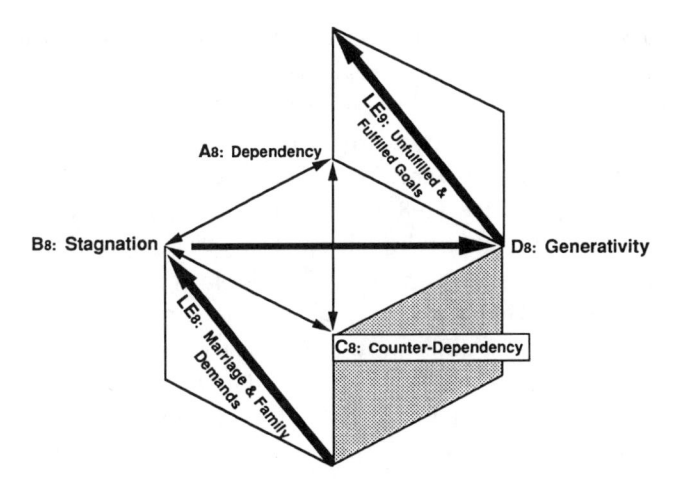

TILT Across the Lifespan: From Mistrust to Trust 111

Figure 5-10 Stage 8: Stagnation *to* generativity versus dependency *or* counter dependency.

for the first time rather than forward. The dynamic of withdrawal to inner space is necessitated by the overwhelming demands of marriage and family life and may be associated with a sense of "burnout," of just going through the motions. This has been associated empirically with personal feelings of worthlessness (Pines & Aronson, 1981).

Erikson defines the core strength at this stage as care, which propels the stagnating middle adult forward along the developmental BED axis into a syntonic state of generativity (D_8). Withdrawal to his or her own resources has freed the generative middle adult to get in touch with an individual sense of creativity (individuation), enabling him or her to enter the role of a mentor for the next generation (attachment), whether in a home or work environment, in a way that integrates care for self and care for others. Shanan (1985) has labeled this midlife personality structure the "active integrated coper"—investment at work is not at the expense of family relationships. A number of studies have explored the difficulties women have had with this transition with regard to role-strain, overload, and generally lowered morale, problems that increase with the births of subsequent children (Dyer, 1963; LeMasters, 1957; Meyerowitz & Feldman, 1966; Rossi, 1968; Russell, 1974; Yalom Linde, Moos & Hamburg, 1968). Levinson and his colleagues have conducted similar research on men (Levinson, 1977; Levinson, Darrow, Klein, Levinson, & Mckee, 1978). They suggest that the demands of the career mentor role raise the same basic generativity issues as those associated with family parenting.

The core pathology for Erikson at this stage is rejectivity, which can be expressed either in what Gutmann et al. (1982) have called dependency (an A_8 structure) or counterdependency (a C_8 structure). Stewart and Salt (1981) have reported that single "agentic" (C_8) working women exhibited ill health in response to stress. In contrast, homemakers with a traditional communal (A_8) orientation responded to stress with depression. However, working wives combining agentic and communal (D_8) orientations experienced no negative effects in response to stress. Similar benefits of combining agency and communion have been reported by Stewart and Malley (1987) and Malley (1989) with regard to both the physical and emotional health of divorcing mothers. Much of the research on this AC clinical axis emerges from the work of Gutmann and his colleagues on the "parental imperative." Gutmann's basic idea that the demands of parenting itself produce traditional sex-role differentiation has found considerable empirical support, even among nontraditional couples (cf., Belsky, 1981; Cowan, Cowan, Coie & Coie, 1978; Hoffman, 1978; Hoffman & Manis, 1978; Lamb, 1978; Shereshevsky, Liebenberg & Lockman, 1973). Gutmann goes even further to suggest associated personality structures, both men and women repressing contrasexual tendencies in the service of parenting. Thus, fathers adapt an "active mastery style" (in exaggerated form, a C_8 detached individuation structure) and mothers a "passive-nurturant style" (an A_8 deindividuated attachment structure). When the nest is emptied, the psychologically repressed style returns with a vengeance (Stein, 1979), women often shifting from passive to active styles and men in the opposite direction, that is, the famous "mid-life crossover" effect (Fiske, 1980; Gutmann, 1975, 1980a, 1980b, 1987; Neugarten & Gutmann, 1958, 1964). This journey, sadly, often represents oscillation along the AC clinical axis (an exchange of symptoms if you will) rather than any true BED development. Such confusion represents one of the great dangers of this particular life stage, producing what Shanan (1985) has labeled "dependent passive copers" (an A_8 structure) or "failing overcopers" (a C_8 structure). Neither of these groups is as happy with his life as is Shanan's D_8 "active integrated" coper group described previously.

Stage 9–Older Adulthood: From Despair to Integrity

Stage 9 in the TILT model (see Figure 5-11) refers to Erikson's older adulthood (approximately ages 65 to 80). The social radius (SR_9) for the older adult has become humankind/my kind—a differentiation of universalistic and particularistic affiliations. It is initiated by the life event (LE_9) of unfulfilled goals (or perhaps now meaningless fulfilled goals), a stressor that forwardly regresses the previously syntonic generative (D_8) middle adult into a profound dystonic state of despair (B_9). All of one's previous achievements have proved meaningless and many of one's dreams are now out of grasp. The B_9 individual has lost the meaning in life (deindividuation) and as such withdraws from social involvements (detachment).

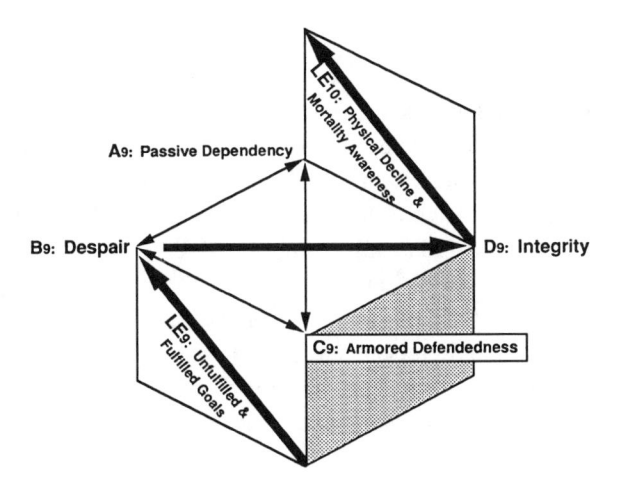

TILT Across the Lifespan: From Mistrust to Trust 113

Figure 5-11 Stage 9: Despair *to* integrity versus passive dependency *or* armored defendedness.

Life has lost its taste. The classic work by Neugarten, Harvinghurst, and Tobin (1968) has labeled adults in this position as unintegrated. Such people have defects in psychological functioning (deindividuation) as well as low levels of role activity and life satisfaction (detachment).

Erikson defines the core strength at this stage as wisdom, which guides older adults forward along the developmental BED axis to a position where they are both individuated and attached. Such a syntonic D_9 individual finds a self-integrity (articulated self-other boundary) based on something more profound than simple fulfilled personal goals and is thus able to reintegrate into humankind (permeable interpersonal walls) with a particularistic affirmation of his or her own kind. Neugarten et al. refer to this position as integrated, which is characterized by a well-functioning ego and a flexible openness with regard to environmental stimuli.

Erikson describes the core pathology at this stage as disdain, which can lead to fixation and oscillation on the clinical AC axis. This can be expressed either in what Neugarten et al. have labeled armored-defended (personalities that are striving, achievement-oriented, and ambitious, with high defenses against anxiety and with the need to maintain strict controls over impulse life) or in what they have labeled passive-dependent (individuals who have strong dependency needs and who seek responsiveness from others). The armored-defended position represents a C_9 structure in my terms (detached individuation), in Erikson's view a jingoistic individual who sacrifices humankind for his own kind. The passive-dependent personality, in contrast, represents an A_9 structure (deindividuated attachment), an individual who in an all-too-embracing universalism sacrifices his own kind for humankind. Indeed, Neugarten (1979) points specifically to the adaptive role of some paranoia for older adults; the self must be fought for against an often increasingly indifferent humankind.

Several more recent studies speak to these same points. Klemmack and Roff (1984) report that older adults with high fear of loneliness (an A_9 structure) are least satisfied with the quality of their lives. Ryff and Heincke (1983) found that healthy older adults perceived themselves to be higher in integrity (D_9) than they had been at previous life stages. Finally, Shanan (1985) points to the greater life satisfaction reported by the aging active coper (D_9) as compared with the aging passive coper (A_9) or the overcoper (C_9) even though he acknowledges the difficulty in maintaining the D structure at more advanced age. Once again, individuals, this time older adults, on the developmental BED axis seem to do better than those on the clinical AC axis.

Stage 10–The Oldest Old: From Incapacitation to Generational Continuity

Stage 10 in the TILT model (see Figure 5-12), the oldest old (approximately ages 80 and older), has not been covered specifically by Erikson nor has it been studied as extensively as some of the earlier adult stages. Peck (1968) represents a classic attempt to extend Erikson's thinking to the oldest old, offering finer distinctions in the second half of life than he felt were made by Erikson. Issues of old age, as distinct from those of middle age, which have been offered by Peck, are

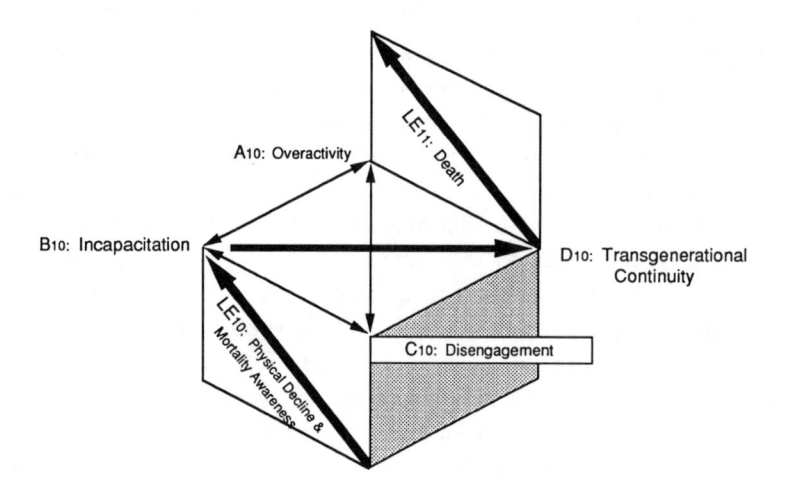

Figure 5-12 Stage 10: Incapacitation *to* transgenerational continuity versus overactivity *or* disengagement.

ego-differentiation versus work-role preoccupation, body transcendence versus body preoccupation, and ego transcendence versus ego preoccupation. Newman and Newman (1987) have tried more recently to extend Erikson's thinking to the oldest old, suggesting the life issue here is "immortality versus extinction." In other papers, Levin (1963) has emphasized depression among the aged, Berger and Zarit (1978) have studied later life paranoid states, and Cath (1966) has differentiated depression and depletion among the elderly.

My model sees the oldest old stage as initiated by the staggering life event or stressor of physical decline and awareness of mortality and life-finiteness (LE_{10}). Gutmann et al. (1982) have labeled it "life cycle shock" or "existential stress" which upsets the syntonic equilibrium (D_9) achieved by the integrity-achieving older adult (Birren, Butler, Greenhouse, Sokoloff, & Garrow, 1971) and forwardly regresses the now oldest old into the helpless dystonic position of incapacitation (B_{10}). A previously healthy older adult may now need a cane or a walker, or even a wheelchair. Memory may fail, as may kidneys. Previously reliable social supports may themselves have died and the individual may become aware of his own limited time. In short, the now oldest old may find themselves both enfeebled (deindividuated) and isolated (detached). What is critical here is how the individual manages to transcend the present-centered integrity of humankind/my kind to deal with the once again expanded social radius (SR_{10}) of present versus future generations. Does the incapacitated or terminal oldest old behave like dying King Berenger the First in Ionesco's (1963) brilliant satire "Exit the King," losing all interest in the present and future world "I am only present in the past?" says the king (p. 50) in response to this his second wife Marie's attempts to console him. When she later (p. 67) points to the expanding future, "the younger generation's expanding the universe, . . . conquering new constellations, . . . boldly battering at the gates of Heaven," Berenger again cuts himself off, "I'm dying, . . . I'm dying, . . . they can knock them flat for all I care." Or does the incapacitated oldest old adult utilize the core strength at this stage, faith, to carve out a historical self (individuation) that allows the individual to connect in a genuine way (attachment) with future generations (D_{10})? Lifton (1973) has called this a "sense of immortality" that overcomes a preoccupation with one's own ego, body, and generation through a faith, a vested interest if you will, in future generations. Indeed Augustine and Kalish (1975) propose that older people and dying people of all ages need to establish some kind of attachment that will be on-going after the death of the body, whether it be through a divine being, being remembered by others, through accomplishments, through progeny, or through association with a cause or ideology. This sense of a transgenerational continuity is deepened by the oldest old taking on the role of transmitter of history to the next generation and helps to prepare the individual for his or her own death, the final life event (LE_{11}).

The core pathology at his stage is what Newman and Newman have labeled doubt, a profound uncertainty that there is anything beyond the present ego, body, and life-finiteness. It tends to truncate the individual's sense of time in the present and may be expressed in one of two forms. One expression is what Cumming and Henry (1961) have labeled disengagement (a C_{10} structure), which is indicated by increased preoccupation with the self and decreasing emotional investments in persons and objects in the environment. When such social withdrawal is voluntary and mutual, it may represent a normal reconsolidation of older adulthood (Lowenthal, Thurnher, & Assoc., 1975). However, when it is not so mutual or voluntary, it may represent a more pathological structure. This structure may also have a paranoiac aspect to it (Berger & Zarit, 1978), which may involve suspicions and accusations of others. The second expression is paraphrased from the work of Havighurst, Neugarten, and Tobin (1968) and may be labeled overactivity (an A_{10} structure), in which people trivialize themselves through mindless activities designed to numb them to their terminal position in the life cycle. While Lawton (1980) has reported that residents of institutions for the aged seek out areas of high activity, Lemon, Bangston, and Peterson (1972) found that activity per se was not significantly related to life satisfaction among new residents of a retirement community. In extreme form, an obsession with overactivity may block the private time necessary to achieve the syntonic D_{10} state of transgenerational continuity and reflect aspects of the depressed state discussed by Levin (1963) and by Cath (1966) with an attendant loss of self-esteem. One recent study (Sonnenberg & Jacobowitz, 1989) points to the greater preponderance of these pathological A and C structures among clinical (depression, personality disorders, paranoia, and anxiety disorders) as opposed to normal older adults. Two other studies (Windle & Sinnott, 1985; Kaplan, Linky, & Jacobowitz, 1987) suggest that a major developmental component of normal older adults (including the oldest old) is the dissipation for both men and women of the rigid gender differentiation evoked at earlier life stages. Here, finally, similar life experiences enable the oldest old to integrate individuation and attachment (the developmental BED axis) in a way not totally determined by rigid gender stereotypes.

With this chapter, I complete the discussion of TILT for individuals. Section C will extend TILT to couples and families.[11]

---

[11] I should emphasize that the normative data collected in America across different age cohort groups did not show age differences with regard to the IAQ subscales.

PART THREE
TILT FOR COUPLES AND FAMILIES

Chapter 6

TILT for Couples: Helping Couples Grow Together[1]

UNIDIMENSIONAL VERSUS BIDIMENSIONAL VIEWS OF FAMILY COHESION

A Unidimensional Model of Family Cohesion

AUTONOMY AND BONDING ARE SEEN AS MUTUALLY EXCLUSIVE

In 1979, Olson, Sprenkle, and Russell offered the following definition of marital and family cohesion: "The emotional bonding members have with one another and the degree of individual autonomy a person experiences in the family system" (p. 5). They suggested that this dimension underlies the varied conceptual frameworks of some of the most influential marital and family theories. They anchor the two ends of the cohesion dimension as follows:

> At the extreme of high family cohesion, enmeshment, there is an over-identification with the family that results in extreme bonding and limited individual autonomy. The low extreme, disengagement, is characterized by low bonding and high autonomy from the family. It is hypothesized that a balanced degree of family cohesion is the most conducive to effect family functioning and to optimum individual development (Olson et al., 1979, pp. 5, 6).

The balanced position is usually healthy and falls between the two pathological extremes. Minuchin (1974, p. 54) described boundaries in enmeshed families as diffuse, in disengaged families as rigid, and in healthy families as clear. Willi (1982) took a similar position, although he introduced the concept of extradyadic boundaries as well. Bowen (1960) also worked with a unidimensional view of

---

[1] An earlier version of this chapter appeared as Kaplan, K. J. (1990), TILT for Couples: Helping Couples Grow Together. *Transactional Analysis Journal, 20*, pp. 229–244. Reprinted with permission from the International Transactional Analysis Association.

119

cohesiveness, assuming pathology at both ends (emotional divorce versus emotional fusion-undifferentiated ego mass), with health in the middle (differentiated self). Olson et al. (1979) worked with the same single dimension, although they broke the scale into four points (disengaged, separated, connected, and enmeshed) rather than three.

Despite this consensus, there remains something problematic about this unidimensional view of cohesion. There seem to be two distinct processes underlying this dimension. The first is bonding or attachment; the second is autonomy or individuation. The psychological literature is replete with evidence regarding each of these processes (e.g., Bowlby, 1969, 1973, on attachment and separation; Kaplan & O'Connor, 1993, and Kegan, 1982, on the "evolving self"; Mahler et al., 1975, on symbiosis and individuation). Yet, the unidimensional definition of cohesion offered by Olson et al. (1979) as an integrating principle seems to assume a necessarily inverse relationship between the two processes—gain in one accompanied by loss in the other. One end of the dimension—enmeshment—involves high bonding and low autonomy; the other end—disengagement—involves low bonding and high autonomy. Both of these extremes are pathological. Instead, a healthy middle category is advocated that reflects, presumably, moderate bonding and moderate autonomy. However, such a definition seems oversimplified and confused given the state of our knowledge and does not allow for the possibility that members of a truly healthy family might possess the capacity for both high bonding and high autonomy (cf. Beavers & Voeller, 1983).

The capacity for high bonding and high autonomy is not a novel idea. Indeed, Olson et al. (1979) echoed the thoughts of Gibran (1968) in defining the middle category as one that allows for separate connectedness. Buber (1957) similarly proposed an informal model that envisions mature individuals as having the capacity for both relation (bonding) and distance (autonomy); Bakan (1966) stressed the dual human needs for agency and communion; and Rank (1936) distinguished fear of death (union) and fear of life (separation). Finally, transactional analysis theory itself has separated the dimensions of "I'm OK—I'm Not OK" and "You're OK—You're Not OK" (Berne, 1961, 1964; Ernst, 1971; Harris, 1969; Kaplan, 1988; Kaplan, Capace et al., 1984). I have discussed this issue at length in previous chapters in the development of the TILT model for individuals. It is extremely relevant to the issue of family process as well.

In spite of the awareness that bonding and autonomy both represent healthy human needs, therapists and researchers often slip into theories that present them as polarities. Even worse, they often make the same mistake clinically, sometimes with disastrous consequences. Olson et al.'s (1979) formal definition of cohesion (as opposed to their informal comments discussed above), views bonding and autonomy as reciprocally antagonistic and reflects this tendency. Olson, Russell, and

Sprenkle (1983) addressed this issue as well as the Beavers and Voeller criticism by dropping the autonomy dimension from their definition of family cohesion. This, however, hardly represents a solution to the problem. The only formal family model I am aware of that has attempted to conceptually distinguish bonding and autonomy is that of Lewis, Beavers, Gosset, and Phillips (1976) from the Timberlawn group. They produced a closeness scale aimed at taking into account both closeness (bonding) and ego boundaries (autonomy). The problem with their approach is that they force both concepts on a single measurement scale.

> Those family systems which, in their communication, reflected vague, amorphous boundaries or fusion were at one extreme of the scale; in the middle portion were those families in which the separateness of the individuals was clear, but associated with considerable interpersonal distance. Families which demonstrated closeness with distinct boundaries were rated at the other end of the scale. (Lewis et al., 1976, p. 85)

Although Lewis et al. reported that their closeness scale differentiated between healthy and dysfunctional families, its unidimensional quality makes it impossible to obtain truly separate measures of bonding and autonomy. This is in marked contrast to the IAQ subscales described in chapter 2 of the present book.

A Bidimensional Model of Family Cohesion

AUTONOMY AND BONDING ARE NOT SEEN AS MUTUALLY EXCLUSIVE

The application of TILT to family cohesion is to treat bonding (attachment) and autonomy (individuation) as two conceptually independent bipolar dimensions. No necessary reciprocal antagonism between these two processes is assumed. The bonding dimension is anchored at one end by attachment (high bonding) and at the other by detachment (low bonding). As such, bonding–attachment represents an interpersonal construct ("distance" from the other) and can be thought of as the barrier or wall between individuals within the family. Once again detachment refers to rigidity of this wall (☐), attachment to its permeability (⋯). The autonomy dimension is anchored at one end by individuation (high autonomy) and at the other by deindividuation (low autonomy). Thus, autonomy–individuation represents an intrapersonal construct ("distance" from the self referring to the contour or boundary defining an individual within the family). Individuation refers to the articulation of this boundary (◯); deindividuation refers to a diffuseness in this regard (⋯).

Figure 1-6 has presented this model in bidimensional space. The ordinate refers to the bonding or attachment dimension, and the abscissa refers to the autonomy or individuation dimension. People may fall into different pairings of autonomy and bonding; Figure 1-6 has graphically illustrated six possible positions. Three of these—A, C, and E—represent points on the cohesion dimension as defined by Olson et al. (1979). Position A represents a state of low autonomy and high bonding. This enmeshed state is characterized by permeable walls and inarticulated boundaries (▦). Position C represents a state of high autonomy and low bonding. This disengaged state is characterized by impermeable walls and articulated boundaries (▣). Position E (the inside square within the middle intersection) represents an in-between state of moderate autonomy and moderate bonding. It is characterized by moderately permeable walls and moderately articulated boundaries (▣).

Three additional positions—B. D, and A/C—emerge from this bidimensional view that have not previously been described. B represents a state of low bonding and low autonomy, characterized by impermeable walls and unarticulated boundaries (▢). D represents a state of high bonding and high autonomy, characterized by permeable walls and articulated boundaries (▦). A/C (the outside square at the middle intersection) represents a position split between enmeshment and disengagement (▣), indicating a conflict on both the autonomy and bonding dimensions. Several important advantages derive from this bidimensional approach to cohesion: (1) It provides the basis for a deeper understanding of health versus pathology than does a unidimensional view, (2) it allows a precise articulation of different couple types, and (3) it suggests a therapy that may "TILT" couples away from pathological toward developmental problems.

Healthy Versus Pathological Cohesion: A Distinction Between Two Axes

The bidimensional view of family cohesion presented here proposes a distinction in terms of axes rather than positions and as a matter of degree rather than a dichotomy. More specifically, two axes have been differentiated in Figures 2-1 and 2-2. The first has been labeled the BED axis (Fig. 2-1), the second, the AC axis (Fig. 2-2). The BED axis has been conceptualized as a developmental axis; each position on the axis (B, E, or D) is seen as healthy, although varying in degree of maturity. The AC axis is conceptualized as a pathological axis, the respective positions (A and C, [A/C]$_{IND}$, and [A/C]$_{ATT}$, and [A/C]$_{TOT}$.) representing increasing levels of pathology. It is important to reemphasize that immaturity is not equivalent to pathology, although it may become so if maturity is not achieved when appropriate for the organism.

Consider first the BED axis of Figure 5-1. The underlying logic of this developmental axis has been applied across the whole life span in chapter 5. Healthy development involves the graduated and integrated replacement of a rigid wall (nonbonding) with an articulated boundary (autonomy). In other words, the subdimensions of bonding and autonomy are not viewed as antagonistic, but as working in concert. In fact, such coordination is postulated to be the sine qua non of healthy development, increases in bonding made possible by increases in autonomy.

According to Mahler et al. (1975) the young infant (0 to 2 months) is in a state of normal autism with no differentiation between the infant and the outside world. In other words, the infant's boundary has not yet been articulated. During this period the mother must serve the infant as a "dual unity with one common boundary," (Mahler et al., 1975, p. 44), a "protective shield" (Khan, 1964, p. 272), or, in terms of this book, an "impermeable wall" to protect the underlying inarticulated boundary. Thus, the autistic infant can be described as occupying Position B. Slowly the processes of separation–individuation emerge. By the age of 2 to 6 months the more differentiating infant begins to define his or her external boundaries by touching fingers and toes (i.e., to moderately articulate his or her boundary). At the same time, the child begins to pull away from mother (i.e., to create a moderately permeable wall). This is characteristic of an E position. Finally, at 10 months the infant begins the practicing phase; the baby is excited about developing his or her own abilities (i.e., articulating his or her boundaries) and by the emerging capacity to do things away from mother (i.e., make the wall fully permeable). This is characteristic of the mature D position.

Chapter 5 has argued that such a progression over these three levels of maturity occurs again and again over the life span, albeit at increasingly complex stages of development. Maturity at one stage of complexity may be sacrificed for temporary immaturity at the next. Thus, a medical student may become less remote and defensive (less rigidity in walls) as he or she becomes more certain of the ability to withstand the emotional and intellectual demands of the profession (greater articulateness in boundaries). However, the remoteness and defensiveness may temporarily return when the former student opens a practice.

The AC axis of Figure 5-2 is very different in this regard. It is, by its very nature, pathological, involving reciprocal antagonism between the subdimensions of bonding and autonomy. Relaxing one's wall prematurely (before one's boundary is sufficiently articulated) produces the embeddedness (nonautonomous bonding) characteristic of Position A. Keeping the wall rigid when that is no longer appropriate (when one's boundary is no longer diffuse) produces the disengagement (nonbonded autonomy) of Position C.

Mahler et al. (1975) provided early childhood examples of A and C pathologies. An example of A is the process of "shadowing" (pp. 133–137), where the child does not let the mother out of his or her sight. The C pathology is exemplified by "darting away" (pp. 133–137), where the toddler continuously runs away from mother, perhaps in an attempt to induce her to chase the child (see Gobes, 1985, for a good discussion of abandonment and engulfment issues).

Both of these positions are narcissistic in the Kohutian sense (Kohut, 1971)— the A position reflecting "idealizing narcissism" ("you are perfect, but I am part of you") (p. 27) and the C position "mirroring narcissism" ("I am perfect") (p. 27). Each position in itself is probably organized at the neurotic level. However, the imbalance of these two polarized positions may produce a tendency to oscillate on either individuation or attachment alone or on both dimensions. Alternation between fusion and isolation in one dimension is characteristic of personalities organized at the borderline level $[A/C]_{IND}$ and $[A/C]_{ATT}$. The first type has been described by Meissner (1984) as the depressive borderline subtype and the second as the paranoid subtype. Finally, oscillation on both dimensions may result in total psychotic splitting between fusion and isolation $[A/C]_{TOT}$, producing constant irreconcilable pressures in both directions.

The distinction between these two axes also should be true for couples. A young couple may become more capable of intimacy with one another as they become certain of themselves. However, *forward regression* (i.e., regression in level in the service of an advance in stage) to a more advanced life style may make the two partners temporarily more defensive. Each position may be healthy at a given point in development. For example, rigid walls (nonbonding) may be necessary to defend diffuse boundaries (nonautonomy). However, the immaturity of BB is preferable to the pathology of a relationship on the AC axis. In contrast, the development of articulated boundaries (autonomy) can allow the possibility of more permeable walls (bonding). In other words, nonbonding is replaced in healthy development by autonomy (BB → EE → DD).

This developmental axis is presented in Figure 6-1. It represents the development of a couple from a state of falling in love to loving. Cell BB is the first level (falling in love) of couple development, with neither party having the capacity for individuation or attachment (i.e., impermeable walls around inarticulated boundaries). Cell EE is the second level (learning to love); both partners are now semiindividuated and semiattached (i.e., moderate walls around moderate boundaries). Cell DD is the third level (loving) of couple development, where both parties have the capacity for both individuation and attachment (i.e., permeable walls around articulated boundaries). Although not represented on the axis, Cell BD is a mixed-stage couple, with one member (D) playing the parent and one playing the child.

The clinical AC axis in Figure 6-2 is quite different. It represents oscillation between enmeshment (A) and disengagement (C). AA represents an enmeshed couple type, CC a disengaged couple type, and AC a rejection–intrusion couple type. All of these positions are neurotic. $[A/C]_{IND}[A/C]_{IND}$, $[A/C]_{ATT}[A/C]_{ATT}$,

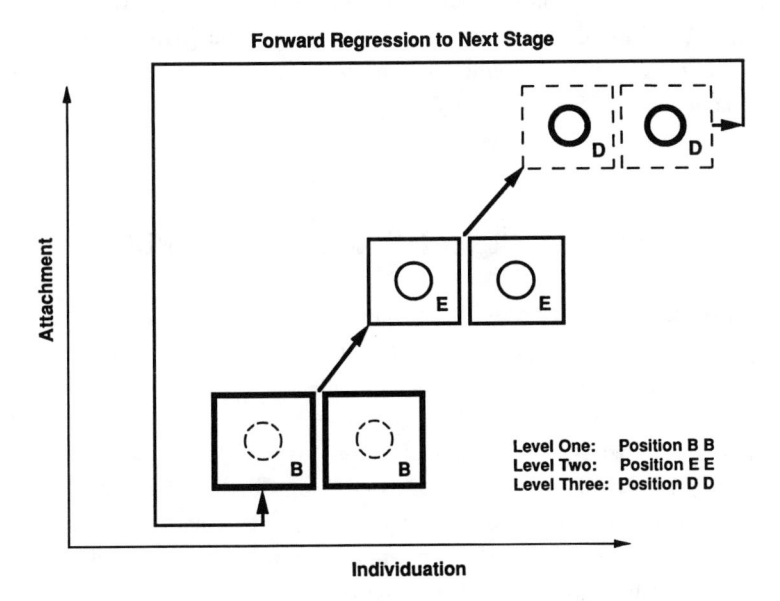

TILT for Couples: Helping Couples Grow Together   125

Figure 6-1   The couple development axis.

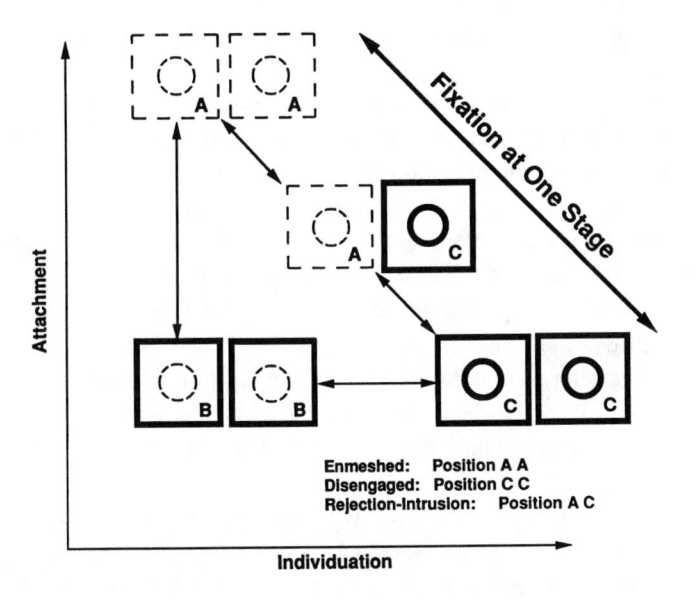

Figure 6-2   The couple pathological axis.

and $[A/C]_{IND}[A/C]_{ATT}$ represent borderline couple types and $[A/C]_{TOT}[A/C]_{TOT}$ a psychotic type. Only the neurotic couple types are specifically represented on the AC axis per se. I will return to these two axes later in this chapter as TILT couple therapy is developed. Let us initially analyze these couple types in terms of need and fear energy.

NEED AND FEAR ENERGY IN COUPLES

Analysis of need and fear energy for couples is parallel to that developed previously for individuals in chapter 3 of this book. However, now the application will be applied to couples rather than to individuals. For simplicity, disregard gender here, denoting one member of the couple as P_1 and the other as P_2. Each of the partners may occupy the various cohesion positions discussed previously. I make several admittedly oversimplified assumptions. First, relationships between a healthy and a pathological partner will not survive. Thus, this discussion is limited to couples with two healthy partners or two pathological partners. Second, pathological couples will remain together only if partners are at the same level of pathology (e.g., two neurotics, two borderlines, or two psychotics.) Finally, healthy couple relationships will survive only if the two partners are at the same level of development (for example, BB, EE, or DD.) I will comment specifically on one interesting exception to this rule—what I call a parent-child (DB) relationship.

Consider first the developmental BED axis. The *regressed* BB couple is portrayed in Figure 6-3. The energy of both members of the couple is invested exclusively in fear, both of individuation and attachment, without expressing need in either direction.

Let us now turn to the *emerging* EE couple (see Figure 6-4). Here both members of the couple have resolved their fears of both individuation and attachment. However, they have not yet developed to the point of asserting healthy needs.

Now consider the *advanced* DD couple type. Here both members of the couple have developed healthy needs for individuation and attachment in addition to having resolved their fears with regard to these two issues. As such, each partner demonstrates the capacity for both individuation and attachment (see Figure 6-5).

Finally consider the mixed level DB type. The D partner is invested in needs while the B partner is fear-dominated. This relationship may not be stable, but it may exist for a certain length of time in terms of a *parent-child* bond (see Figure 6-6).

B

B

FI = Fear of Individuation   NI = Need for Individuation
NA = Need for Attachment   FA = Fear of Attachment

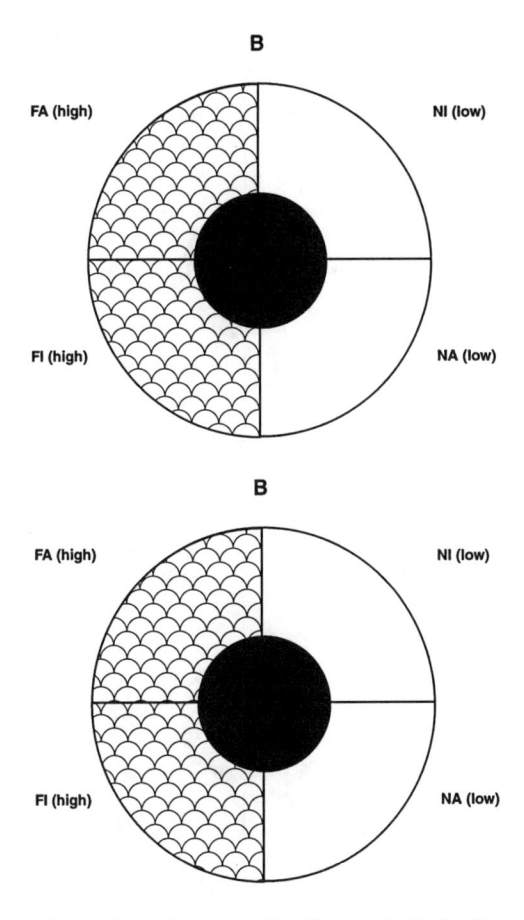

Figure 6-3   BB couple.

What is true in all of these developmental positions is that each partner maintains his or her own balance between individuality and attachment. A partner may be fear-dominated on both dimensions or neither, or may be need-dominated on both or neither, but this pattern is similar for individuation and attachment. As we shall see below, this does not necessarily apply to partners in clinical couple types.

Let us first consider the new couples types: AA, CC, AC. In the *enmeshed* AA couple, both partners display an imbalance in needs and fears. They are polarized in the direction of attachment at the expense of individuation. Each partner displays

128 *TILT for Couples and Families*

E

FA (low) NI (low)

FI (low) NA (low)

E

FA (low)) NI (low)

FI (low) NA (low)

FI = Fear of Individuation   NI = Need for Individuation
NA = Need for Attachment   FA = Fear of Attachment

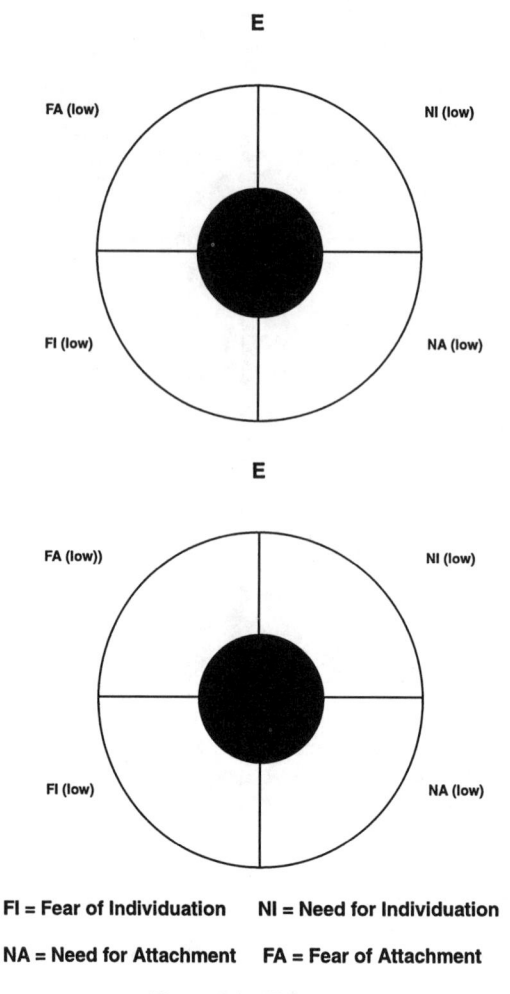

Figure 6-4 EE couple.

a high need of and low fear of attachment and simultaneously low need of and high fear of individuation (see Figure 6-7).

Couples in the disengaged CC position show a polarized imbalance in the direction of individuation. Each partner displays a high need of and low fear of individuation. At the same time, each partner displays a low need of and high fear of attachment (see Figure 6-8).

The *rejection-intrusion* AC couple represents a complementary process between the two partners. Although the A partner is imbalanced toward attachment and the C partner toward individuation (see Figure 6-9), on the couple level they show a

TILT for Couples: Helping Couples Grow Together 129

FI = Fear of Individuation   NI = Need for Individuation
NA = Need for Attachment   FA = Fear of Attachment

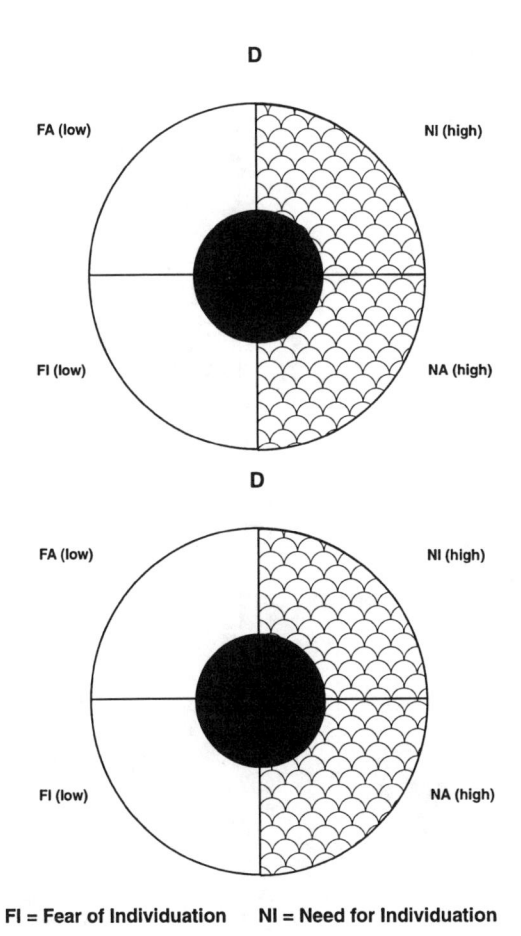

Figure 6-5   DD couple.

balance between these two issues. This may explain the particular durability of this couple type.

We now turn to an examination of the three borderline couple types: [A/C]$_{IND}$ [A/C]$_{IND}$, [A/C]$_{ATT}$[A/C]$_{ATT}$, and [A/C]$_{IND}$[A/C]$_{ATT}$. In the *depressive borderline* [A/C]$_{IND}$[A/C]$_{IND}$ couples, the two partners each show conflict between needs and fears with regard to individuation but not to attachment. In other words, each partner shows a high need and a high fear of individuation and a low need and a low fear of attachment (see Figure 6-10).

The two partners in the *paranoid borderline* [A/C]$_{ATT}$[A/C]$_{ATT}$ couple each show conflict between needs and fears with regard to attachment but not to

130 TILT for Couples and Families

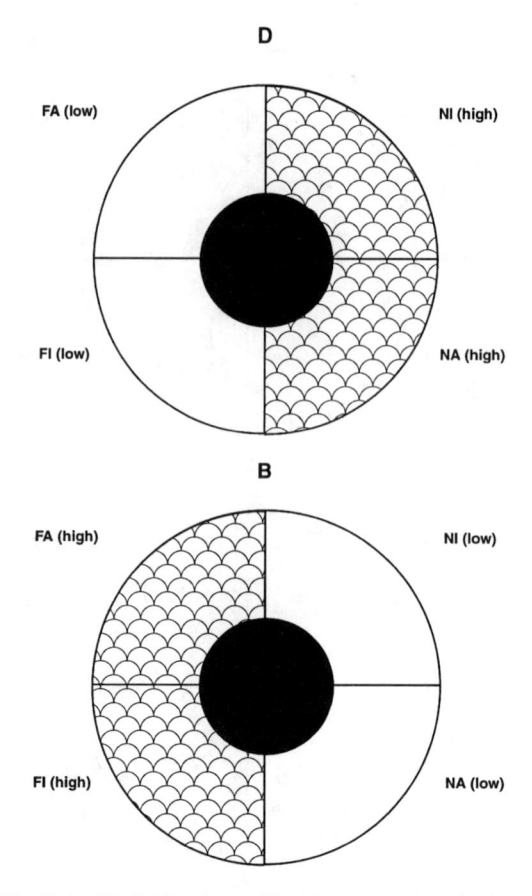

D

FA (low)   NI (high)

FI (low)   NA (high)

B

FA (high)   NI (low)

FI (high)   NA (low)

FI = Fear of Individuation   NI = Need for Individuation
NA = Need for Attachment   FA = Fear of Attachment

Figure 6-6   DB couple.

individuation. In other words, each partner shows a high need and a high fear of attachment and a low need and a low fear of individuation (see Figure 6-11).

In the *mixed borderline* $[A/C]_{IND}[A/C]_{ATT}$ couple type, the two partners show a complementary pattern. The $[A/C]_{IND}$ partner shows conflict with regard to individuation and the $[A/C]_{ATT}$ partner with regard to attachment. This couple pattern seems to distribute the conflict across the two partners in the couple, giving this couple type a certain cohesiveness (see Figure 6-12).

The partners in the *psychotic* $[A/C]_{TOT}[A/C]_{TOT}$ couple each show conflict with regard to both individuation and attachment. Each partner shows high needs and high fears with regard to both individuation and attachment (see Figure 6-13).

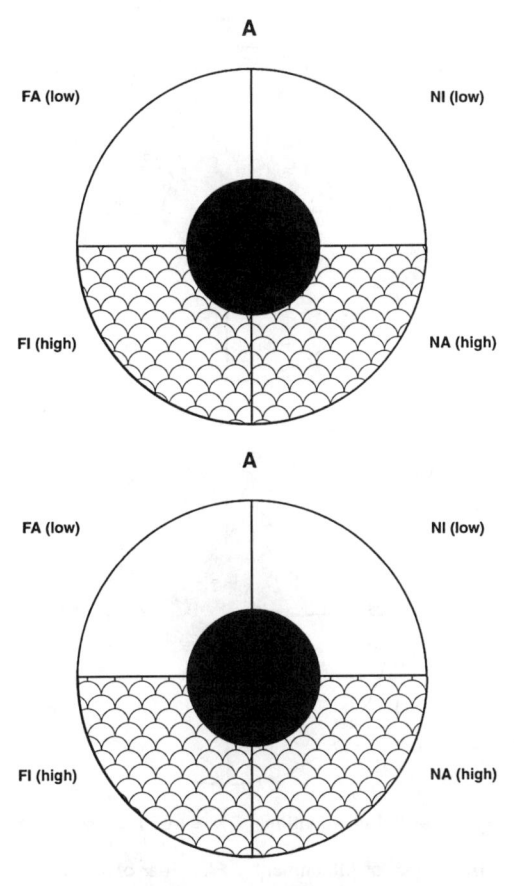

TILT for Couples: Helping Couples Grow Together 131

A

FA (low)   NI (low)

FI (high)   NA (high)

A

FA (low)   NI (low)

FI (high)   NA (high)

FI = Fear of Individuation   NI = Need for Individuation
NA = Need for Attachment   FA = Fear of Attachment

Figure 6-7 AA couple.

COHESION AND COUPLE TYPE: A BIDIMENSIONAL DISTANCING ANALYSIS

Another problem emerges when the attempt is made to extend an individual psychological model to couples and families. It is terminological. Simply, therapists who work with individuals typically use different terms from those used by marriage and family therapists. For example, the former might speak of narcissistic, borderline, and psychotic pathology, whereas the latter describe marriages and families as enmeshed, disengaged, or as rejection–intrusion types. The language

132 TILT *for Couples and Families*

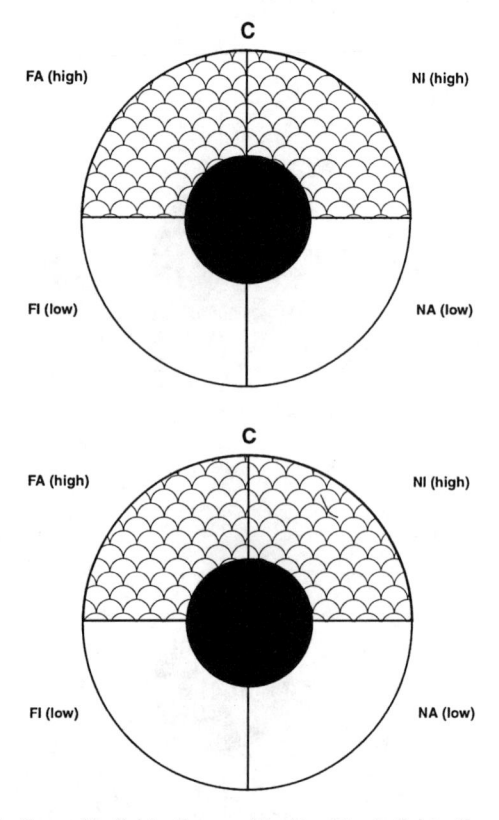

FI = Fear of Individuation   NI = Need for Individuation
NA = Need for Attachment   FA = Fear of Attachment

Figure 6-8   CC couple.

system introduced in this section is aimed at bridging this gap by using the same interpersonal distancing terms to characterize individual and couple positions.

Individual Distancing Patterns

In Chapter 3, individual distancing patterns were presented to the right of the respective positions (Table 3-1 and Figures 3-9 through 3-16). Persons with different capacities for bonding and autonomy should be expected to react differentially to invariant approach and withdrawal probes on the part of a hypothetical other. For simplicity, the "focal person" is represented as P and the "other" as O.

The developmental axis. Let us first consider the healthy BED axis in Figure 2-1 and Table 3-1. Positions B, E, and D differ in maturity. B is immature, E is

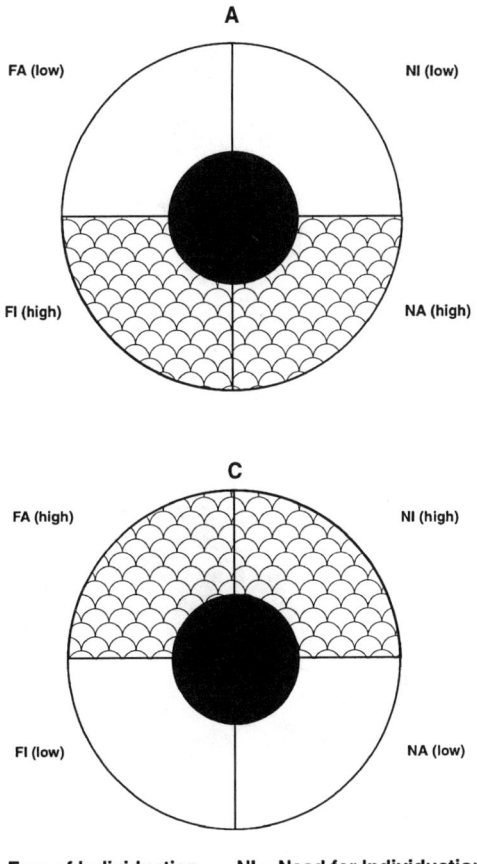

TILT *for Couples: Helping Couples Grow Together* 133

A

FA (low)   NI (low)

FI (high)   NA (high)

C

FA (high)   NI (high)

FI (low)   NA (low)

FI = Fear of Individuation   NI = Need for Individuation
NA = Need for Attachment   FA = Fear of Attachment

Figure 6-9   AC couple.

semimature or emergent, and D is mature. A P in Position B is "immature" in that he or she is unable to be either bonded or autonomous and will thus block overtures of both approach and withdrawal on the part of O. O's approaches are likely to elicit fears of attachment, with P withdrawing in response. O's withdrawals, in contrast, may elicit fears of individuation, with P approaching in response. In position E, P is semimature. He or she is moderately bonded and moderately autonomous and characterized as emergent. As such, he or she is likely to remain stationary in response to both approach and withdrawal on the part of O. Finally, the D position describes a "mature" P who has the capacity for both high bonding and high autonomy. He or she should thus respond to O's overtures of approach with

134   *TILT for Couples and Families*

Figure 6-10 (A/C)_{INDIVIDUATION} (A/C)_{INDIVIDUATION} couple.

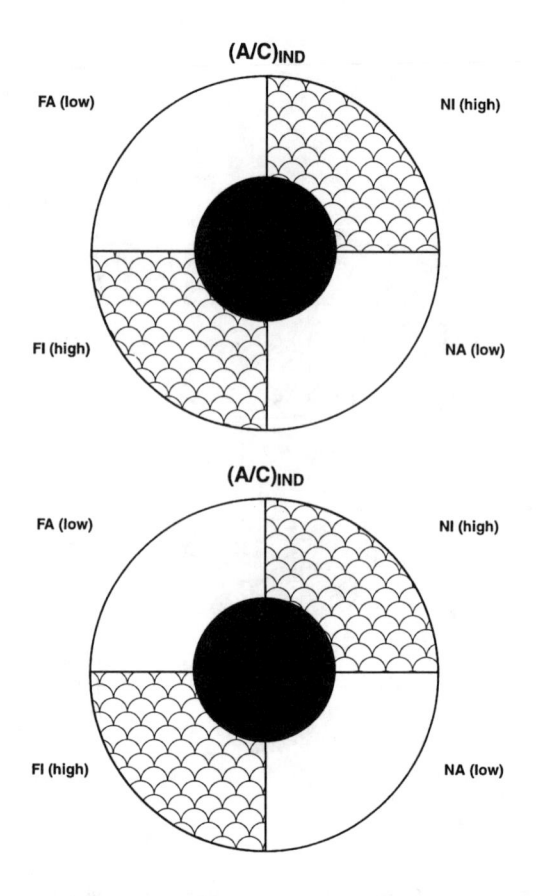

FI = Fear of Individuation   NI = Need for Individuation
NA = Need for Attachment   FA = Fear of Attachment

his or her own approach, and O's overtures of withdrawal with his or her own withdrawal.

The clinical axis. Now consider the Clinical AC axis in Figure 2-2 and Table 3-1. First consider the neurotic A (enmeshed) and C (disengaged) positions. In Position A, P has a fear of individuation but a need for attachment. As such, he or she should match O's approach overtures, but block those of withdrawal. This results in a noncontingent approach (enmeshed) pattern, with P approaching regardless of the direction of O's initial distance move. In position C, in contrast, P has a need for individuation but a fear of attachment. As such, he or she should match O's withdrawal overtures but attempt to block those of approach. This results in a

TILT for Couples: Helping Couples Grow Together   *135*

Figure 6-11 (A/C)_{ATTACHMENT} (A/C)_{ATTACHMENT} couple.

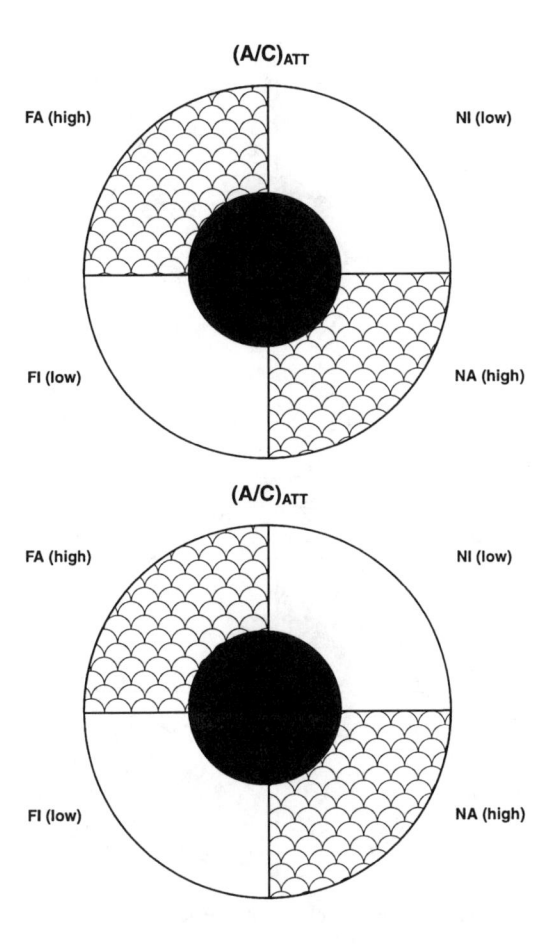

FI = Fear of Individuation   NI = Need for Individuation
NA = Need for Attachment   FA = Fear of Attachment

noncontingent avoidance (disengaged) pattern, with P withdrawing regardless of the direction of O's initial distance move. Both of these patterns are characterized as neurotic.

Now let us consider the two borderline positions [A/C]$_{IND}$ and [A/C]$_{ATT}$. The first borderline type represents the depressive position and the second, the paranoid position. The [A/C]$_{IND}$ position reflects a P who is indifferent with regard to attachment or bonding, having neither needs nor fears of it, but highly ambivalent with regard to individuation or autonomy, simultaneously needing it and fearing it. Thus, a P in this position should remain stationary in response to O's approach.

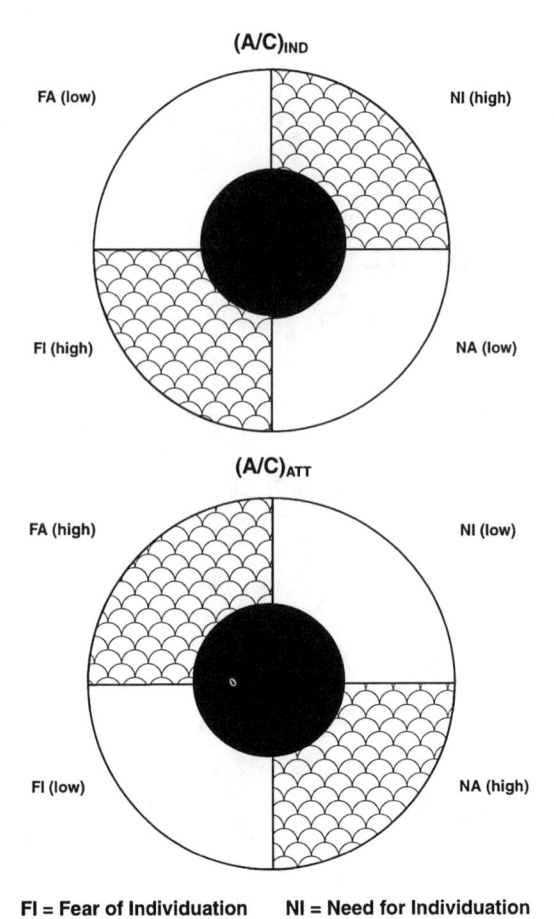

(A/C)_{IND}

FA (low)   NI (high)

FI (high)   NA (low)

(A/C)_{ATT}

FA (high)   NI (low)

FI (low)   NA (high)

FI = Fear of Individuation   NI = Need for Individuation
NA = Need for Attachment   FA = Fear of Attachment

Figure 6-12 (A/C)_{INDIVIDUATION} (A/C)_{ATTACHMENT} couple.

However, with regard to O's withdrawal, P should show a conflicted response pattern, simultaneously pushing closer and pulling away.

The [A/C]_{ATT} position displays the opposite pattern. Here P is ambivalent with regard to attachment and indifferent with respect to individuation. He or she should show conflicted responses toward any approach probe on the part of O. P may vacillate back and forth, simultaneously pulling forwards (reflecting a need for attachment) and pushing backwards (reflecting a fear of attachment). In contrast, P should remain stationary in response to O's withdrawal, neither needing individuation nor fearing it. Individuation is simply not much of an issue for a person in this position.

TILT for Couples: Helping Couples Grow Together 137

(A/C)_{TOT}

FA (high)   NI (high)

FI (high)   NA (high)

(A/C)_{TOT}

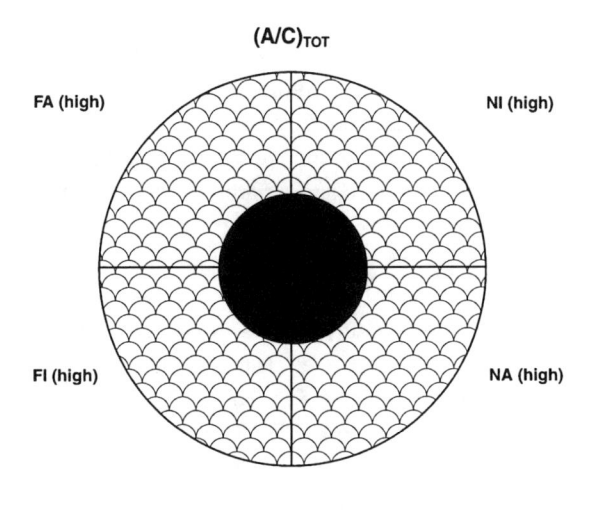

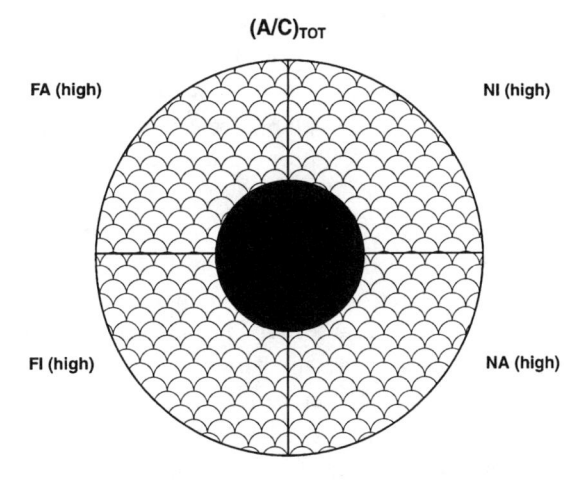

FA (high)   NI (high)

FI (high)   NA (high)

FI = Fear of Individuation   **NI = Need for Individuation**
NA = Need for Attachment   **FA = Fear of Attachment**

Figure 6-13 (A/C)$_{TOTAL}$ (A/C)$_{TOTAL}$ couple.

Finally, consider the psychotic position [A/C]$_{TOT}$. An individual in this position is ambivalent with regard to both autonomy and bonding, having high needs and high fears toward both individuation and attachment. A P in this position will show conflicted pushes and pulls toward any probe on the part of O, whether it be approach or withdrawal. In other words, an individual in this position should be in a constant state of approach–avoidance conflict.

Couple Distancing Patterns

Once again, gender is disregarded, denoting one member of the couple as P_1 and the second as P_2. Each of the partners may occupy the various cohesion positions discussed previously. I reemphasize my admittedly oversimplified assumptions. First, marriages between a healthy and a pathological partner will not survive. Thus, this discussion is limited to couples with two healthy partners or two pathological partners. Second, pathological couples will remain together only if partners are at the same level of pathology (e.g., two neurotics, two borderlines, or two psychotics). Finally, marriages of healthy couples will survive only if the two partners are at the same level of development (for example, BB, EE, or DD). Again, I will comment specifically on one interesting exception to this final rule, what I call a compensating or a parent-child couple (DB). These couple patterns are presented in Figure 6-14.

The developmental axis. Let us first consider the developmental couple types (BB, EE, DD, and DB) presented in Figure 6-14. One of the peculiarities of beginning a relationship is that it forwardly regresses separately mature individuals into a temporarily immature BB state. This is the "falling in love" state experienced by new lovers. The present analysis diagnoses them as rushing together in a mutual flight from autonomy. Each may feel liberated from aloneness; however, neither is secure enough in himself or herself to tolerate genuine intimacy. Each loves his or her idealization of the other. Together they engage in a *regressed (immature) reciprocal* relationship, conflict emerging when the partners in the couple get too intimate with each other or too remote (see Figure 6-15). Each of the parties maintains an impermeable wall because his or her boundary is not yet articulated.[2]

Position EE represents the second stage of healthy couple development, moving past the falling-in-love state. Now each partner is semiindividuated and semiattached. Neither fears nor needs either bonding or autonomy. Each is in a half-way position on all fronts and may be characterized as emergent. Together they engage in what appears to be a static relationship, neither partner desiring too much intimacy or too much space (see Figure 6-16). This is called an *emerging reciprocal* or *holding* relationship.[3]

Position DD represents the third stage of healthy couple development. Finally the partners have come to love each other as the other really is. This position represents two mature, highly individuated and attached partners, who need both bonding and autonomy. As such, they will engage in an *advanced (mature)*

---

[2] This is similar to the "symbiotic–symbiotic" couple type described by Bader and Pearson (1983, p. 30).

[3] This is similar to the "practicing–practicing" couple subtype described by Bader and Pearson (1983, p. 31).

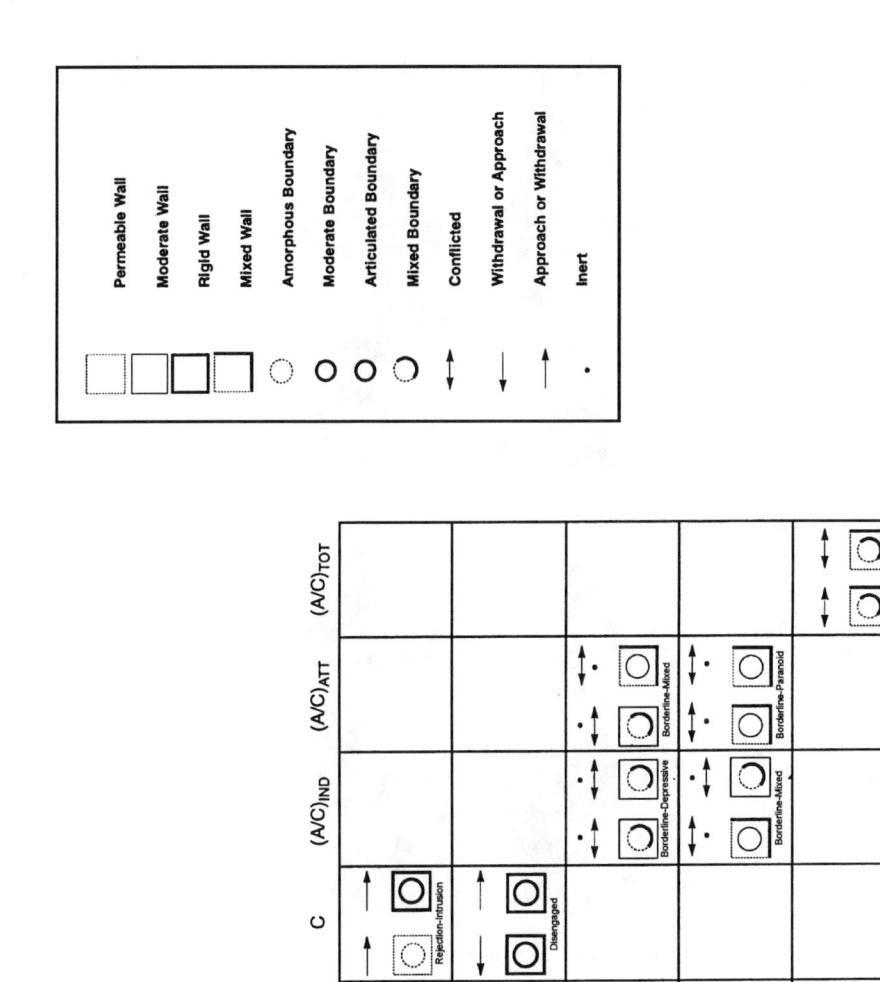

Figure 6-14 Couple distancing patterns.

Figure 6-15 BB: regressed reciprocal couple.

reciprocal relationship in which they coordinate mutual desires for intimacy ("we-ness") and space ("I-ness") (see Figure 6-17). Walls become permeable with more articulated boundaries.[4]

Position DB represents a parent-child relationship. One partner (the D) in each relationship is mature—at the third level of development; the other (the B) is immature—at the first level. D will offer bonding and autonomy; B will block both. The result is a compensatory pattern (see Figure 6-18). The less mature B partner will block the more mature partner's offers of either bonding or autonomy.[5]

---

[4] This describes the "mutual interdependence–mutual interdependence" subtype described by Bader and Pearson (1983, p. 31).

[5] This is similar to the "symbiotic–practicing" couple type described by Bader and Pearson (1983, p. 31).

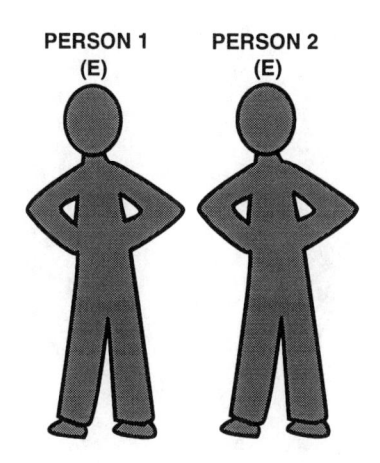

Figure 6-16 EE: energetic, reciprocal couple.

All other possible healthy couples involve one partner who is at Position E and the other at either Position B or D (either BE or DE). Such a pairing will invariably produce a noncontingent indifferent pattern and, as such, is not specifically delineated in Figure 6-2.

The clinical axis. Consider now the purely clinical types in Figure 6-2. First, there is the neurotic level of pathology: couples consisting of two As, two Cs, or one of each. In Position AA, both parties are afraid of autonomy but not of bonding (i.e., they are attached but not individuated). Gobes (1985) described these individuals as having abandonment issues. Minuchin (1974, p. 54) calls this an *enmeshed* or *embedded* relationship, conflict emerging when the parties in the couple become too remote from each other (see Figure 6-19). Each party's wall is too permeable to protect his or her inarticulated underlying boundaries, and each is looking for the omnipotent other to save him or her from himself or herself (i.e., they are both idealizing narcissists [Kohut, 1971]).

In Position CC, both parties are afraid of bonding but not of autonomy (i.e., they are individuated but not attached). Each has engulfment issues (Gobes, 1985). As such, they will engage in what Minuchin (1974, p. 54) calls a *disengaged* or *isolated* relationship, conflict emerging when the parties in the couple become too intimate with each other (see Figure 6-20). Each party maintains an impermeable wall around an articulated boundary, and each has an overly grandiose sense of self (i.e., both are mirroring narcissists).

Position AC represents what Napier (1978, p. 11) labeled a *"rejection-intrusion"* relationship and what Willi (1982, p. 76) called a *"narcissistic collusion."* One person, C, is the mirroring narcissist, afraid of entrapment and engulfment (Gobes, 1985) by his/her partner and looking to become the ideal self of the partner.

Figure 6-17 DD: advanced reciprocal couple.

The other person, A, in contrast, is the idealizing narcissist, afraid of individual responsibility and abandonment (Gobes, 1985) by the other partner and looking for a substitute self in that partner. The C partner is so grandiose because the A partner is effusively adoring. In behavioral terms, the A partner continually approaches (desires a "we-ness") and the C continually avoids (wants an "I-ness") (see Figure 6-21).

Now let us consider the borderline level of pathology: couples consisting of two $[A/C]_{IND}$s, two $[A/C]_{ATT}$s, or one of each. In couple type $[A/C]_{IND}[A/C]_{IND}$, both parties can be characterized as depressive borderlines and the relationship as a *depressive borderline* relationship. Each is ambivalent regarding individuation and indifferent regarding attachment. If the attachment issue is evoked, both parties will remain stationary, showing neither needs nor fears. However, if the individuation

TILT for Couples: Helping Couples Grow Together 143

Figure 6-18 DB: compensatory couple.

issue is evoked, both parties will show highly conflicted and vacillating responses, reflecting their needs and their fears. They will simultaneously show pushes toward each other and pulls away from each other (see Figure 6-22).

Now let us consider couple type [A/C]$_{ATT}$[A/C]$_{ATT}$, two paranoid borderlines engaged in a *paranoid borderline* relationship. Here, both parties are indifferent regarding individuation and ambivalent regarding attachment. If the individuation issue is evoked, both parties will remain stationary. However, if attachment is evoked, the ambivalent needs and fears of each partner will be reflected in conflict between approach and withdrawal (see Figure 6-23).

The above two couple types, then, will vacillate between mutual equanimity and conflict, dependent on whether issues of attachment or individuation are evoked. Consider, in contrast, a *mixed borderline* couple type of one depressive borderline

144 *TILT for Couples and Families*

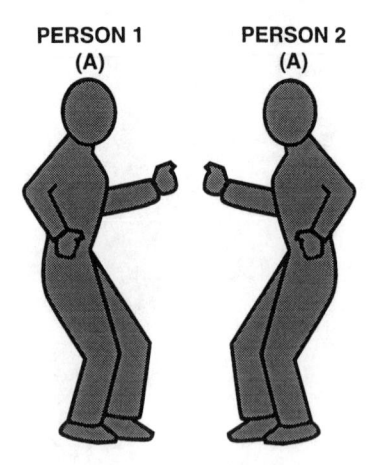

Figure 6-19 AA: enmeshed couple.

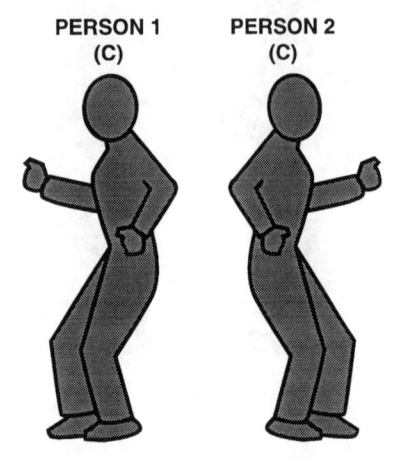

Figure 6-20 CC: disengaged couple.

and one paranoid borderline: $[A/C]_{IND}[A/C]_{ATT}$. If the attachment issue is evoked, the $[A/C]_{ATT}$ partner will show conflicted pushes and pulls while the $[A/C]_{IND}$ partner will remain stationary. If the individuation issue is evoked, in contrast, it is the $[A/C]_{ATT}$ partner who will remain stationary while the $[A/C]_{IND}$ partner shows conflicted vacillation. In either case, one partner will always be in conflict and the other will show equanimity (see Figure 6-24).

Finally, let us consider a *psychotic* couple: $[A/C]_{TOT}[A/C]_{TOT}$. Here both parties are mutually conflicted, whether the issue involves individuation or attachment. In other words, this relationship will be continuously chaotic, with each partner continuously in conflict (see Figure 6-25).

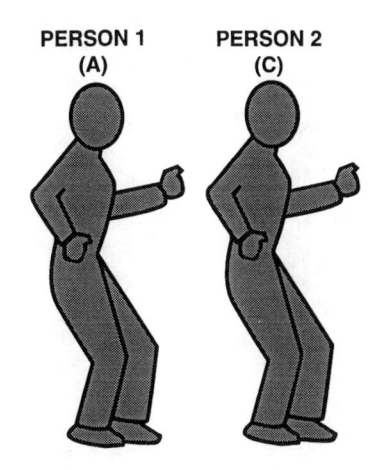

Figure 6-21 AC: rejection–intrusion couple.

TILT FOR COUPLES: A PROGRAM FOR RESPONSIVE COUPLE GROWTH

A Model for Couples

This chapter has been insistent on a bidimensional definition of cohesion that represents health as a separate developmental axis rather than as a moderate position on an essentially pathological unidimensional axis. Several examples can illustrate this distinction for couples. Carole complains that Michael goes out too much with friends on his time off from work (the entire weekend). Michael complains that Carole wants him to spend all his spare time with her (leaving him no time on the weekend to go his own way). A unidimensional therapist may see both parties as pathological—Carole as enmeshed (high bonding, low autonomy) and Michael as disengaged (low bonding, high autonomy). The therapist might hammer out a practical compromise (moderate bonding, moderate autonomy) allowing Michael and Carole one day on their own each weekend and one day together. However, this solution does not really address the underlying problem. In contrast, the bidimensional therapeutic goal is to restructure the situation to enable both Carole and Michael to express their respective identities in the company of the other.

In another example Dan complains that he feels exploited because he has spent too much time (6 hours) looking for a present for Judy, and he resents her for it. However, on a prior occasion he felt guilty and selfish for spending only a half-hour looking for a present. A unidimensional perspective might view Dan's behavior on the first occasion as disengaged (Position C) and on the second occasion as

Figure 6-22 (A/C)$_{IND}$ (A/C)$_{IND}$: borderline depressive couple.

enmeshed (Position A), with a potential solution simply to spend a middle ground of 3.25 hours looking for a present for Judy. In contrast, a bidimensional perspective would focus on the more basic question of what it means for Dan to feel exploited. Perhaps he could create a personal gift for Judy that would represent a deep expression of himself, with the time it took to make the gift simultaneously representing individuation and attachment.

With both of these couples, a unidimensional therapeutic goal might be to achieve an EE resolution to an AC conflict. However, a bidimensional goal ultimately involves the potential for a DD relationship, even if the couple must initially regress to BB. Problems such as these have prompted the application of

TILT for Couples: Helping Couples Grow Together 147

Figure 6-23 $(A/C)_{ATT}$ $(A/C)_{ATT}$: borderline paranoid couple.

TILT to couples. The outlines of this program emerge in the multistage, multilevel approach to couple growth already presented in Figures 6-1 and 6-2.

Three aspects of this approach should be emphasized. First, there is no route between any position on the AC axis and Cell DD. Cells AA, CC, and AC represent dead ends in terms of moving ahead. The only possibility for growth involves regression back to Cell BB and coordinated advance through Cell EE to Cell DD. Second, the attainment of Cell DD (Level 3) at one level opens up the possibility of forward regression to a more advanced stage. However, this more advanced stage must be entered at BB (Level 1)—that is, the beginning—and the process must be undergone again. Third, all of these moves involve coordination of the two partners

Figure 6-24 $(A/C)_{ATT}$ $(A/C)_{IND}$: borderline mixed couple.

or the couple will disintegrate. For example, the regression of two A persons, two C persons, or one A person and one C person to B must be coordinated, just as must be their advance to E and then to D and finally their reentry at Cell B at a more advanced stage.

The logic underlying this approach is that healthy couple growth involves the coordinated and graduated replacement of interpersonal walls by self–other boundaries. Taking the walls down prematurely (i.e., before the boundaries are strong enough)—as in AA—or leaving them up too long (i.e., after the boundaries have already formed)—as in CC— leads to the respective pathological outcomes of embedded and isolated structures. Splitting these dysfunctions according to stereotyped male and female socialization (male C and female A) leads to the narcissistic

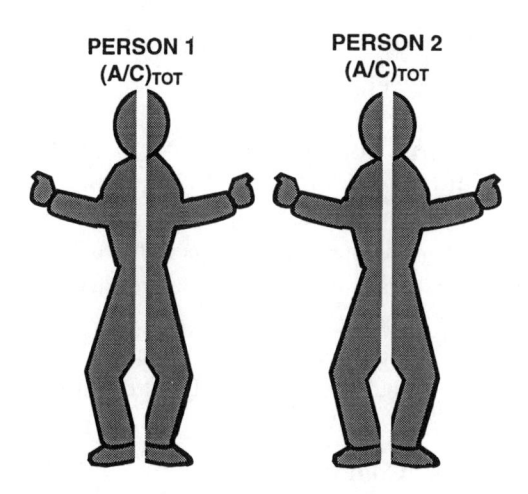

Figure 6-25 $(A/C)_{TOT}$ $(A/C)_{TOT}$: psychotic couple.

collusion of the AC relationship where the idealizing wife (A) intrudes and the mirroring husband (C) rejects. The unsatisfactory aspects of the more severe AC couple pathologies speak for themselves and will not be discussed further here. It is clear that only unsatisfactory oscillations and collusions are possible for couples on the AC axis unless both partners are regressed back to the BB position and TILTed forward on the BED axis in an integrated, coordinated, and noncollusive manner.

Some implications of this model are quite disturbing. The striving of many couples on the AC axis to escape their positions may simply change or reverse the nature of the collusion, bringing neither member of the couple closer to the D position (individuated attachment). For example, the enmeshed AA couple (deindividuated attachment) striving for individuation is likely to flip into the equally unsatisfactory isolated CC position. Likewise, the isolated CC couple (detached individuation) is likely to flip into the equally unsatisfactory enmeshed AA position. A similar flip may occur between the depressive borderline $[A/C]_{IND}[A/C]_{IND}$ couple (conflict on individuation) and the paranoid borderline $[A/C]_{ATT}[A/C]_{ATT}$ couple (conflict on attachment.)

Finally, in the rejection–intrusion AC couple the liberation of a traditional enmeshed female partner (A) may flip her into the C position; likewise, the liberation of the traditional isolated male partner (C) may flip him into the A position. This is exactly the finding of Neugarten and Gutmann (1958) on midlife shifts in sex roles. The A and C positions are simply reversed without solving the basic collusion; individuation is achieved at the expense of attachment and vice versa. A similar reversal may be expected between the two partners in the mixed borderline $[A/C]_{IND}[A/C]_{ATT}$ couple. A depressive borderline female partner $[A/C]_{IND}$ may flip into the paranoid borderline position and a paranoid borderline male partner $[A/C]_{ATT}$ may flip into the depressive borderline position without any real solution to the basic collusion.

Finally, a psychotic $[A/C]_{TOT}[A/C]_{TOT}$ may be completely trapped unless it finds some way of TILTing off of the AC axis and getting reoriented ahead on the BED axis. This, of course, is true of all of the examples given of couples on the AC axis. However, this therapy requires a coordinated regression from a more advanced level on the AC axis to a more primitive level on the BED axis (BB), and to the then sometimes frustratingly slow progression through Level EE to Level DD, and finally, after Level DD has been attained, a willingness to advance to a more complicated stage with the regression to Level BB that such growth entails.

The Goals of TILT for Couples

The TILT program has four goals: (1) regression of a couple off of the AC collusive axis back to BB, (2) integrated progression through EE to DD, (3) forward regression to BB at the next advanced stage, and (4) coordination between the two members of a couple at each of the above points.

Regression. It is no easy task to convince a couple on the AC axis to give up the quick fix of full attachment (A) or individuation (C) to return to the seemingly hopeless BB position. The allure of the AC relationship is especially difficult to give up. Yet, this is exactly what TILT requires. A persons must temporarily put up walls, and C persons must temporarily eliminate their boundaries. Therapeutic interventions designed to foster this process include, in an AA couple, encouraging both people to disengage from overconcern about their partners' problems. In a CC couple both members are encouraged to loosen their hyperidentities. In an AC couple, the A member is encouraged to disengage from overinvolvement with the partner, and the C member is encouraged to loosen his or her hyperidentity. The following examples illustrate these points by the neurotic couples portrayed in Figure 6-2.

The AA couple. Mr. and Ms. A present with mutual complaints regarding a lack of space in the relationship. They each feel smothered by the demands of the other. The therapist does not, at this point, advise the partners to begin to assert their identities. If either tries, he or she will go to the other extreme, isolating himself or herself from the other in the name of identity (i.e., becoming a CC couple). Instead, Mr. and Ms. A are encouraged to temporarily withdraw from one another without asserting their respective identities (i.e., regression to BB) in order to provide mutual walls that allow each to avoid the other's demands and expectations. According to the TILT program, neither Mr. or Ms. A is ready for moves in such areas as career or school. However, they are able to disconnect from one another, as frightening as this may seem to individuals in their position.

The CC couple. Mr. and Ms. C present with mutual complaints regarding a lack of intimacy in the relationship. They each feel isolated. The TILT program does not, at this point, advise either to become closer to one another. If either tries, he or she will go to the other extreme, blurring his or her sense of self in the name of intimacy (i.e., becoming an AA couple). Instead, TILT simply encourages both Mr. and Ms. C to temporarily blur their pseudoidentities without establishing intimacy with one another (i.e., regress to BB). The point is to lessen the parties' own involvement with self, creating the isolated condition while the protective walls are still maintained. Neither Mr. or Ms. C is ready for activities such as becoming more responsive to one another or taking each other's needs more into account. However, they are each able to disengage somewhat from their own concerns, as frightening as that may be to people in their condition.

The AC couple. Mr. C and Ms. A present with symptoms that fit the rejection-intrusion pattern described earlier. Mr. C feels smothered and wants more space. Ms. A feels isolated and wants more intimacy. Although the temptation is great, TILT does not at this time advise Mr. C to put himself more into the relationship and Ms. A to develop her own interests. If possible, such moves would simply reverse the roles between Mr. C and Ms. A (Mr. C becoming an A and Ms. A a C) without establishing the desired balance in either of them. Instead, TILT encourages Mr. C to temporarily blur his pseudoidentity without increasing his push toward intimacy and Ms. A to temporarily withdraw from Mr. C without asserting her own identity (i.e., attempts to regress the couple to BB). The point is to erase the oppositional set between self- and other involvement. Regression for each of them, from both the A and C positions, may provide the initial balance to make integrated individuation and attachment moves possible.

Integrated stage progression. It is not easy to convince a couple at BB to give up the immediate gratification of full attachment (AA) or full individuation (CC). It may be even harder to convince a BB couple to give up the seeming completeness of an AC relationship. The deficits of each partner are disguised by the collusion between them. Indeed, this has been the implicit contract beneath many apparently successful marriages, the individual deficits only becoming manifest when the couple disintegrates through death of one partner, divorce, or separation.

TILT discourages the immediate fix of full attachment (A) and individuation (C), instead encouraging the partners in a BB couple to each do a little bit of both (EE), which ultimately leads to full individuation and attachment for each (DD). However, this takes time and patience and must proceed one step at a time. *What is required is the selection of interpersonal behaviors that are simultaneously individuating and attaching and a couple environment that permits and supports this*. Finding such behaviors may require some creativity. Giving creatively requires compatability and a mutual redefinition of the situation. Each, for example, can use his or her talents to create a personal present for the other. Thus, as the relationship matures, a context emerges containing a repertoire of actions that are simultaneously individuating and attaching.

THE ACT OF CREATING IS INDIVIDUATING.
THE OFFERING OF THAT CREATION TO THE OTHER
IS ATTACHING.

The three major problems of this stage are: (1) giving up quick attachments (Cell A moves) and/or individuations (Cell C moves), (2) finding a repertoire of behaviors that simultaneously individuate and attach (Cell E moves), and (3) a couple environment that permits and supports this process. Such slow but integrated progress pushes a couple eventually to the DD position and involves giving up mutual walls one step at a time with graduated increases in self–other boundaries.

Forward regression. The process described above recurs throughout the life cycle for the healthy couple, at increasingly more complicated stages of development. This involves the third challenge for TILT: preparing a couple that reaches the third level (Cell DD) at Stage X to move ahead to Stage X + 1 even though this involves a regression back to the first level (Cell BB). Such moves occur often in life in a natural way in reaction to environmental stressors. For example, a couple who dated for 3 years may decide to live together, a couple used to living together may marry, and a couple may move to a new city with a faster environment. The TILT system suggests that in each of these cases the couple will experience regression in level in the process of advancing in stage. Thus, it is called forward regression. Walls become temporarily less permeable as boundaries become less articulated. The therapist's job is to encourage couples to pay attention to the "itch" that signals that they have outgrown their stage, even though they have reached a healthy level there, with impermeable walls around articulated boundaries. In their advance as a couple they will encounter environmental stressors (e.g., marriage, moving, job change) and must expect to have to erect temporary walls once again.

Coordination. The moves of the two partners in a couple must be coordinated. For example, if one partner in a BB couple moves to E; while the other jumps at the quick fix of an A or C position, the couple may disintegrate, psychologically if not physically. If one member of an AC couple is willing to regress to B while the other is not, a similar disruption may occur. Finally, if one member of a DD couple is willing to forwardly regress to level B at a more advanced stage of development while the other member is not so willing, the couple may transform into an unstable

TILT for Couples: Helping Couples Grow Together 153

and compensatory relationship (DB). The therapist must simultaneously consider the needs of the couple as well as the needs of the individual partners. To this end, the therapist must encourage each partner to pace his or her growth and regression moves and even his or her "TILT" off the axis to remain synchronous with those of the partner. Chapter 7 will present specific clinical examples of couples undergoing TILT therapy to demonstrate how this process plays out in concrete examples.

Chapter 7

Psychotherapy Illustrations for Couples

The present chapter presents actual clinical cases illustrating the different TILT couple types described in chapter 6. Let us initially consider couples falling on the developmental BED, in order of maturation. First, we examine the *regressed* BB couple type, then the *emerging* EE couple type, and finally the *advanced* DD couple. We also examine a couple falling into the mixed *parent–child* BD position.

DEVELOPMENTAL CASES

Regressed Couple Type BB: Peter and Anne

Regressed couple type BB is characterized by two partners each with high fears and low needs of individuation and attachment. Consider the case of Peter and Anne, who at the time they first entered treatment had been married for 7 years. It was the second marriage for each, both Peter and Anne having been deserted by their previous partners. Peter complained that Anne continuously bossed him around, giving him orders. She would become frustrated when he did not comply, typically withdrawing and avoiding sexual relations. Anne, in contrast, complained that her husband behaved like an overgrown adolescent, preferring to spend time with male friends rather than with her. Anne also complained that Peter preferred spending time with his son from his first marriage rather than with Anne and their daughter. Peter's initial diagnosis was dysthymic disorder (300.4) and Anne's was an Axis II diagnosis of dependent personality disorder (301.6) The responses of Peter and Anne on the IAQ indicated that there was truth to both their complaints. Both scored as Position B, having high fears of both individuation and attachment (high FI and high FA) and very low needs on both issues (low NI and low NA).

Peter, for example, showed agreement (3) with the statements "Being in close relationships often keeps one from doing what one wants to do" (high FA) and "It makes more sense to fit in than be conspicuous (high FI) but disagreement (1) with the statements "I have a great need for sharing my feelings with other people" (low

NA) and "Ultimately I have to do things my own way" (low NI). Anne showed essentially the same IAQ pattern: She agreed (3) with the statements "If I open myself to others I'll get hurt" (high FA) and "A highly responsible position is too much of a burden" (high FI). Anne disagreed (1) with the statements "The best part of parties is the chance to make new friends" (low NA) and "I express what I think even if I know my position is extremely unpopular" (low NI).

The relationship between Peter and Anne seemed inconsistent. They would be getting along at a moderate level of intimacy. As they would spend more time together, a fight would occur over what objectively seemed to be a very minor event. They then would spend a week not talking to each other and come to therapy mutually miserable. They would use the session as the basis for reconciliation. Then the whole process would begin again. From a TILT perspective, they would withdraw from each other as intimacy increased (evoking their joint fears of attachment) and approach each other as distance increased (evoking their joint fears of individuation). The goal of therapy was to move the couple ahead to Position EE on the BED dimension without having either of them run off to a quick fix solution on the AC axis.

During the course of therapy, Peter and Anne and began to overcome their fears of individuation and attachment without asserting their needs in these areas. They learned to coexist. Anne became less demanding and Peter less abandoning. At the time of this writing, they were slowly beginning to assert their needs in a more positive way. Peter learned to express his individuality within the relationship, rather than running away to his friends. Anne began to express her needs for space more directly rather than do things to drive Peter away.

The change in their IAQ responses during the course of therapy reflected this pattern. Peter now strongly disagreed (0) with the statement "Being in close relationships often keeps one from doing what one wants to do" (low FA) and was now uncertain (2) regarding the statement "It makes more sense to fit in than be conspicuous" (uncertain FI), and "Ultimately I have to do things in my own way" (uncertain NI). Peter now showed slight agreement (3) with the statement "I have a great need for sharing my feelings with other people" (high NA). Anne too showed changes. She now strongly disagreed (0) with the statements: "If I open myself to others I'll get hurt" (low FA) and "It makes more sense to fit in than to be conspicuous" (low FI). Anne now was uncertain (2) regarding the statements: "The best part of parties is the chance to make new friends" (uncertain NA) and showed mild agreement (3) with the statement: "I express what I think even if I know my position is extremely unpopular" (high NI).

In summary, the prognosis for this couple is very good. In TILT terms they have progressed from Position BB to EE and have just entered the beginning of Position DD (see Figure 7-1).

Figure 7-1 Peter and Anne.

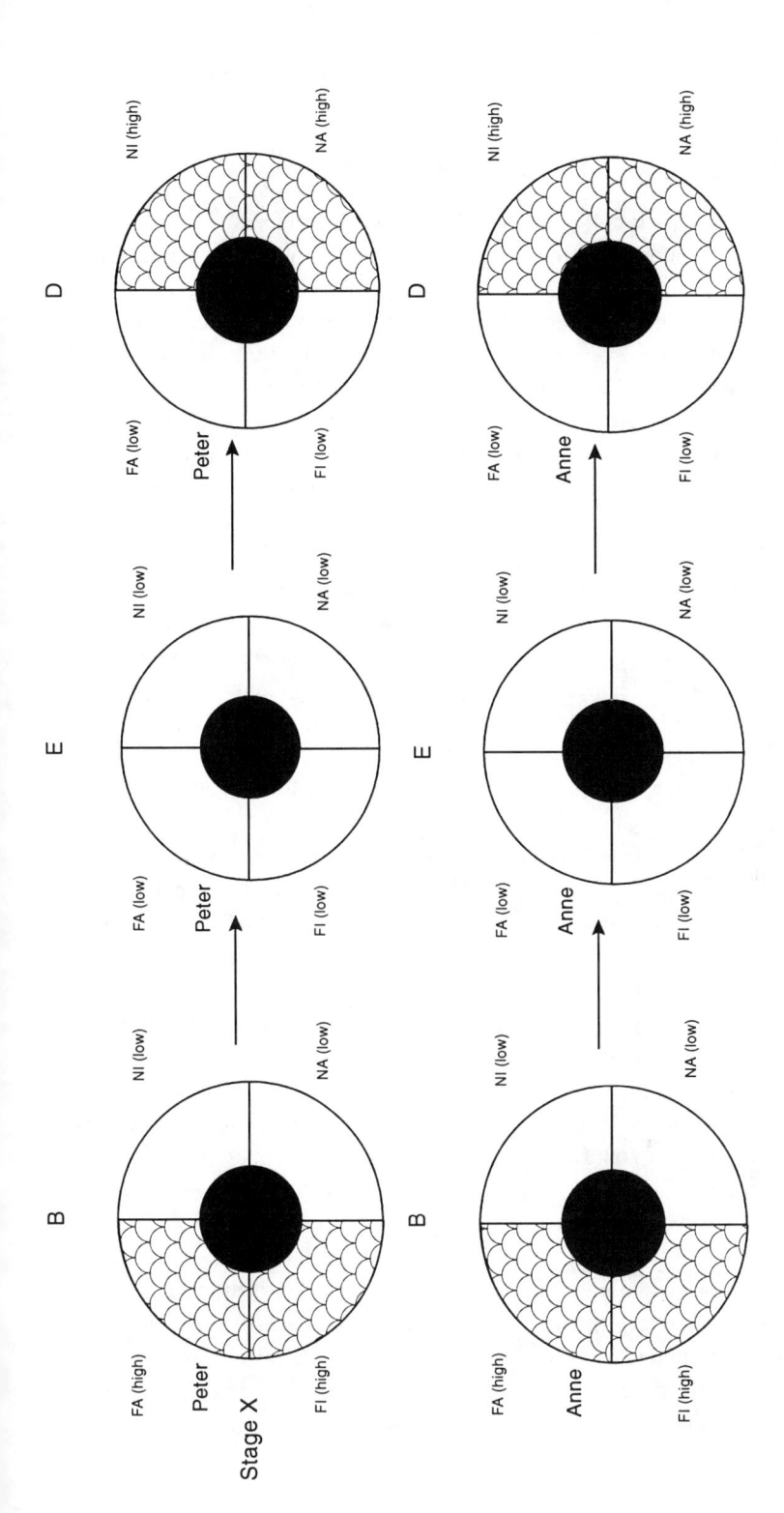

FI = Fear of Individuation NI = Need for Individuation
NA = Need for Attachment FA = Fear of Attachment

Emerging Couple Type EE: Nancy and Robert

Emerging couple type EE is characterized by low needs and fears of both individuation and attachment on the part of both members of the couple. At the time they first entered treatment, Nancy and Robert had been married for 15 years. They had two children. Nancy was 39 years old and had a history of alcoholism and depression. Much of this seemed to have been precipitated by a childlike set of expectations. Nancy had a history of being unable to follow through on her own career initiatives. For example, Nancy never finished her undergraduate degree, though she obviously was of high intelligence. She blamed her husband Robert for blocking her in her career objectives and showed resentment toward him for his involvement in his own career. Nancy's initial Axis II diagnosis was a dependent personality disorder (301.6)

Robert was a highly conscientious but somewhat moralistic man in his early forties. He was diagnosed on Axis II with an obsessive–compulsive personality disorder (301.4). Robert, an oldest son, came from a highly demanding family of origin, with parents who seemed to demand an inordinate amount of success from him. Their love for him seemed to be conditional on his success. Robert, who appeared to be a basically sensitive man, tended to sabotage his career development at various opportunities. He then tended to blame his wife for his career setbacks and kept her at arm's length while he plunged blindly ahead.

Many of these conflicts seemed to have diminished with time. Now, however, they were replaced by an eerie quiet, with Nancy and Robert each living their own private lives. While they no longer blamed each other for their failures, as they had previously, neither party felt very much in love with the other, nor especially drawn to the other's company.

Responses on the IAQ shed light on this process. Both Nancy and Robert fell into the E position showing low fears of individuation and attachment, but also low needs with regard to their two issues. For example, Nancy disagreed (1) with the statement "Love is often more trouble than it's worth" (low FA) but also disagreed (1) with the statement "You are not worth much if you are only occupied with your own concerns" (low NA). Nancy also showed indifference with regard to individuation. She disagreed (1) with the statement "It makes more sense to fit in than be conspicuous" (low FI) and with the statement "I don't hesitate to fight for my own opinions with those I am close to" (low NI). Robert showed the same essential pattern; disagreeing (0) or (1) with the statements "I believe everyone has an obligation to find their own way in life" (low NI); "I feel very secure when I have a close friend stronger than myself to rely on" (low FI); "Relating to others is essential to coming to know oneself" (low NA); and "If I open myself up to others I will get hurt" (low FA).

Therapy attempted to keep Nancy and Robert focused on their marriage even though not much seemed to be happening within it. The temptation of relationships with outside parties was especially enticing. In the course of therapy, Nancy and Robert decided on a trial separation in which each would be free to see others. During the course of the separation Nancy completed her long-postponed degree and Robert began to put quality time into his relationship with his children.

Their responses on the IAQ showed significant changes with regard to the "need" items. Now Nancy showed mild agreement (3) with the statement "You are not worth much if you are only occupied with your own concerns" (high NA) and strong agreement (4) with the statement "I don't hesitate to fight for my own opinions with those I am close to" (high NI). Robert showed a similar pattern of change. He now showed mild agreement (3) with the statements "I believe everyone has an obligation to find their own way in life" (high NI) and "Relating to others is essential to coming to know oneself" (high NA).

At the time of this writing Nancy and Robert have decided to try to put their marriage and family back together. Older and wiser, the two of them seem to be moving ahead into a DD marriage. They seem ready to express healthy interpersonal needs. Prognosis is excellent (see Figure 7-2).

Advanced Couple Type DD: Tom and Christine

Advanced couple type DD is characterized by mutuality of high needs of individuation and attachment. Consider Tom and Christine, who came into treatment complaining of growing pains in what until recently had been a very happy marriage. Both Tom and Christine had been married previously. While Christine's divorce was amicable, Tom's had been quite traumatic, involving estrangement from his children. After the divorce Tom plunged himself into his work as an attorney and was very successful. He was alone for a number of years and finally met Christine, a woman nine years his junior. Since he met her, Tom reported being happier than he ever had been in his life. He considered Christine to be his best friend as well as his wife.

Christine, in contrast, had dated a number of people since her divorce and had lived with her daughter for a number of years. She had continued to work in jobs with no hope for advancement despite her obvious intelligence. She indicated that she too was very happy now. She felt she had found a very deep lifetime companion in Tom.

Examination of Tom and Christine's IAQ scores placed them in a mature DD couple position. Each of them had high needs for individuation and attachment as well as low fears of each issue. Tom, for example, strongly agreed (4) with

160 *TILT for Couples and Families*

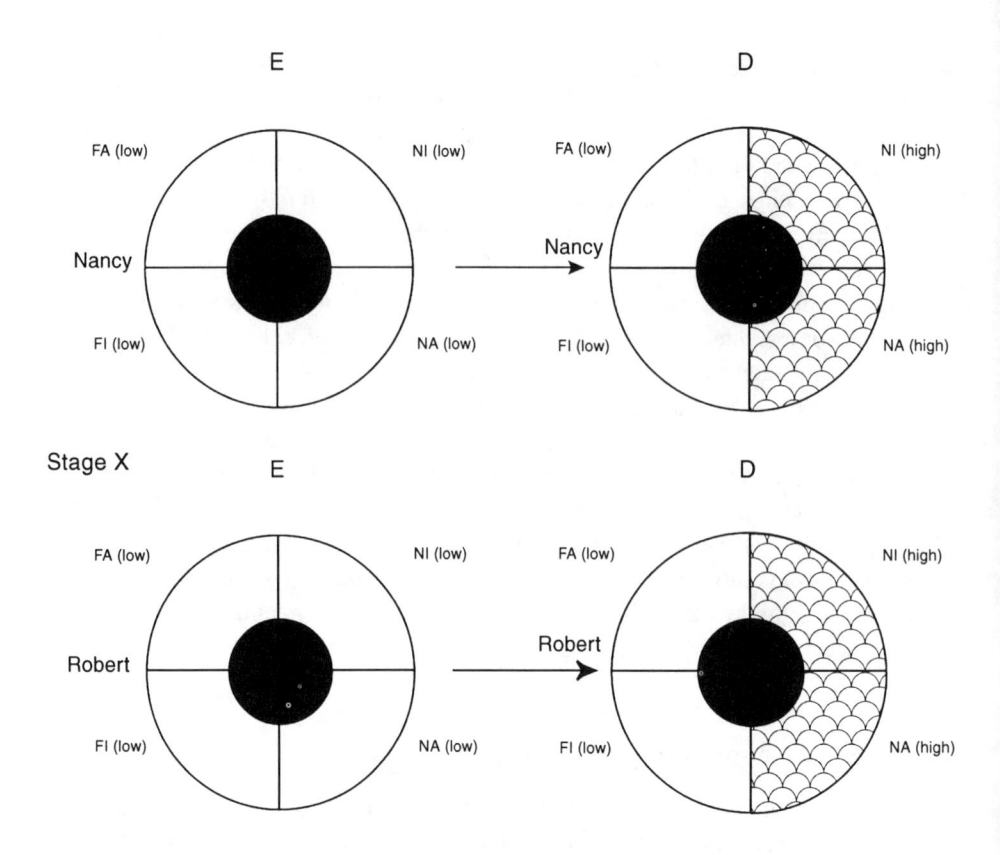

Figure 7-2 Nancy and Robert.

FI = Fear of Individuation   NI = Need for Individuation
NA = Need for Attachment   FA = Fear of Attachment

the statements "You are not worth much if you are only occupied with your own concerns" (high NA) and "If I am not for myself I can't expect anyone else to be for me" (high NI). Christine showed agreement (3) with these two statements and in addition showed strong agreement (4) with the statements "I feel fulfilled when I'm involved in what is going on with other people" (high NA) and agreement (3) with the statement "I don't hesitate to fight for my own opinions with those I am close to" (high NI). Both Tom and Christine disagreed (1) with the statements "If I open myself to others I'll get hurt" (low FA) and "Paying attention to your own feelings is typically destructive for a relationship" (low FI).

Their marriage gave each of them the mutual support to begin to explore their own interests, and it was this very growth that had put them into disruptive situations. Tom, with Christine's strong encouragement, had begun to attempt a rapprochement with a son from his first marriage. The boy came to live with them but proved to be a pathological liar and thief. He would take money from them and then lie about it. Christine perceived Tom as weak when dealing with his son. Ultimately, Christine refused to have the boy live with them any longer, though she was more than willing for Tom to subsidize him to live in his own apartment. She interpreted Tom's need for attachment as a fear of individuation.

At the same time, Christine completed a doctoral program in counseling psychology, a program she had begun with Tom's blessing. She now began spending a large number of evenings and weekends away from the house in an attempt to build up her practice, something that Tom seemed to resent. He was very encouraging about her seeing patients during the week but he wanted evening and weekend hours to be for them. He seemed to interpret Christine's need for individuation as fear of attachment.

Tom and Christine's situation was ironic, but not atypical of good marriages. The very strength of their relationship had put them into a place of mutual conflict. They were now in a period when each had high fears of individuation and attachment (Position BB). Both entered therapy with a diagnosis of dysthymic disorder (300.4). The approach of therapy was to help them forwardly regress from DD at one life stage to BB at the next without succumbing to an imbalance between individuation and attachment. In other words, TILT therapy was aimed at having them stay the course without veering off to quick fix solutions on the AC clinical axis.

As therapy proceeded, Christine learned to be sensitive to Tom's distinction between working during the weekdays and on evenings and weekends. Tom, in turn, began to realize that as a new clinician Christine could not necessarily choose the hours that she saw people. Tom also began to appreciate Christine's distinction between his son being with them and in a separate apartment with Tom's subsidy. Tom began to realize that Christine was not trying to block his relationship with his son. The change in Christine and Tom's IAQ patterns was fascinating. Initially, they both began to agree (3) with the statements "If I open myself up to others, I'll get hurt" (high FA) and "Paying attention to your own feelings is typically destructive for a relationship" (high FI). However, as therapy progressed, they returned to their earlier position of disagreement (1) with these two statements (low FI and low FA).

The prognosis for this couple is very good. By the time of this writing Tom and Christine had begun to overcome their fears of individuation and attachment in the context of factoring in Christine's emerging career and Tom's relationship with his son from his first marriage. In TILT terms, they had forward regressed from DD to BB at a more advanced lifestage and were now moving ahead to Position EE (see Figure 7-3).

Figure 7-3 Tom and Christine.

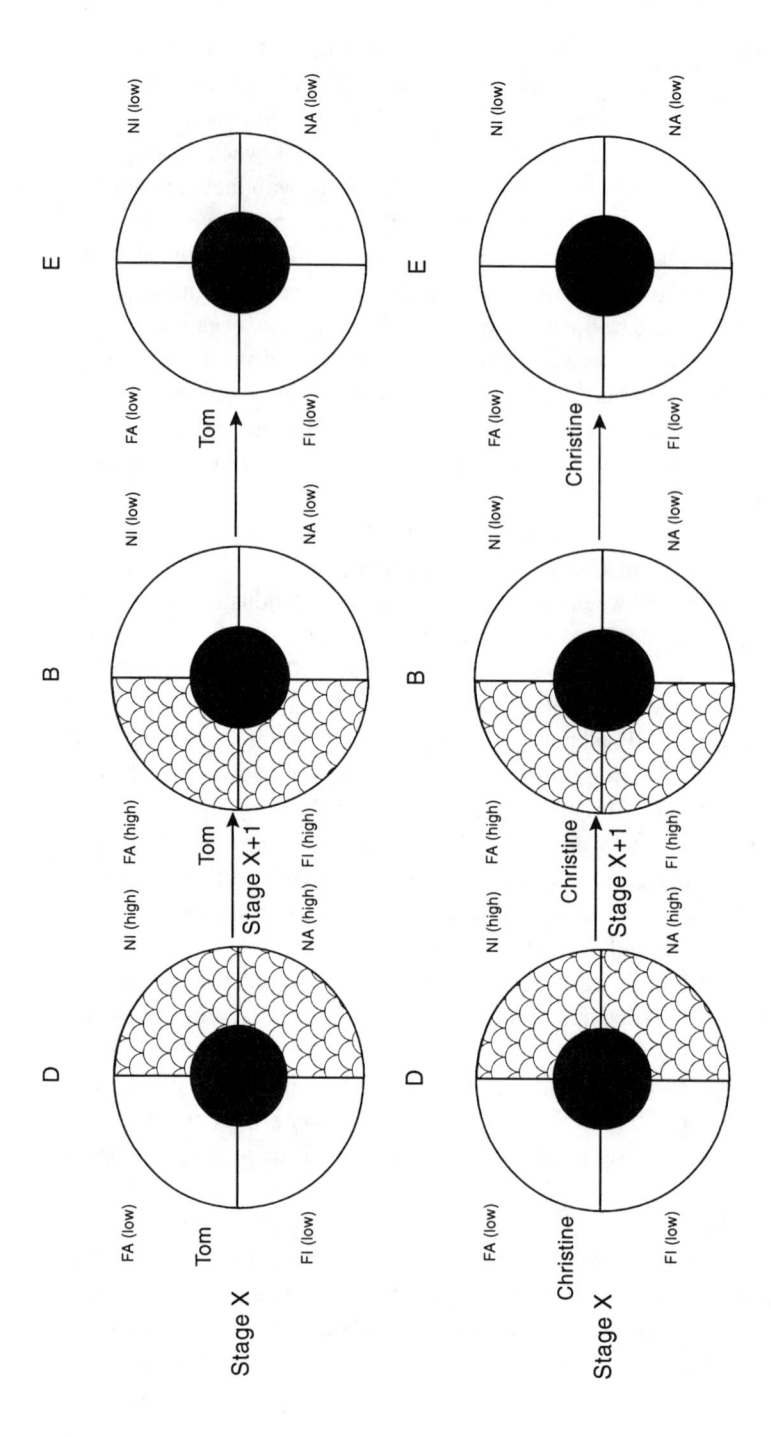

FI = Fear of Individuation   NI = Need for Individuation
NA = Need for attachment   FA = Fear of Attachment

Mixed Parent–Child Couple Type DB: Danielle and Brad

The mixed parent–child couple type DB is characterized by a nonmutuality between the two partners. Consider the case of Danielle and Brad. The fourth developmental couple relationship is not balanced as are the first three. Here one member, Danielle, a French teacher in a private school, is in a D position and the other, Brad, a veterinarian five years younger than Danielle, is in a B position. Danielle's IAQ responses indicated high needs for individuation and attachment and low fears on both dimensions. Brad's pattern was the opposite. He was fear-dominated and did not have developed needs. Brad typically met any show of affection on the part of Danielle with rejection or sullen withdrawal. At the same time, he became highly abusive when Danielle attempted to take space for herself. Whenever she made plans to visit her family in France, he would become highly anxious and do what he could to disrupt her trip. When she acknowledged his feelings and invited him to travel with her and "make a vacation of it," he refused to go.

This pattern was reflected in their IAQ responses. Danielle agreed (3) with the statements "I have a great need for sharing my feelings with other people" (high NA) and "We should act on our own best judgments even if other people strongly disagree" (high NI), while strongly disagreeing (0) with the statements "I think people always try to control others" (low FA) and "I try to avoid being on my own" (low FI). Brad showed exactly the opposite pattern. He strongly agreed (4) with the statements "I think people always try to control others" and "If I open myself to others I'll get hurt" (high FA) and agreed (3) with the statement "A highly responsible position is too much of a burden" (high FI). Brad disagreed (1) with the statements "I have a great need for sharing my feelings with other people" (low NA) and "I don't hesitate to fight for my own opinions with those I am close to" (low NI).

The beginning of therapy coincided with a planned trip to France by Danielle. As always, Danielle invited Brad to go. As always he refused, yet bitterly complained that Danielle was going without him. While Danielle was away, Brad began an affair with an old girl friend. When Danielle returned, she suspected Brad was involved with someone else because of a sudden irregularity in his behavior patterns. Brad denied it but continued to behave erratically. Ultimately Danielle confronted him with evidence that Brad could not deny and with the help of the therapist gave Brad the option of giving up his relationship or moving out.

At this stage Brad became very frightened and swore he would give up the relationship if only Danielle would let him come back. The therapist advised Danielle against this course of action because the pattern would likely repeat itself. Instead, the therapist recommended separate living quarters on a temporary basis. However, Danielle agreed to let Brad come back on the condition he give up the other woman. Brad enthusiastically agreed but within a month was seeing the other woman again. At this point, Danielle ordered Brad out of the house and filed for divorce. Danielle soon terminated therapy, having made the adjustment to a single life. Her IAQ responses showed a temporary regression back to B at her more advanced stage and a slow moving ahead to E. For example, after the separation, Danielle came to strongly endorse (4) the statement "If I open myself up to others, I'll get hurt" (high FA) and came to disagree (1) with the statement "I have a great need for sharing my feelings with other people" (low NA). With time, however, Danielle's agreement with the first statement was replaced by uncertainty (uncertain FA) while her response to the second remained the same (low NA).

Brad continued to flounder, trying to make his other relationship work. However, his dependency manifested itself openly as an A and he seemed to be in the process of driving his new partner away with his clingingness. For example, while he continued to disagree (1) with the statement "I don't hesitate to fight with my opinions with those I am close to," (low NI) he now came to strongly agree (4) with the statements "I try to avoid being on my own" (high FI) and "I have a great need for sharing my feelings with other people" (high NA). At the time of this writing, Brad precipitously discontinued therapy (see Figure 7-4).

This case should serve as a warning as to the potential volatility inherent in a parent–child DB relationship and only serves to reinforce the working assumption that successful relationships must involve couples at the same level of development even within the developmental BED axis. Let us now turn to an examination of clinical couples presenting on the AC axis.

CLINICAL CASES

First I will discuss three neurotic couple types AA, CC, and AC. Then I will discuss three borderline couple types, $(A/C)_{IND}$ $(A/C)_{IND}$, $(A/C)_{ATT}$ $(A/C)_{ATT}$, and $(A/C)_{IND}$ $(A/C)_{ATT}$. Finally, I will focus on a psychotic couple: $(A/C)_{TOT}$ $(A/C)_{TOT}$.

Neurotic Enmeshed Couple Type AA: Herb and Brenda

Neurotic enmeshed couple type AA is characterized by mutuality of high needs for attachment and fear of individuation. Consider Herb and Brenda, who at the time they entered treatment were each 43 years old. Herb was a physician specializing in internal medicine and was diagnosed at intake as having an Anxiety Disorder (300.00). Herb presented with low self-esteem as manifested by continuous

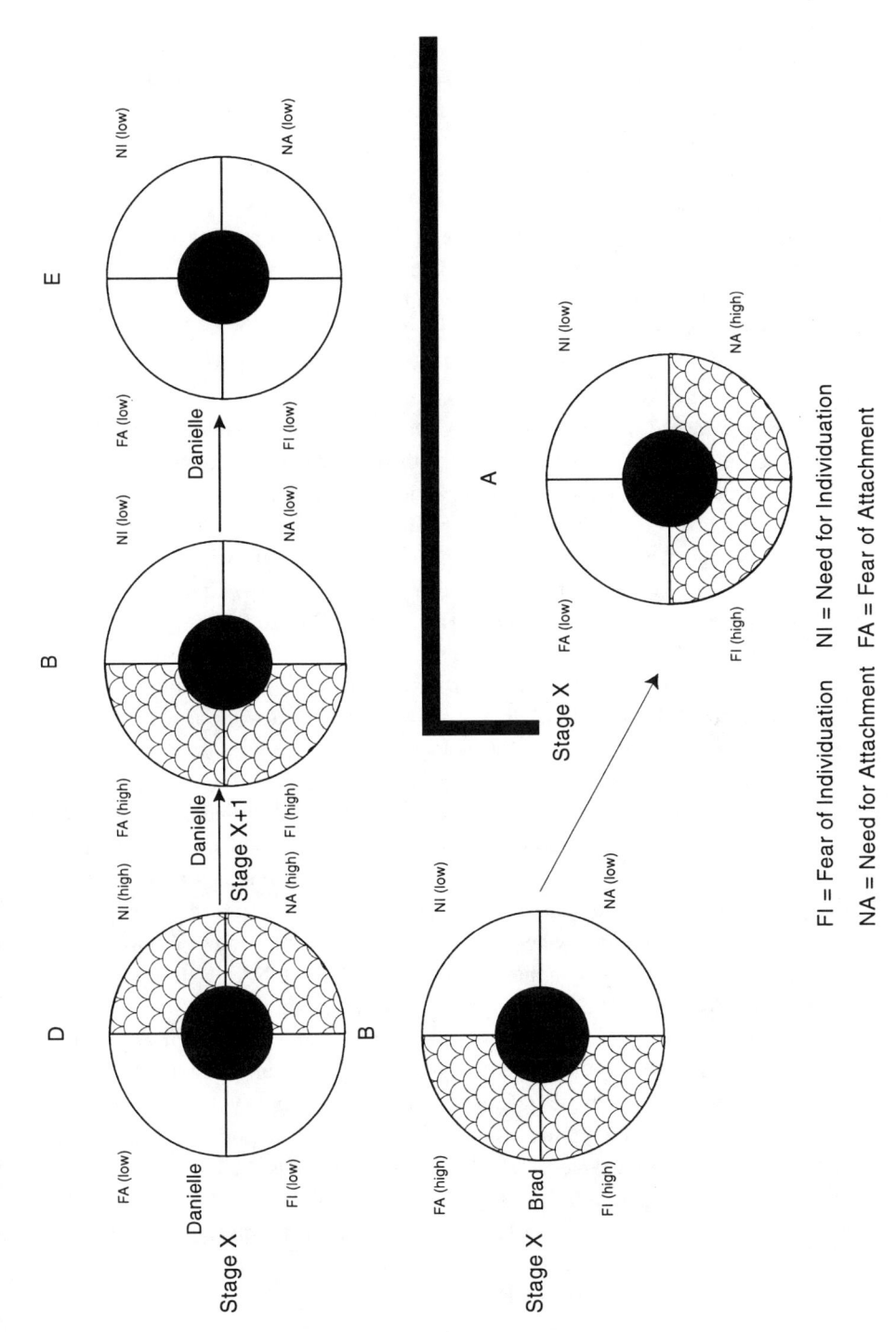

FI = Fear of Individuation   NI = Need for Individuation
NA = Need for Attachment   FA = Fear of Attachment

Figure 7-4 Danielle and Brad.

165

self-disparaging remarks, and by anxiety as indexed by general fatigue, restlessness, and trouble falling asleep. Herb also showed depression as reflected in a general loss of interest in his activities.

Brenda was a substitute librarian and teacher and lived with her husband and their two children. She was slightly obese and quite pessimistic. Brenda's affect was flat and she had difficulty concentrating. She was diagnosed with dysthymic disorder (300.4) and was taking the antidepressant drug Prozac. Brenda reported conflict with her husband and difficulties in communicating with him, a problem that seemed to have existed for at least several years.

Therapy revealed significant issues in the childhoods of Herb and Brenda contributing to their respective problems. Herb's father had been an architect and builder, and his mother had been the bookkeeper in the firm. Both of Herb's parents were now retired. Although he worked with his parents in their business when he was young, he had always felt pushed by them to be a doctor. Even though he "chose" the profession they wanted for him, he always felt inferior to his younger brother. Herb had very few relationships before he met his wife.

Brenda's father was in advertising, and her mother was a housewife. Brenda was close to her father but felt constantly criticized by her mother. Although she was very bright Brenda consistently sabotaged any chances she had for a serious career. Although her grades were quite good as an undergraduate, Brenda chose not to go on to obtain a postgraduate degree. Brenda seemed to feel she could not handle any serious career, instead deciding to raise her family and work as a substitute teacher and librarian for the public school system. Nevertheless, Brenda blamed her husband for this decision, claiming that he was threatened by her success.

Many of these patterns are revealed in the IAQ scores for Herb and Brenda. Both fell into the enmeshed (A) position, showing high needs for attachment and high fears of individuation. At the same time, both displayed low fears of attachment and low needs for individuation. For example, Herb strongly agreed (4) with the statements "I feel inadequate when people disapprove of me" (high FI) and "One should go out of his/her way to maintain friendships" (high NA). Herb disagreed (1) with the statements "I believe everyone has an obligation to find their own way in life" (low NI) and "Being in a close relationship often keeps one from doing what he/she wants to do" (low FA). Brenda's response configuration was very similar. She agreed (3) with the statements "Paying attention to your own feelings is typically destructive for a relationship," "I try to avoid being on my own" (both high FI) and with the statement "The best part of parties is the chance to make new friends" (high NA). Brenda strongly disagreed with the statements "I prefer not to get too close to others" (low FA) and "I express what I think even if I know my position is extremely unpopular" (low NI).

During the course of treatment, Herb developed medical problems and was no longer able to function in his job as an internist. He was transferred by the state of

Michigan to a well-paying but boring desk job in Flint that involved a two-and-a-half hour daily commute (round trip) from his home in a Detroit suburb. Herb felt that the best course of action was to rent an apartment in Flint for the weekdays, an act that would also serve to diminish contact between Brenda and him, and thus reduce the endless conflict and bickering. Brenda agreed with this decision.

To their suprise, the enforced separation only made them more anxious and dependent on each other. They quarreled a great deal over seemingly insignificant issues, yet clung to each other at the same time. They blamed each other for having to do things alone. Neither could stand to be on his or her own. Yet, their very fear of individuation blocked them from having a healthy relationship when they were together.

TILT therapy attempted to tilt Herb and Brenda to the BED axis, where they would temporarily build up walls (Position BB) to begin to develop stronger self–other boundaries. Subsequent IAQ responses on the part of both Herb and Brenda indicated an increase in fear of attachment and a decrease in need for attachment. Herb, for example, now indicated uncertainty (2) with regard to the statement "Being in a close relationship often keeps one from doing what he/she wants to do" (uncertain FA) and disagreement (1) with the statement "One should go out of his/her way to maintain friendships" (low NA). Brenda showed a similar change, now agreeing (3) with the statement "I prefer not to get too close to others" (high FA) and showing uncertainty regarding the statement "The best part of parties is the chance to make new friends" (low NA).

The enforced separation between them provided the opportunity for some growth on the BED axis. Slowly Herb and Brenda began to do things with their individual time without blaming the other for not being there. While they were not yet capable of any real intimacy, they seemed better able to tolerate each other's company without exploding. For example, both Herb and Brenda showed reduction in their IAQ "fear" scores, Herb coming to disagree (1) with the statement "I feel inadequate when people disapprove of me" (low FI) and Brenda now becoming uncertain (2) regarding the statement "I prefer not to get too close to others" (uncertain FA) and disagreeing (1) with the statement "I try to avoid being on my own" (low FI). They had not yet learned to express healthy needs with each other. In TILT terms, Herb and Brenda had first TILTed back to the BB position and were now moving ahead to couple Position EE (see Figure 7-5).

Neurotic Disengaged Couple Type CC: Henry and Mary

Neurotic disengaged couple type CC is characterized by mutuality of high need for individuation and fear of attachment. Henry and Mary came into therapy with complementary complaints about their marriage. Mary complained that Harry continuously withdrew from family decisions regarding their two young children.

Stage X

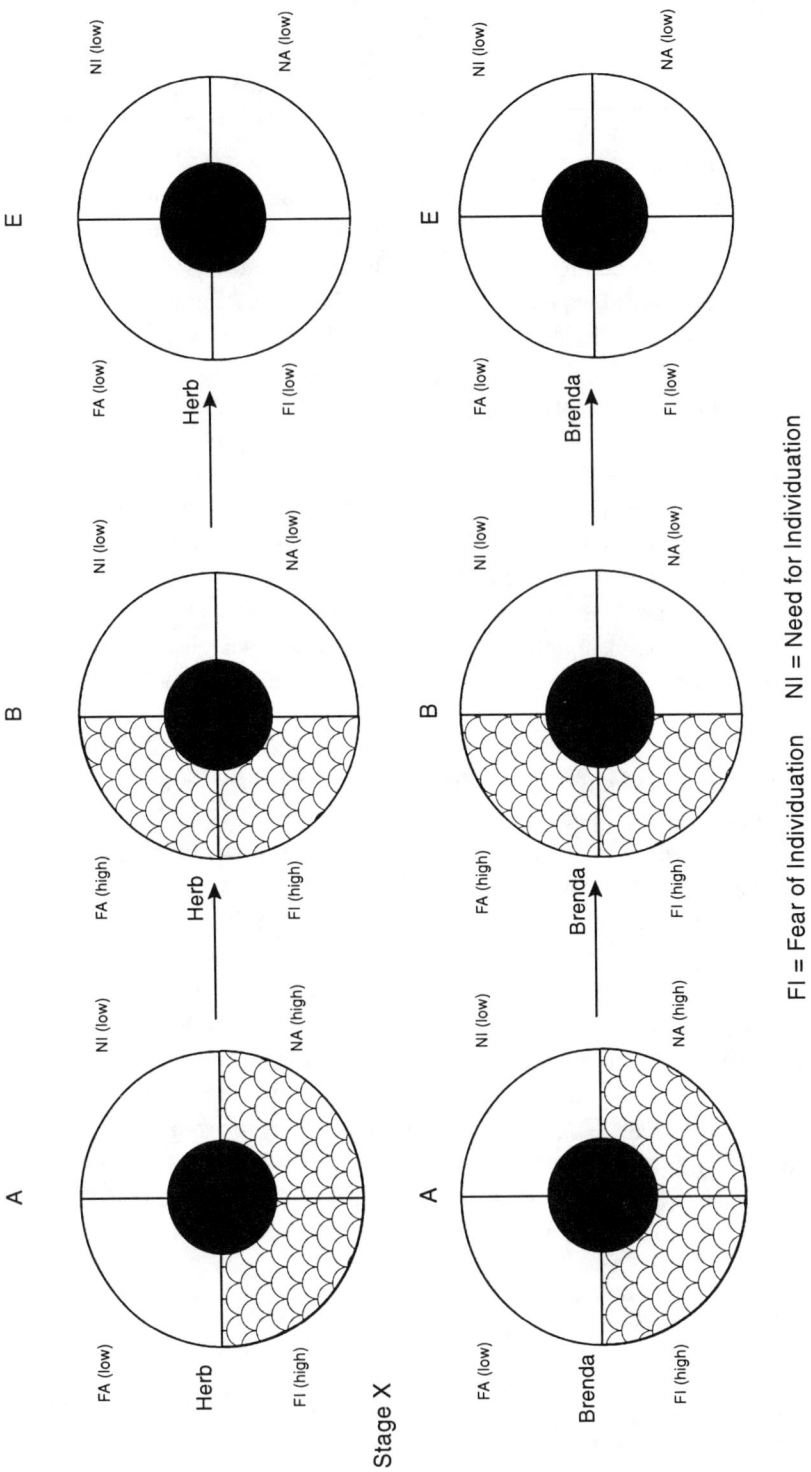

FI = Fear of Individuation   NI = Need for Individuation
NA = Need for Attachment   FA = Fear of Attachment

Figure 7-5 Herb and Brenda.

Henry complained that Mary continually judged him as inadequate and refused to have a sexual relationship with him.

Investigation of the family backgrounds of both partners indicated that they had come from difficult childhoods. Henry was raised in Puerto Rico in a strict, large, Catholic family. Henry's father was a barber, his mother stayed at home to take care of the children. Therapy revealed that Henry's father was domineering and sadistic, whereas his mother was masochistic.

Henry reported several fights with his father, one when he tried to protect his mother from his father's anger. His family of origin rarely spent time together. At the age of 12, Henry moved with his mother and one brother to New York City, never seeing his father again. As a young man, Henry avoided dating because he was so afraid of repeating his father's experience. This history was reflected in Henry's IAQ pattern. He clearly fell into a disengaged (C) position, having a high need for individuation and fear of attachment and low fear of individuation and need for attachment scores. For example, Henry agreed strongly (4) with the statements "I believe everyone has an obligation to find their own way in life" (high NI) and "I prefer not to get too close others" (high FA), although disagreeing (1) with the statements "I try to avoid being on my own" (low FI) and "I have a great need for sharing my feelings with other people" (low NA). Henry's initial Axis II diagnosis was a schizoid personality disorder (301.20).

Mary's family background seemed different on the surface. She was raised in a free-thinking, seemingly happy, family in Michigan. Her father was a Unitarian minister and her mother a school teacher. However, Mary's father turned out to be very ineffectual, losing his pulpit without a fight when his church merged with another larger Unitarian church, ministered by a much younger and less experienced man. In Mary's eyes, her father did not sufficiently fight for himself and for his family. Mary's father never had a full-time job again, leaving Mary's mother with the major responsibility for raising income for the family. Mary had a very strong distrust of the dependability of men in a marriage and felt her mother had been trapped into the role of provider as well as homemaker. Mary's IAQ profile reflects these experiences. Like her husband, Mary displayed a disengaged (C) pattern showing high need for individuation and fear of abandonment and low need for attachment and fear of individuation. Mary agreed very strongly (4) with the statements "The price of a close relationship is that it keeps you from truly being yourself" (high FA) and "I believe everyone has an obligation to find their own way in life" (high NI). She disagreed (0) with the statements "Relating to others is essential to coming to know oneself" (low NA) and "I feel very secure when I have a close friend stronger than myself to rely on" (low FI). Mary's initial Axis II diagnosis was a paranoid personality disorder (301.0).

As a couple, Henry and Mary displayed a classic disengaged stance, feeling comfortable at a fairly remote distance from each other. They seemed to have sensed the fear of intimacy in one another and chosen each other for the very qualities they now found intolerable. Mary was angry at Henry's remoteness from the family. Yet, she was unable to trust herself to become dependent on any man. Henry was angry at Mary's sexual unresponsiveness. Yet, Henry was afraid to become too close to any woman lest he become abusive, as he remembered his father as being. In short, Henry and Mary presented as a disengaged (CC) couple, each pseudo-individuated with a natural fear of attachment.

TILT therapy involved TILTing Henry and Mary back to a BB position as a first step in tilting them ahead on the BED axis. This first step in therapy was predicated on both Henry and Mary giving up their pseudoboundaries while maintaining their protective walls. To do this, the therapist encouraged Henry to question seriously his adaptation to his parents' marriage and to experience the loneliness he had felt his whole life, all this while remaining somewhat remote from his wife. Now Henry, for example, became uncertain regarding (2) the IAQ statement "I try to avoid being on my own" (uncertain FI). Mary, in contrast, was helped to see her obsession with self-sufficiency and independence as a defense. Slowly Mary began to realize that she could not be as self-sufficient as she might want to be. She now admitted (4) that "I feel secure when I have a close friend stronger than myself to rely on" (high FI).

At the time of this writing Henry and Mary had tilted from Position CC on the AC axis to Position BB on the BED axis, this move setting the stage for healthy neurological development along the BED axis. In this regressed position, Henry and Mary mutually resisted both attachment and individuation. The ultimate aim of therapy was to produce a relationship that would provide a mutuality of attachment and individuation needs on the part of the two partners for each other and themselves. At the time of this writing, they were still at the regressed BB position (see Figure 7-6).

Neurotic Rejection–Intrusion Couple Type AC: Laura and Hal

Neurotic rejection–intrusion couple type AC is characterized by nonmutuality between the two partners. One member of this relationship is an A exhibiting enmeshing behaviors and the other is a C exhibiting disengagement behaviors. Consider the prime example of Laura and Hal. Laura and Hal had been married for 15 years at the time they entered therapy. They had two children together. Hal, 59, had been married previously with one child. Laura, 48, had never been married before.

Laura and Hal met while they were both working for a company. Hal was vice-president of the company and was married. Laura, single, came in as a young researcher. After a considerable period of turmoil, Hal filed for divorce and married Laura. During the course of the marriage Hal operated in a fairly rigid dictatorial

Psychotherapy Illustrations for Couples 171

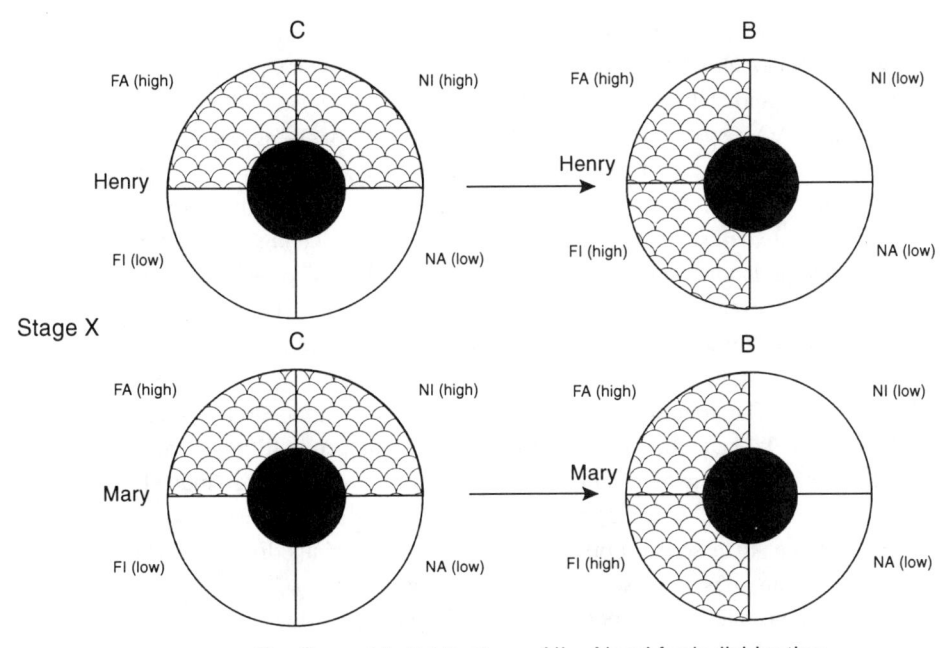

Stage X

FI = Fear of Individuation   NI = Need for Individuation
NA = Need for Attachment   FA = Fear of Attachment

Figure 7-6   Henry and Mary.

manner. He made most of the day-to-day decisions regarding where to live and how to handle the finances. Laura was quite dependent in these areas, and was unable even to assert herself in terms of the religious upbringing of their children. (Laura was Jewish, Hal Baptist), something she continuously complained about in therapy, but did nothing to change. A precipitating presenting issue at the onset of therapy was Hal's impending retirement and Laura's increasing dissatisfaction with her dependent role. Hal also had begun to drink heavily.

Laura's diagnosis was dysthymic disorder (300.4). Hal's was anxiety disorder nos (300.0) complicated by achohol abuse (305,00). The pattern of initial IAQ scores for Laura and Hal confirm the above diagnosis. Laura scored initially as an enmeshed personality (A). She displayed high fear of individuation and need for attachment. For example, she indicated strong agreement (4) with the statements "I have a great need for sharing my feelings with other people" and "I try to help people out with their problems even if it is inconvenient for me" (both high NA), but also with the statements "It is important for me to meet other people's expectations of me" and "I let people I respect shape my decisions" (both high FI). Laura also disagreed (1) with the statements "If I open myself to others I'll get hurt" and "Love is often more trouble than it's worth" (both low FA), but also with the statements "I express what I think even if I know my position is extremely unpopular" and "Ultimately I have to do things my own way" (both low NI).

Hal's IAQ response pattern was the opposite, strongly agreeing (4) with the statements "Ultimately I have to do things my own way" (high NI) and "Love is often more trouble than it is worth" (high FA), whereas he strongly disagreed (2) with the statements "I have a great need for sharing my feelings with other people" (low NA) and "I let people I respect shape my decisions" (low FI).

Therapy revealed the dominant interpersonal pattern between Laura and Hal. Laura would come to Hal for help in a particular problem in which she felt insecure. Hal would help her, but in a manner that left her feeling more incompetent than previously. The goal of TILT therapy in this particular case was to regress both Laura and Hal back into a BB position as an initial step in tilting them off of the clinical axis. This involved convincing Laura to stop asking for so much help (i.e., to temporarily put up walls) and for Hal to be less certain that he knew all the answers (i.e., to lessen his boundaries). This was especially difficult as Hal tended to become anxious when someone disagreed with him.

Treatment made the impossibility of this goal self-evident. Through therapy, Laura was able to seek a temporary separation, continuing to live with the younger of the two children (the older child attended the state university in another city). She has now filed for divorce and is slowly building a single life with its ups and downs. Laura's later responses to the IAQ reflected this later pattern. Immediately after her separation, Laura came to strongly agree (4) with the statements "If I open myself up to others, I'll get hurt" and "Love is often more trouble than it's worth" (high FA). With time, however, Laura returned to her previous level of disagreement (1) with these two statements. This time, however, Laura's need for attachment score was lower. She now disagreed (1) with the statement "I try to help people out with their problems even if it is inconvenient for me" (low NA). Her responses to NI items remained low. In TILT terms, Laura tilted from A to B and was slowly moving ahead to E.

Hal, in contrast, lived alone and continued to feel very anxious. He drank heavily and refused to come back into treatment. From all indications, he remained in the C position, although it was not possible to obtain later IAQ measures as he moved out of state and broke off all contact with the therapist (see Figure 7-7).

Borderline Depressive Couple Type (A/C)$_{IND}$ (A/C)$_{IND}$: Lester and Rosemary

In the borderline depressive couple type (A/C)$_{IND}$ (A/C)$_{IND}$, both partners are conflicted with regard to individuation, showing both high fears and needs with

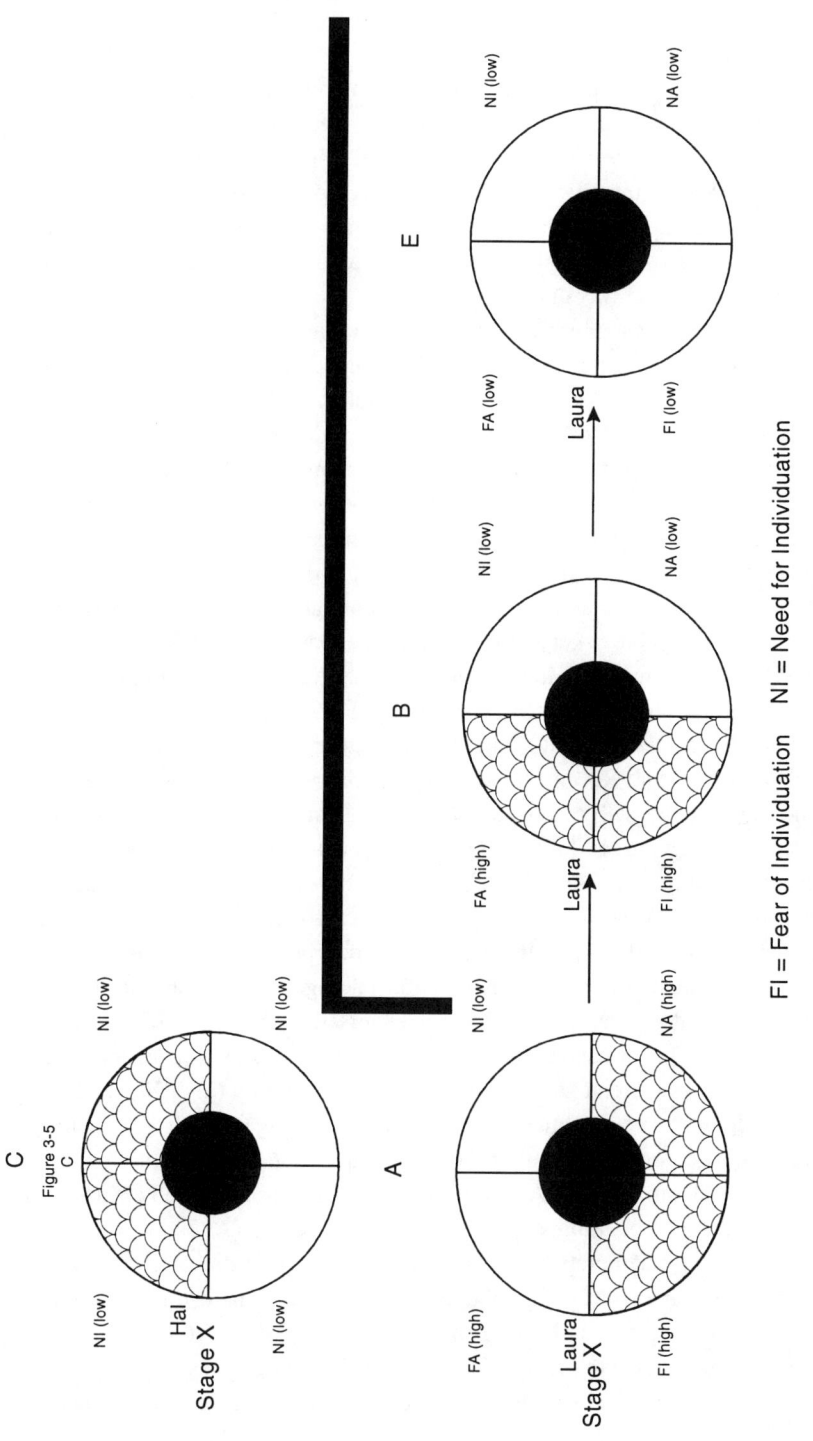

FI = Fear of Individuation NI = Need for Individuation
NA = Need for Attachment FA = Fear of Attachment

Figure 7-7 Laura and Hal.

173

regard to this issue. Consider Lester and Rosemary, who came into treatment because of continuous conflict in their marriage regarding plans for Lester's retirement. Lester, a career executive for a large paper products company, was in his midfifties and quite overweight. He had been passed over for promotion by his company after he had made a series of geographical moves to accommodate his superiors. He was disillusioned and was now considering early retirement. He complained that he was unable to make joint retirement plans with his wife, who he claimed always avoided the topic. Lester's initial diagnosis was an Axis II obsessive–compulsive personality (301.40) with depressive undertones (311).

Rosemary had devoted herself to being a mother and wife. Even after their children had left home, Rosemary never worked more than part-time. She felt dragged by her husband from town to town in the pursuit of his career and complained bitterly that she never had a chance to develop her own. However, it became abundantly clear that Rosemary often manufactured excuses to keep from getting a serious job. For example, she insisted on going to stay with her widowed daughter and grandson in another state for a month at a time and used this as an excuse for not being able to get a job. She would become agitated when confronted on this subject. Rosemary's initial diagnosis was an Axis II dependent personality disorder (301.6) with recurrent depressive undertones (311)

Examination of Lester and Rosemary's IAQ patterns confirmed the above diagnoses. Both Lester and Rosemary displayed conflict on the individuation dimension and indifference with regard to attachment. Lester agreed strongly (4) with the statements "A contract delineating each person's rights and obligations is an essential part of any love relationship" (high NI). However, Lester also agreed (3) with the statement "A highly responsible position is too much of a burden" (high FI). Lester disagreed (0 or 1) with items such as "If I open myself to others, I'll get hurt" (low FA) and "I prefer to use my free time talking to other people" (low NA).

Rosemary's pattern was very similar. She endorsed (3) the items "If I am not for myself, I can't expect anyone else to be for me" (high NI) and "I feel very secure when I have a close friend stronger than myself to rely on" (high FI). She was largely indifferent to attachment items, strongly disagreeing (0) with the statement "I prefer not to get too close to others" (low FA) and "I prefer to use my free time talking to other people" (low NA). Initially, Lester and Rosemary fell clearly into the borderline couple position, depressive subtype $(A/C)_{IND}$ $(A/C)_{IND}$.

During the course of therapy the degree of Rosemary's resentment toward Lester became apparent as well as her great dependence on him. She had not wanted to move from place to place, indicating she felt "like a gypsy." Yet, she never was able to put her foot down to prevent this but instead protested passively. Lester, in contrast, pretended he "had it all together" but in fact would have been terrified to make any of these moves alone.

Now that Lester's career dream had failed, Rosemary felt empowered to challenge him directly. At the same time, his career failure left Rosemary feeling very vulnerable, as she unconsciously had blocked any chance for an independent source of income. Talk of retirement frightened her and she avoided such discussions with all her power.

The aim of TILT therapy was to regress Lester and Rosemary back to the BB position by exposing their respective needs for attachment as fears of individuation and working to eliminate them and move the couple ahead to Position EE on the BED axis. At the time of this writing, Rosemary seemed to be ready to face this issue, admitting that she agreed (3) with the statement "I prefer not to get too close to others" and "If I open myself to other people, I'll get hurt" (both high FA) and becoming uncertain (2) about the statements "A contract denoting each person's rights and obligations is an essential part of any love relationship" and "If I am not for myself, I don't expect anyone else to be for me" (uncertain NI). Rosemary seemed to be aware that her need for individuation was a pseudodefense against her unresolved fear of attachment. However, Lester did not show such awareness and remained fixed in his borderline stance. Although Lester and Rosemary were still together, the prognosis was uncertain at the time of this writing (see Figure 7-8).

Borderline Paranoid Couple Type $(A/C)_{ATT}$ $(A/C)_{ATT}$: John and Virginia

The borderline paranoid couple type $(A/C)_{ATT}$ $(A/C)_{ATT}$ is characterized by mutuality and conflict with regard to attachment, with each member of the couple showing high needs and high fears with regard to attachment. Consider John and Virginia, both in their late 40s, who came into therapy to attempt to save what seemed to be their dying marriage. John, a school teacher for many years, was diagnosed with a dysthymic disorder (300.4) with a secondary Axis II diagnosis of a schizoid personality disorder (301.20). Virginia's primary diagnosis was an Axis II borderline personality disorder (301.83).

John complained about the lack of a sexual relationship between Virginia and himself. However, therapy revealed John's longstanding impotence problem. Although John stressed the importance of passing down family traditions, he also admitted feeling manipulated by his mother when he was growing up. Virginia, in turn, voiced complaints regarding John not having been there to help with the kids. At the same time, she continuously made disparaging comments about John's parenting style. She also had gained a considerable amount of weight. Therapy revealed a great distrust on the part of Virginia toward her own father and suggested the possibility of abuse in her childhood.

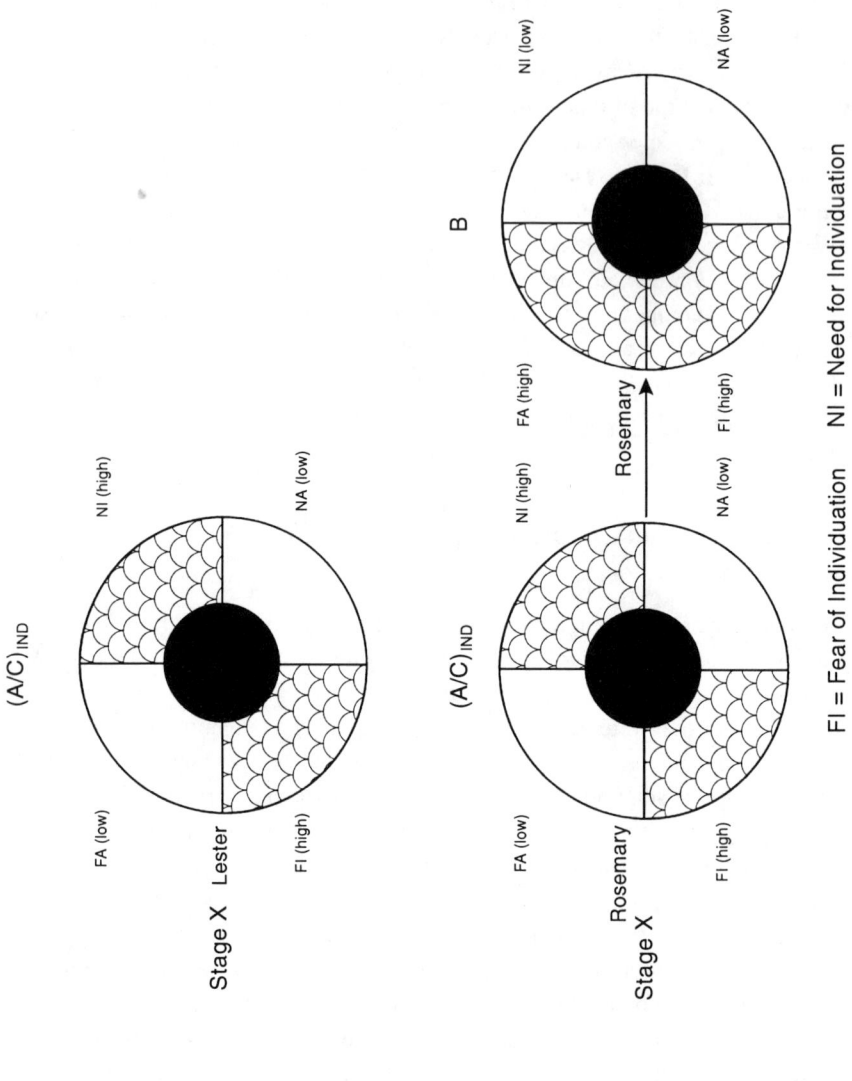

Figure 7-8 Lester and Rosemary.

Examination of the IAQ scores for John and Virginia revealed that they both were very conflicted regarding attachment, both needing it and fearing it at the same time. Individuation, in contrast, did not seem to be a very important issue for either one of them. Both John and Virginia strongly endorsed (4) the statement "I have a great need for sharing my feelings with other people" (high NA). John also strongly endorsed (4) the similar statement "It should be legally negligent not to help an accident victim" (also high NA). At the same time John also endorsed (3) the statement, "I prefer not to get too close to others" and "If I open myself up to others I will get hurt" (both high FA), whereas Virginia strongly endorsed the statement "Love is often more trouble than it's worth" and "I think people always try to control others" (both high FA).

Both John and Virginia strongly disagreed (0) with the statement "I try to avoid being on my own" (low FI). John also disagreed strongly (0) with the statement "A contract delineating each person's rights and obligations is an essential part of any love relationship" (low NI) whereas Virginia disagreed (1) with the statement "I don't hesitate to fight for my own opinions with those I am close to" (low NI). In TILT terms, they were locked into a borderline couple position, paranoid subtype $(A/C)_{ATT}$ $(A/C)_{ATT}$.

During the course of treatment, John considered leaving the teaching profession to go into an independent business. Ironically, Virginia began to explore the possibility of operating her own preschool. John was uninterested in Virginia's venture, Virginia was mildly encouraging about John's business, but advised him not to give up his teaching job.

John and Virginia separated but did not divorce. They continued to do things together as friends and to take an interest in each other's life. However, they seemed to have no interest in resuming a marriage, though John, on the surface, made overtures in this direction. John began a business venture involving entertainment items while continuing to teach. Virginia began her preschool program.

The aim of TILT therapy was to regress both John and Virginia back to Position BB, which involved the awareness that their need for attachment was really a masked fear of individuation. Given that this fear was faced directly, the reasoning was that both Virginia and John, together or separately, might begin to move ahead on the BED developmental axis.

At the time of this writing, both John and Virginia have regressed back to Position B. John became quite uncertain (2) regarding the statement "I have a great need for sharing my feelings with other people" (uncertain NA) but now admitted (3) "I try to avoid being on my own" (high FI). Virginia now disagreed (1) with the statement "I have a great need for sharing my feelings with other people" (low NA) and strongly agreed (4) with the statement "I feel very secure when I have a close friend stronger than myself to rely on" (high FI). They are still separated and John, at least, is beginning to contemplate divorce. To follow through, however, a reduction of fear of individuation is essential, something that hopefully will come about through TILT therapy, with both patients progressing to the E position (see Figure 7-9).

Borderline Mixed Couple Type (A/C)$_{ATT}$ (A/C)$_{IND}$: Karen and Ron

In the borderline mixed couple type (A/C)$_{ATT}$ (A/C)$_{IND}$ there is dissymmetry in the issue of conflict. One partner is conflicted with regard to individuation whereas the other is conflicted with regard to attachment. Consider Karen and Ron, who came into therapy in the midst of a highly problematic relationship. Karen, diagnosed as an Axis II narcissistic personality disorder (301.81) with paranoid features, was a highly intelligent woman in her midforties who seemed to want intimacy with Ron, her boyfriend, yet was afraid of it. Ron was diagnosed as a dependent personality disorder (301.6) on Axis II with secondary aspects of depression.

Karen came from a high-achieving family. Her father had been a very successful attorney and her mother had been a homemaker who Karen felt had not really developed herself. Karen felt her parents were not very close. Karen became a very prominent advertising executive for a national firm. In her mind, this cost her a first marriage. Her first husband refused to move with her to another state when she was offered a well-deserved promotion in a regional firm office. She stayed on at the lesser job and in her marriage only to discover that her husband was having an affair with a mutual friend.

Karen went through a very bitter divorce and stayed alone for a number of years, nurturing her career and vowing never to make the mistake of sacrificing her career for a man again. Eventually Karen met Ron, a social worker, who was eight years her junior. After dating him steadily for several months, she was again offered a major promotion in another firm in a state some 800 miles away. Although she was very happy with Ron, she decided to take the new job. Ron was willing to move with her but was unable to practice in the new state as he was not licensed in it. Nevertheless, Karen was adamant in her decision to move and was unwilling to support Ron until he got situated. She moved alone and Ron commuted on a semiweekly basis.

Examination of Karen's IAQ pattern indicated a fundamental conflict on the issue of attachment, displaying both a high need and a high fear with regard to it. For example, Karen strongly agreed (4) with the statement "I have a great need for sharing my feelings with other people" (high NA) but also with the statements "Being in close relationships often keeps one from doing what he/she wants to do" and "If I open myself to others I'll get hurt" (high FA). No such conflict occurred for Karen with regard to individuation, displaying a low need and a low fear toward

Figure 7-9 John and Virginia.

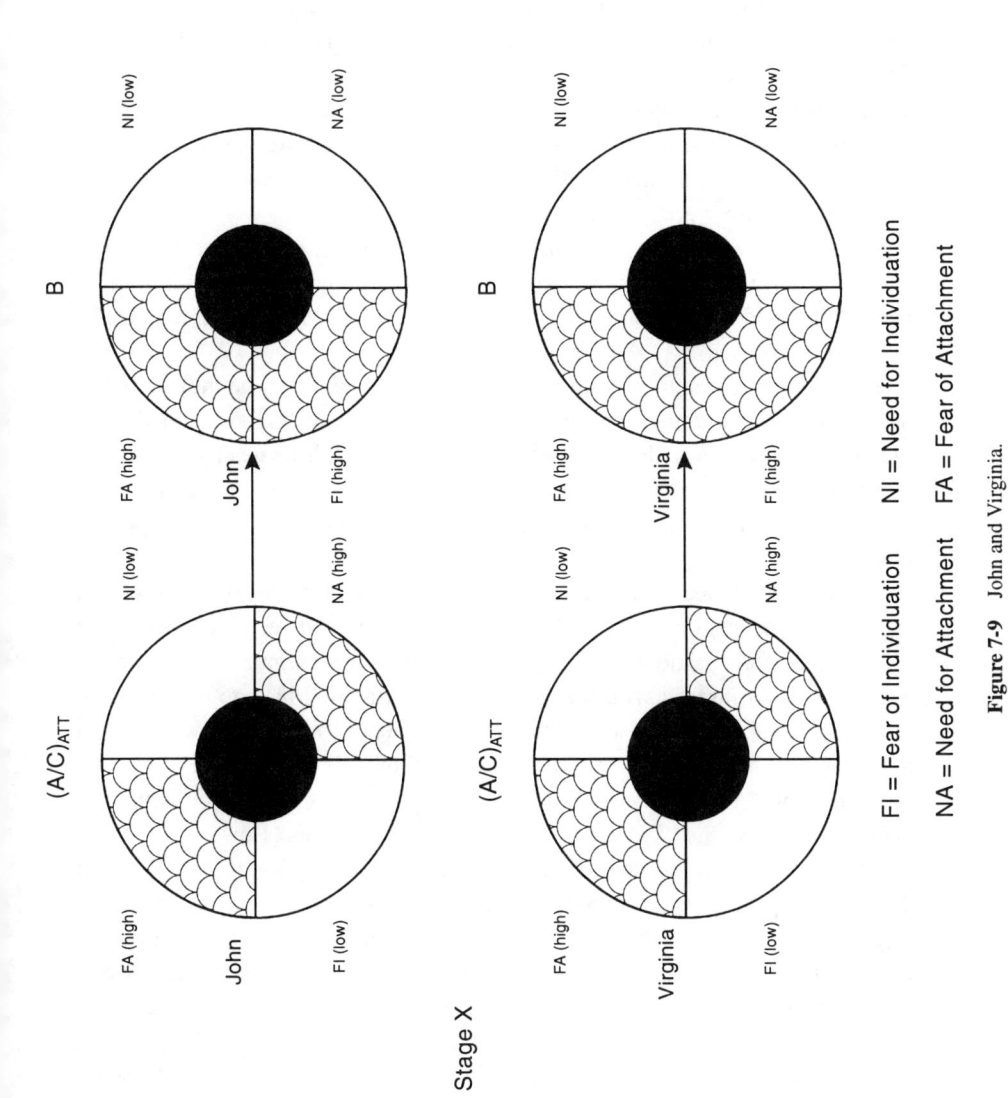

this issue. For example, Karen disagreed with the statements "I express what I think even if I know my position is extremely unpopular" (low NI) and "I try to avoid being on my own" (low FI).

Ron was in a very different place. He was the youngest child from a large family and the first to obtain a college degree. A successful career was very important for him, but yet he seriously questioned his abilities, choosing to work as a social worker on a modest salary rather than go on and train as a clinical psychologist. He had dated a number of women, but none of them were as professionally advanced as himself and certainly none of them were in Karen's league, whose salary was two and a half times greater than his own.

After Karen left for her new job, Ron commuted for almost a year. Finally, he agreed to move to Karen's new state and to work at whatever he could until he became licensed as a social worker. Given this agreement, Karen agreed for Ron to move in with her.

Ron came into treatment with Karen some six months after he moved in with her. They were fighting constantly over Karen's demandingness and the fact that Ron had neither seriously looked for a full-time job (instead working in a part-time job leading nowhere), nor had taken any steps to become licensed as a social worker. At the same time, Ron was putting a lot of time into fixing up the house.

Examination of Ron's initial IAQ scores indicated a tremendous conflict with regard to individuation, both needing it and fearing it, and very little affect with regard to attachment, neither needing it nor fearing it very much. For example, Ron strongly (4) agreed with the statement "Ultimately, I have to do things my own way" (high NI) but also (4) with the statement "I feel secure when I have a close friend stronger that myself to rely on" (high FI). Ron disagreed (1) with the statement "I feel fulfilled when I am involved in what is going on with other people" (low NA) and "I prefer not to get too close to others" (low FA).

Therapy revealed the complicated interaction between Karen and Ron. In TILT terms, Karen was a borderline personality, paranoid type, whereas Ron was a borderline personality, depressive type. On individuation issues, Ron was ambivalent and Karen indifferent. Thus, Ron would continuously blame Karen for being the cause of giving up his career. At the same time, he would run away from any chances to develop it. Individuation for Karen was not problematic. She approached her career realistically, showing no great enthusiasm for it but also not sabotaging herself.

On attachment issues, in contrast, the opposite pattern emerged. Here Karen showed great conflict while Ron seemed quite indifferent. On the one hand, Karen complained that she was not as close to Ron as she wanted. On the other, it was clear that Karen did not trust Ron enough to let herself be close to him; that indeed, she had set this pattern up by forcing Ron to choose between her and his career.

For Ron attachment seemed largely a nonissue. He did not seem to crave greater closeness with Karen, not objecting to her busy work schedule, nor did he block her desires for greater closeness, something she herself would sabotage.

The goal of TILT therapy was to regress both Ron and Karen back to Position BB on the BED axis. Therapy focused on Karen's attachment conflict, wanting closeness with her boyfriend but fearing it, and also on Ron's individuation conflicts, in which he wanted more of his own career but simultaneously ran away from it. Karen and Ron were seen individually in an attempt to resolve issues from their respective families of origin.

Therapy seemed to be making progress, but the entire process came to an abrupt halt when Karen discovered Ron had become addicted to cocaine and had become emotionally involved with a fellow user, who was also a prostitute. This incident unfortunately confirmed Karen's basic mistrust of men, and she immediately asked Ron to move out, which he did within a month. Karen continued therapy in an attempt to minimize the impact of this issue and resolve her attachment conflict. At the time of this writing, Karen was exploring the nature of her parents' marriage and trying to understand her mother's feelings. Ron was referred to an addiction counselor with the hope that this incident might propel him to begin to resolve his individuation conflict. At the time of this writing, Karen can be described as regressing from position $(A/C)_{ATT}$ back to B. She admitted to a fear of individuation much like her mother's. She agreed (3) with the statement "I try to avoid being on my own" (high FI) while coming to question her previously indicated need for attachment. She indicated uncertainty (2) regarding the statement "I have a great need for sharing my feelings with other people" (uncertain NA). Ron, however, showed no such changes and was still at Position $(A/C)_{IND}$ at the time he left therapy (see Figure 7-10).

Psychotic Couple Type $(A/C)_{TOT}$ $(A/C)_{TOT}$: Jenny and Vince

The psychotic couple type $(A/C)_{TOT}$ $(A/C)_{TOT}$ is characterized by both partners being conflicted with regard to both individuation and attachment. Consider Jenny and Vince, who came into therapy in the midst of a turbulent, often violent marriage. The precipitating event was an explosive fight in which Jenny had taunted Vince regarding his inadequate sexual functioning and then locked him out of the house. The temperature was below freezing, and Vince was outside without a coat. Vince had tried to reenter the house through an open window in the kitchen, but Jenny had slammed the window down on his hand. Vince reported crying out in pain, his hand being badly bruised, upon which Jenny opened the door, embraced him, and put ice on his hand. Jenny's initial diagnosis was an Axis II narcissistic personality disorder (301.81) and Vince's was an Axis II obsessive–compulsive personality disorder (301.4).

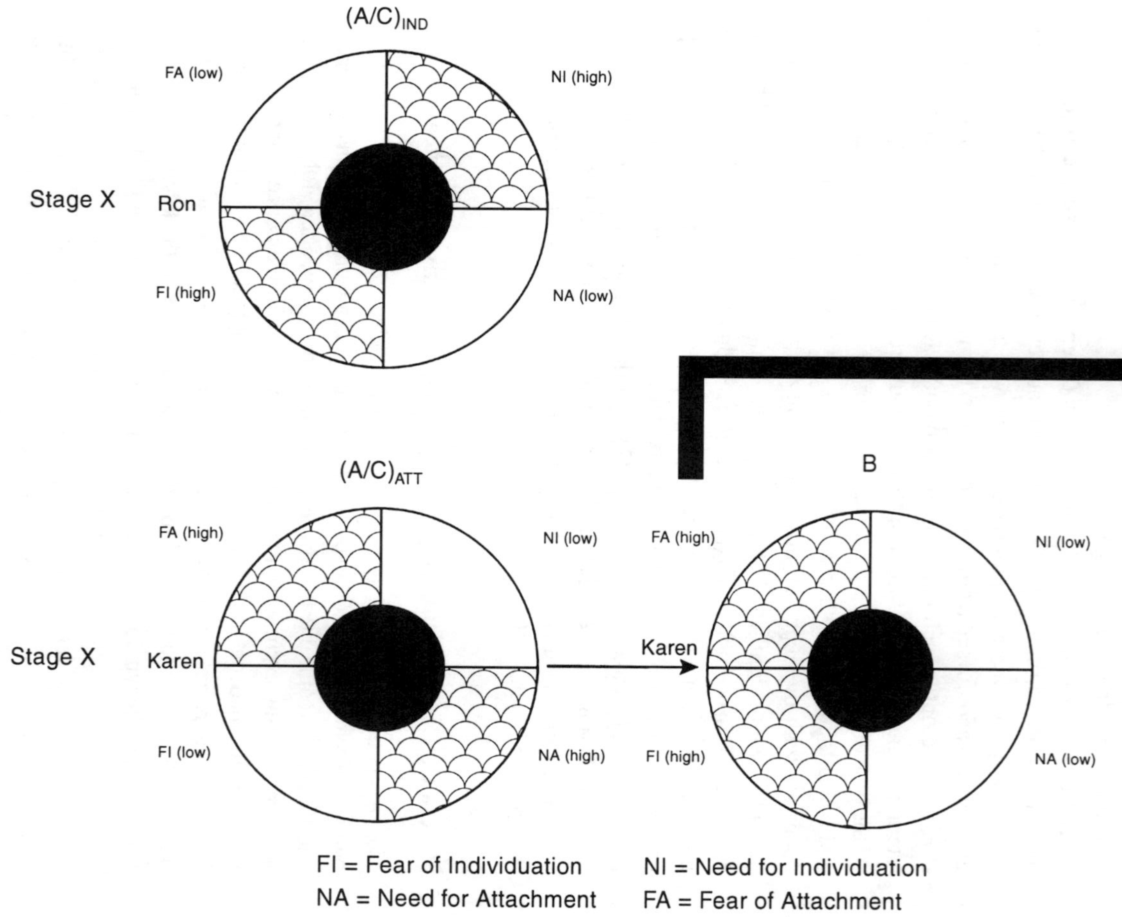

Figure 7-10 Karen and Ron.

Examination of the IAQ responses of Jenny and Vince shed greater light on the underlying dynamic. Both Jenny and Vince displayed conflict on both individuation and attachment issues, each of them simultaneously needing and fearing both closeness and separation. Jenny, for example, showed strong agreement (4) with the statements "I feel very secure when I have a close friend stronger than myself to rely on" (high FI) and "I believe everyone has an obligation to find their own way in life" (high NI). She also agreed (3) with the statements "If I open myself to others I'll get hurt" (high FA) and "I have a great need for sharing my feelings with other people" (high NA). Vince's pattern was identical, although he endorsed somewhat different items. Vince agreed (3) with the statements "I try to avoid being on my own" (high FI) and "I have to do things my own way" (high NI). He also strongly agreed (4) with the statements "You are not worth much if you are only occupied with your own concerns" (high NA) and "I think people always try to control others" (high FA).

The relationship between Jenny and Vince revealed perpetual conflict no matter what the underlying issue. Vince, a biochemist at a major university, showed great conflict regarding an offer to go into a private company that would have tripled his salary. He wanted to very much yet was afraid. Worse, he blamed Jenny for pushing him to do it, yet creating so much conflict in the house that he would be unable to manage it. Jenny had finished law school yet delayed taking the bar exam. She blamed Vince for making her life unbearable.

The situation was equally chaotic regarding attachment. Vince continuously complained about the lack of a sexual relationship in the marriage, yet refused to agree to a comfortable king-sized bed that Jenny wished to buy. As a result, Jenny continued to sleep on a separate couch in the downstairs den and Vince continued to complain about the lack of intimacy. Jenny, in turn, complained that Vince did not spend more time with her and their son, yet often went with her son to sleep at her parents' home.

This pattern of mutual pushes and pulls created a chaotic family pattern, which manifested itself in continuous bickering, cold wars, and occasional physical outbursts. The situation was also quite damaging to Jenny and Vince's 4-year-old son. He received very inconsistent parenting manifested in shifting alliances with one parent against the other and very irregular bedtimes. In TILT terms, Jenny and Vince were clearly a psychotic couple type $(A/C)_{TOT}$ $(A/C)_{TOT}$.

The aim of TILT therapy was the following: to regress both Jenny and Vince back to Position BB on the BED axis. Vince began to explore issues in his family of origin regarding conflictual individuation and attachment patterns. His father, a very successful lawyer, had died of a heart attack while in his forties. Vince believed his father's death was caused by his father's love for his wife and his subsequent overwork, which was designed to keep her happy. His mother had

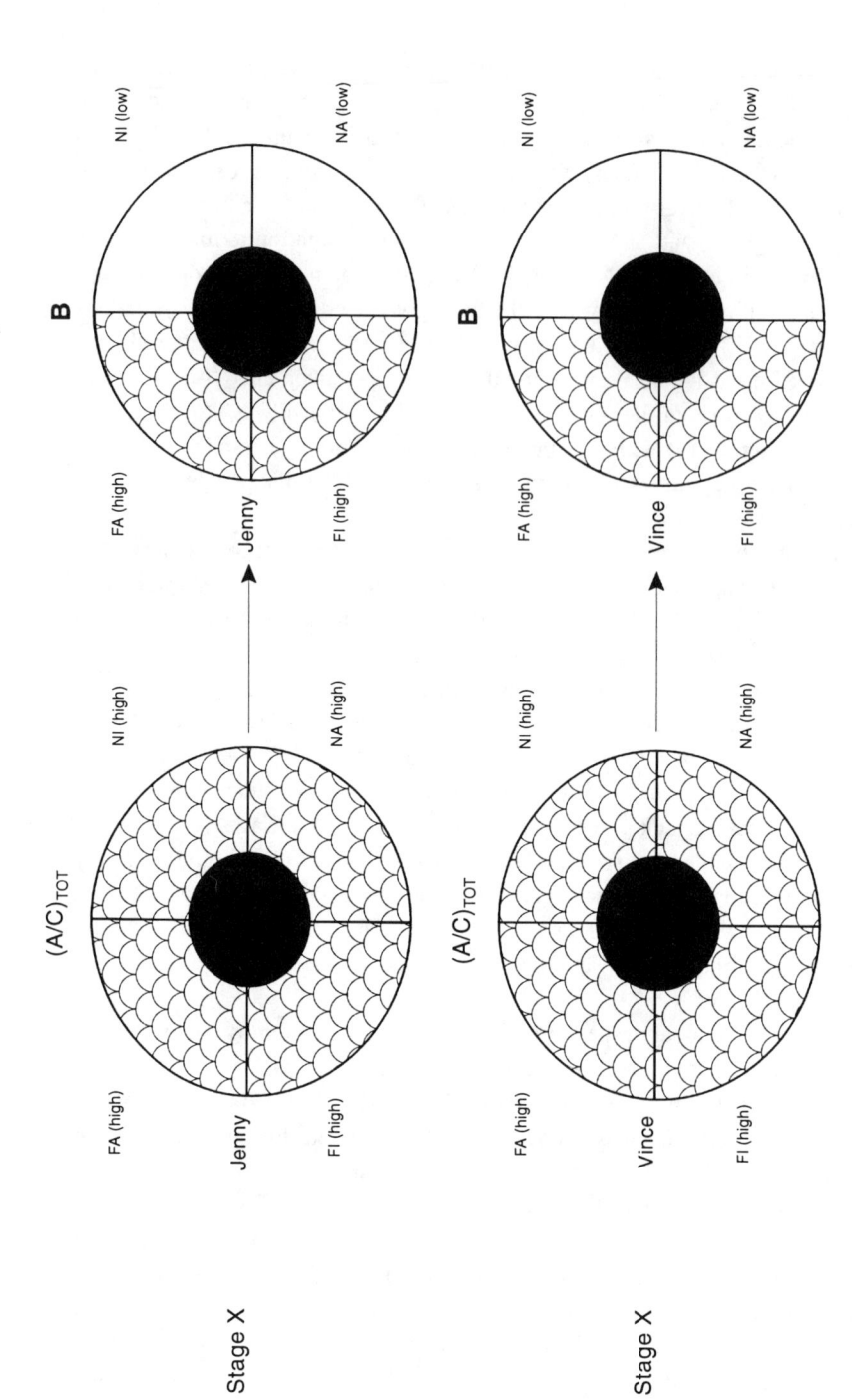

Figure 7-11 Jenny and Vince

never developed a career of her own. Vince felt compelled to be successful, yet he was afraid of it. He felt compelled to be a devoted husband, yet he was afraid of it. Slowly, Vince developed the insight necessary to see his problem in a different light. He realized his own wife was not dependent the way his mother had been. He felt less compelled to be successful and the source of strength for his wife. At this point, he showed uncertainty (2) regarding the statements "I have to do things my own way" (uncertain NI) and "You are not worth much if you are only occupied with your own concerns" (uncertain NA).

Jenny was a much tougher nut to crack. She had had a disastrous first marriage to a successful business executive. She had worked to put him through business school. However, he subsequently left Jenny for a younger woman. As a result, Jenny felt tremendously conflicted regarding both attachment and individuation. She was frightened of getting too close, yet she needed love. She was frightened of being left on her own, yet needed a career. She seemed to be afraid that preparing for being alone would bring it about.

As a result of continued treatment, Jenny became more relaxed regarding individuation and attachment. She now disagreed (1) with the statements "I believe everyone has an obligation to find their own way in life" (low NI) and "I have a great need for sharing my feelings with other people" (low NA).

In TILT terms, Jenny and Vince had regressed from a psychotic $(A/C)_{TOT}$ $(A/C)_{TOT}$ marriage to a BB position on the BED axis. They still had fear of both individuation and attachment but were not longer conflicted on the issue. Hopefully further therapeutic work will move them ahead to Position EE (see Figure 7-11).

IMPLICATIONS FOR CHILDREN

Discussions in this book have not yet touched on the position of children in these different couple types. For example, a couple organized at the neurotic level (AC) may produce a child or adolescent who vacillates in borderline fashion between the two positions or who psychotically introjects this conflict (A/C). In other words, children may represent a more serious level of pathology than do the parents. A goal of family therapy may be to transform this type of family into a healthy one in which both parents are D (DD) and the child is B, avoiding the temptations of premature bonding (A) or autonomy (C). This, of course, may involve a temporary regression on the part of the parents to BB (AC → BB) before they are able to move ahead (BB → EE → DD). The therapist must shield the child (D) during this troubled time, allowing him or her to be a child (B). Chapter 8 will present an empirical study that investigates the relationship between marital patterns and completed adolescent suicide.

Chapter 8

TILT for Families: A Family Study on Adolescent Suicide

PARENTS AND CHILDREN: A THEORETICAL EXTENSION

Chapter 8 presents a study on the role of families in preventing and/or promoting adolescent suicide, as an illustration of how TILT can be applied to families. The underlying approach of this chapter is to define adolescent suicide and other self-destructive behaviors in terms of incongruent combinations of individuation and attachment as displayed on the AC axis. Developmental growth and constructive behaviors, in contrast, are conceptualized in terms of congruent growth of individuation and attachment along the developmental BED axis.

First the analysis of couple types developed in the previous two chapters is extended to families as a whole. This extension, of course, necessitates a specification of what types of children emerge from the different couple types discussed previously.

Let us begin with some admittedly oversimplified axioms. First, it should be emphasized again that

IMMATURITY IS NOT PATHOLOGY

The following axioms assume no corrective therapeutic intervention into the family dynamics: Children raised by couples on the developmental BED axis should themselves develop on the BED axis, whereas children raised by couples on the clinical AC axis should likewise develop on the AC axis. In other words

HEALTHY COUPLES SHOULD PRODUCE HEALTHY CHILDREN

PATHOLOGICAL COUPLES SHOULD PRODUCE PATHOLOGICAL CHILDREN

Table 8-1
Children of different TILT couple types

Parental couple TILT type	Child TILT type
Developmental axis	
(Regressed) BB	B
(Emerging) EE	B or E
(Mature) DD	B, E, or D
(Parent–child) DB	B
Clinical axis	
(Neurotic)	
Enmeshed AA	A (or possibly C)
Disengaged CC	C (or possible A)
Rejection-intrusion AC	A, C, $(A/C)_{IND}$, $(A/C)_{ATT}$ or $(A/C)_{TOT}$
(Borderline)	
Depressive $(A/C)_{IND}$ $(A/C)_{IND}$	$(A/C)_{IND}$ [or possibly $(A/C)_{ATT}$]
Paranoid $(A/C)_{ATT}$ $(A/C)_{ATT}$	$(A/C)_{ATT}$ [or possibly $(A/C)_{IND}$]
Mixed $(A/C)_{IND}$ $(A/C)_{ATT}$	$(A/C)_{IND}$, $(A/C)_{ATT}$ or $(A/C)_{TOT}$
(Psychotic)	
$(A/C)_{TOT}$ $(A/C)_{TOT}$	$(A/C)_{TOT}$

Children on the developmental BED axis are likely to be at the same developmental level (B, E, or D) as their least-developed parents or lower. In other words

**IN HEALTHY FAMILIES, CHILDREN ARE
NO MORE DEVELOPED THAN THEIR PARENTS**

Children on the clinical AC axis are likely to be at the same level of pathology (neurotic, borderline, or psychotic) as their parents or higher. In other words

**IN PATHOLOGICAL FAMILIES, CHILDREN ARE
NO LESS PATHOLOGICAL THAN THEIR PARENTS**

A taxonomy of child types likely to emerge from the different couple types is presented in Table 8-1. This table describes a number of frequently observed family patterns and some that are less frequently observed. Let us briefly examine these configurations one by one. First the "balanced" developmental (BED) axis will be discussed, and then the "imbalanced" clinical (AC) axis.

THE DEVELOPMENTAL (BED) AXIS

TILT regards all of these developmental positions as healthy (in the sense of being balanced between individuation and attachment) but at different levels of maturity (in the sense of being fear-dominated or need-dominated) and as open to development in this regard (from fears to needs).

The regressed BB family. The partners in a BB couple are not able to tolerate individuation or attachment. They are dominated by fears with regard to these two issues. A child in this family is likely to show this same pattern (i.e., also be at Position B).

The emerging EE family. Here the parents have overcome their fears of individuation and attachment but they have not yet learned to assert healthy needs. A child in this family is likely to copy the parents' pattern (i.e., Position E) or be at the more regressed fear-dominated position discussed directly above (i.e., Position B).

The mature DD family. Here the parents have overcome their fears with regard to individuation and attachment and can express healthy needs with regard to both issues. The child coming from this family configuration may likewise be in a mature D position or may be less developed on this same developmental axis, falling into the emerging (E) or regressed (B) positions discussed above.

The parent-child BD family. This represents the most problematic and unstable of any couple on the BED developmental axis. Here one partner (D) is need-dominated while the other (B) is fear-dominated. It is highly unlikely that a child emerging from this situation will be anything but fear-dominated (i.e., be at Position B), being limited by the developmental level of the less mature partner.

Again, it should be emphasized that the children emerging in all of the above cases are essentially healthy in the sense that they are balanced in terms of individuation and attachment. Thus, in the course of normal development, these children are likely to develop along the BED axis. B children will overcome their fears and become E children. E children will learn to express their needs and become D children.[1]

THE CLINICAL (AC) AXIS

It should be emphasized again that TILT regards all of the following clinical positions as unhealthy (in terms of being imbalanced between individuation and attachment), unstable (in the sense of oscillating between enmeshed and disengagement polarities), and blocked to development without therapeutic intervention (i.e., being tilted onto Position B on the BED axis.)

---

[1] It may be possible that a child emerging from this relationship will veer toward attachment or individuation and thus fit on the clinical AC axis. However, this remains conjecture at the present time.

The neurotic enmeshed (AA) family. Both partners in the parental couple have fears of individuation blurred with needs for individuation. Lack of space should be an issue for a child in this family. He or she is likely to repeat this pattern and become an enmeshed personality (Position A) or may possibly rebel in protest and become disengaged (Position C).

The neurotic disengaged (CC) family. Here both parents have needs for individuation coupled with fears of attachment. Lack of closeness should be the primary issue for children growing up in this family. A child may repeat this pattern, becoming a disengaged personality (Position C), or may possibly take the opposite tack and crave affection at all costs, becoming an enmeshed personality (Position A).

The neurotic rejection-intrusion (AC) family. Here one partner in the parental couple is enmeshed (A) and the other is disengaged (C). The child experiences one partner continuously approaching and the other withdrawing. The A partner perceives the C as rejecting and the C perceives the A as intruding. In such a conflictual situation, the child may identify with one parent or the other (A or C positions), remaining at the neurotic level. However, it is also possible that the child will attempt to resolve this conflict by bridging the two positions. With therapeutic intervention, this child seems a likely candidate to regress to Position B on the developmental axis. Without such help, however, he or she is likely to be pulled simultaneously in the direction of enmeshment and disengagement, either on individuation or attachment [the borderline depressive positions $(A/C)_{IND}$ and paranoid position $(A/C)_{ATT}$] or both [the psychotic $(A/C)_{TOT}$] position.

The borderline depressive $[(A/C)_{IND} (A/C)_{IND}]$ family. The partners in a borderline depressive marriage are mutually conflicted regarding individuation, both needing and fearing it, and indifferent toward attachment. The child from such a depressed configuration may adopt this ambivalence regarding individuation, remaining a borderline depressive personality $[(A/C)_{IND}]$. It also is possible that the child may switch his or her ambivalence to the attachment issue, transforming to the borderline paranoid $[(A/C)_{ATT}]$ position.

The borderline paranoid $[(A/C)_{ATT}(A/C)_{ATT}]$ family. The partners in a borderline paranoid marriage are mutually conflicted regarding attachment, both needing and fearing it, and indifferent toward individuation. The child in this paranoid configuration may emulate the parents and remain in the borderline paranoid position $[(A/C)_{ATT}]$ or may possibly convert his or her ambivalence to the opposite individuation dimension, falling into the borderline depressive $[(A/C)_{IND}]$ position.

The borderline mixed $[(A/C)_{IND}(A/C)_{ATT}]$ family. The partners in a borderline mixed configuration are complementary. One is depressive and ambivalent about individuation issues whereas the other is paranoid, ambivalent about attachment issues. The child in such a marriage may emulate one parent or the other (remaining) at the borderline level [either $(A/C)_{IND}$ or $(A/C)_{ATT}$]. Alternatively, the child may attempt to maintain loyalty to both parents and attempt to bridge this difference. Although this makes such a child a good candidate for being tilted back to B on the BED developmental axis, this is unlikely to occur without therapeutic intervention. More likely, this child will become even more pathological, becoming ambivalent with regard to both issues [$(A/C)_{TOT}$].

The psychotic [$(A/C)_{TOT}$ $(A/C)_{TOT}$] family. The partners in a psychotic couple are ambivalent regarding both individuation and attachment, needing and fearing both. The child in such a chaotic relationship is likely to remain psychotic [$(A/C)_{TOT}$] without outside intervention to shield him or her from the pathological family dynamics. Many of these clinical patterns are quite subtle. However, from the perspective of TILT, they are all pathological in the sense of being imbalanced between individuation and attachment. Furthermore, without outside intervention (TILTing these children back to Position B on the BED axis), these children are likely to remain in the same (or worse) pathological positions as adults and thus repeat this family pathology when they themselves become parents.

The implications of the TILT approach to family development are straightforward. Children raised by developmental BED parents are likely to be healthier than children raised by the clinical AC parents. With this in mind, we turn to an original literature review and empirical study linking parental marital style to completed adolescent suicide.

FAMILY FACTORS IN ADOLESCENT SUICIDE

A number of studies have investigated the role of family in suicide. Several researchers have emphasized the clustering effect of suicide in some biological families (Egeland & Sussex, 1985; Farberow & Simon, 1969; Tsuang, 1983). One explanation for these effects is simply genetic. However, other explanations are possible as well. It is possible that family members of a suicide victim are at greater risk for suicide because a genetic predisposition for specific psychiatric disorders (e.g., mood disorders) runs in the family, and the latter predisposition raises the risk for suicide. For example, Pitts and Winokur (1964) showed that 68% of 37 psychiatric patients with a family history of suicide had an affective disorder. Roy (1983) showed that 56% of 243 psychiatric inpatients with a family history of suicide had a current primary depressive disorder and 84% had a history of major depressive disorder.

These results are very important in alerting us to the potential mediating role of psychiatric disorder in studies examining family influences on suicide. However, an exclusive focus on parental and family psychiatric history per se does not pay sufficient attention to the important question of how parental and family patterns (aside from parental psychiatric history) may affect the suicidal risk of an individual (cf., Durkheim, 1897/1951; Freud, 1917/1957a; Heilig, 1980). This is especially germane for an adolescent who must depend on a secure family base to allow development of his or her own identity (cf., Haim, 1970; Stierlin, 1974). Indeed, federal statistics have indicated that the suicide rate for adolescents and young adults has risen rapidly since the middle of the twentieth century (Anderson, Kochanek & Murphy, 1995). Even more strikingly, attempted suicides in this age group may actually be 120 times as great (Finch & Poznanski, 1971).

A number of empirical studies have stressed the importance of secure parental patterns beginning in early infancy. Ainsworth (1972) stresses the importance of an "attachment-exploration" balance proceeding from a "secure base" (also cf., Brazelton et al., 1974; and Stern, 1977). Empirical results have demonstrated stable developmental patterns in this regard across the early years of life (e.g., Arend et al., 1979; Main, 1973; Hoffman, 1977). Children receiving secure parenting seem to be more resilient than those coming from more insecure families. The implications of this consistent developmental pattern are quite striking for adolescent suicide. The life task for adolescence involves separation from one's parents (Stierlin, 1974) and the achievement of a secure identity (Erikson, 1968, 1980). This task is facilitated by parental permission and support for this individuation process and hindered by parents who are threatened and attempt to block it.

The supportive family is one that itself has a balance between attachment and individuation (exploration) while a nonsupportive family is likely to show imbalance between these two forces, presenting the adolescent with the alternatives between enmeshment and estrangement. An adolescent emerging from a secure family base that provides the balance between attachment and individuation (exploration) should be more resilient and thus at lesser risk for suicide than one coming from an insecure base. In TILT terms, adolescents emerging in families falling on the developmental BED axis should be at lesser risk for suicide than those emerging from families falling on the clinical AC axis. The present chapter will examine two types of evidence to test this hypothesis. First, the results of published studies linking family structure variables to adolescent suicide will be examined. Second, data will be presented from an original study designed to test this hypothesis. For the purpose of simplicity, I limit the analyses to two developmental couple types (BB and DD) and three clinical couple types (AA, CC, and AC).

The healthy developmental couple types each involve congruence between individuation and attachment and do not involve polarization of either partner.

1. A regressed BB couple where neither parent is able to tolerate much intimacy or separation, but where there is still congruence between these two forces. Each parent is defended but not polarized into enmeshed or disengaged

positions. This is seen as a temporary position, setting the stage for healthy maturation into the mature position described directly below.
2. An advanced DD couple where both parents are able to tolerate both intimacy and separation (cf., Jourard & Friedman, 1970).

The pathological incongruent types involve incongruence between individuation and attachment and are polarized as follows:

3. An enmeshed (AA) couple where both parents are attached without being individuated (Durkheim, 1897/1951; Minuchin, 1974; Olson et al., 1979).
4. A disengaged (CC) couple where both parents are individuated without being attached (Durkheim, 1897/1951; Minuchin, 1974; Olson et al., 1979).
5. A rejection-intrusion (AC) couple where one partner is enmeshed and the other is disengaged (Durkheim, 1897/1951; Napier, 1978; Willi, 1982).

The logic behind these predictions is straightforward. Children of BB and DD couples are likely themselves to develop on the BED axis. These positions are not likely to be suicidal. In contrast, children of AA, CC, and AC couples will, without outside intervention, probably remain on the AC axis. In Emile Durkheim's classic work on suicide (1897/1951), all of these positions are potentially suicidal. Durkheim distinguishes between *egoistic*, *altruistic* and *anomic* suicides. Durkheim's egoistic suicide is insufficiently integrated with his outside environment. In TILT terms, this clearly represents the disengaged C position. The altruistic suicide, in contrast, is insufficiently differentiated from his environment. This represents the enmeshed A position in the TILT model. Finally, the anomic suicide for Durkheim is potentially the most lethal and involves confusion in boundaries between the individual and his outside environment. This parallels the A/C positions described in the TILT model.

In summary, TILT hypothesizes that children of parents on the AC axis are more likely to be suicidal than those of parents on the BED axis. This prediction can be reversed as well. A sample of completed adolescent suicides has a higher proportion of A and C parents than a control sample of nonsuicidal adolescents. Let us now turn to the empirical evidence.

A TAXONOMY

The author in collaboration with Marshall Maldaver (Kaplan & Maldaver, 1993) reviewed some 85 studies that linked family structure variables of the type discussed above to adolescent suicidal behavior. In these studies, judgments of enmeshment and disengagement had to be inferred from self-report measures, behavioral

Table 8-2
Frequency of studies linking family variables to adolescent suicidal behavior

Family variables	No effect on adolescents	Psychiatric disorder only	Suicidal attempts behavior and ideation	Completed suicides	Total
Specified parental marital types					
Advanced reciprocal	—	—	—	—	—
Regressed reciprocal	—	3	5	—	8
Embedded	—	4	5	—	9
Isolated	—	3	19	3	25
Rejection–intrusion	5	14	23	1	43
Total	5	24	52	4	85

descriptions, and/or individual psychiatric diagnoses. Thus, for example, a psychiatric diagnosis of dependent personality disorder was classified as enmeshed and a diagnosis of a paranoid personality type as disengaged. These judgments were made by two research assistants who were instructed as to the above definitions of family type but who remained unaware of the underlying hypotheses of the authors or the specific results of a particular study linking the family structure variables to suicidal outcome.

Table 8-2 summarizes the relative frequencies of the reviewed empirical findings. The abscissa is graded in terms of increasing severity of outcome: (1) no effect, (2) psychiatric disorder with no suicidal behavior, and (3) unsuccessful suicidal attempts, behavior, and ideation, and (4) completed suicide. The ordinate is classified in terms of the five parental patterns discussed above. Attempted adolescent suicide occurs most frequently (76%) in the disengaged (CC) parental pattern, followed respectively by the regressed (BB) parental pattern (62%), the enmeshed (AA) parental pattern (56%) in suicide studies reporting the rejection–intrusion (AC) parental pattern (53%). No attempted suicides are reported for the advanced (DD) parental pattern. With regard to completed suicides, the most frequent marital pattern is disengaged (12%), followed by the rejection–intrusion pattern (2%). The enmeshed parental pattern is most lethal with regard to adolescent psychiatric diagnosis (44%), followed by the regressed pattern (34%), the rejection–intrusion pattern (33%), and finally the disengaged parental pattern (33%). Overall, the literature review supports the notion that the congruent parental styles (at least the advanced reciprocal pattern) are consistently associated with less adolescent pathology (ranging from psychiatric disorder through completed suicide) than are the incongruent marital styles ($p < .05$). The regressed reciprocal parental pattern is associated with higher degrees of adolescent pathology than might be expected from a simple congruency prediction.

Consider some illustrations of the suicidogenic effects of these dysfunctional marital types. Consider first the case of disengaged parents. Corder, Page, and Corder (1974) found that parents of adolescent attempters were perceived as stringent disciplinarians, disengaged, and unable to communicate with their children. McIntire and Angle (1973) report that 56% of children who poisoned themselves indicated a loss of communication with their parents (see also the studies of Chia, 1979; Garfinkel, Froese, & Hood, 1982; Parnitzke & Regel, 1973; Sathyavathi, 1975).

Consider now the enmeshed parental type. Hill (1970) compared the mothers of suicidal and nonsuicidal adolescent girls on a measure of empathy, finding that the mothers of the suicidal subjects were the least empathic and most symbiotic of all groups. Richman (1978) found a polarity between symbiosis and disengagement in the work of Litman and Tabachnik (1968), Wold (1968, 1970), Sarwer-Foner (1969), and Boszormenyi-Nagy and Spark (1973). Related work has been reported by Cassorla (1984), Friedman, Corn, Hurt, Fibel, Schalick, and Swirsky (1984), and Housman (1981).

The rejection–intrusion parental type is also lethal. Wenz (1978) reports greater anomie and conflict among families of 55 suicides than among those of 55 matched controls. Similar results were obtained by McKenry, Tishler, and Kelly (1982), who found family conflict to be greater among adolescents attempting suicide than among controls. The reader is also referred to the work of Kosky (1983), Pfeffer (1981), and Wenz (1979). While these results are not definitive in themselves, they are certainly suggestive of the utility of the individuation–attachment approach in the study of family structure and adolescent suicide. We now turn to an original empirical study of completed adolescent suicide, an underrepresented outcome variable in the above literature review.

AN EMPIRICAL STUDY

An original study (Kaplan & Maldaver, 1993) addressed more directly the relationship between parental marital pattern and completed adolescent suicide. Parental marital patterns were divided into three types: (a) healthy (each parent congruent between individuation and attachment), (b) pathological (each parent incongruent between individuation and attachment), and (c) mixed (one healthy parent and the other pathological parent (whether enmeshed or disengaged). The study specifically hypothesized that families of completed adolescent suicides would show a higher preponderance of pathological marital types and a lower frequency of

Table 8-3
Characteristics of the sample from Cook, Lake, and DuPage Counties
(1987–1988)

	Suicide families	Comparison families
Number contacted	25	25
Number responded	18	25
Number intact	15	21
Number reconstituted	3	3
Widowed or divorced	3	4
Male adolescents	16	23
Female adolescents	2	2
White	16	23
Black	2	2

healthy marital types than would those of matched controls. It was expected that differences between the two groups would be minimized with regard to the mixed marital types.

The index or suicide group (see Table 8-3) consisted of 25 parental couples of a sample of consecutive completed suicides in 1987 and 1988 aged 15 to 19 inclusive in a three-county area surrounding Chicago. They were referred to the investigators by the county coroner's office (in Lake and DuPage counties) and the medical examiner (in Cook County) as part of an ongoing psychological autopsy study conducted by researchers at Rush-Presbyterian-St. Luke's Medical Center in Chicago. The parents in the suicide group were approached from three to six months after the death of their children. Eighteen of the 25 pairs of parents contacted agreed to participate in this "family" part of the study. Sixteen of the adolescent suicides were males and 2 were female with a mean age of 17.23 at the time of the suicide. The modes of death were gunshot wounds (8), carbon monoxide (6), hanging (2), jumping (1), and drug overdose (1). Sixteen of the families were Caucasian and 2 African-American. Fifteen of the families involved intact marriages (ongoing marriage of biological parents) and 3 involved reconstituted marriages.

The comparison or control group (again see Table 8-3) consisted of the parents of 25 control adolescents matched to the 25 suicides in terms of age, gender, and race. The control families were also matched in terms of intactness and geographical proximity (six blocks away from an urban or suburban suicide family, four miles away for rural cases). The control sample consisted of 23 males and 2 females with a mean age of 17.36. Twenty-three of the families were Caucasian and 2 were African-American. Twenty-one of these parent pairs were intact, 3 were reconstituted, and only 1 represented a presently divorced single parent (again see Table 8-3).

The most important measures obtained by this study for the TILT model are as follows.

The Individuation–Attachment Questionnaire (IAQ). A 40-item version of the IAQ was employed in this study. As described previously in chapter 2, it is designed to yield four separate attachment and individuation scores: NI, or the need to make one's own decisions; FI, or the fear of making one's own decisions; NA, or the need to form close relationships; and FA, or the fear of forming close relationships. Congruencies or nondiscrepancies between individuation and attachment scores (either both high or both low) placed that individual as healthy; incongruencies or discrepancies between these scores (one high and the other low) placed the individual as pathological. Healthy couples consist of two healthy partners, mixed couples consist of one healthy partner and one pathological one; pathological couples consist of two pathological partners.

Family Adaptability and Cohesion Evaluation Scales (FACES). FACES is a traditional family measure developed by Olson and his colleagues (1979, 1980, 1982, 1983). Families are assessed on two basic dimensions. The first is family cohesion, which assesses the degree to which members are separated from or connected to others in their family. This assumes an inverse relationship between separation and connection. The second dimension is family adaptability, which is defined as the ability of a marital or family system to change its power structure, role relationships, and relationship rules in response to situational and developmental stress.

Child Behavior Checklist-Parent Version (CBCL-P). The CBCL-P (Achenbach & Edelbrock, 1983) provided a measure of psychopathology. It provides a parental description of the level of psychopathology among the subjects to be studied that may be compared with empirically established population norms.

Group Differences in Age of Parents

In an unexpected effect, the parents in the suicide group were significantly older than those of controls who had themselves been matched in age to the suicided adolescents. This was true for both mothers (mean ages 47.3 to 43.3, $p < .05$) and for fathers (mean ages 52.9 to 47.5, $p < .05$).

Group Differences in Parental Marital Pathology

The degree of parental pathology as diagnosed by the IAQ self-report systematically differed between the suicide and control group. As can be seen in Figure 8-1, 16.7% (3) of the 18 suicide families had two healthy parents (congruency between individuation and attachment), 44.4% (8) had a mixed parental pattern—one

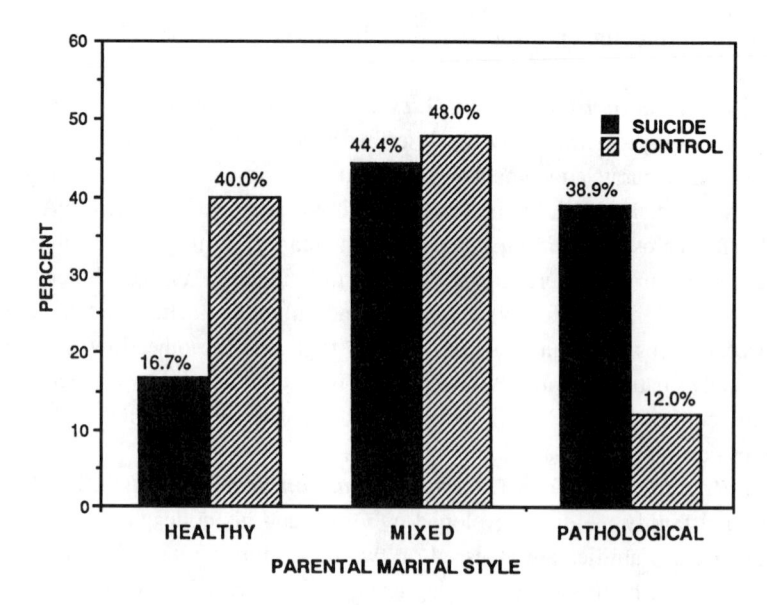

Figure 8-1 Marital pathology and completed adolescent suicide.

healthy (congruent) parent and one pathological parent (incongruency between individuation and attachment)—and 38.9% (7) had two pathological (incongruent) parents. The 25 control families showed a dramatically opposite pattern. Forty percent (10) of these families had two healthy parents, 48% (12) had a mixed (one healthy and one pathological) parental pattern, and only 12% (3) had two pathological parents. The chi-square describing this interaction equals 5.16 (2 d.f.) and is significant at the .075 level.[2]

None of the FACES pathology measures provide the discriminating power offered by the IAQ. For example, neither parent's perceptions of the FACES family pathology score was significantly different in the two groups. Both mothers and fathers tended to perceive their families as nonpathological (moderate on a unidimensional distance measure) whether they were in the suicide or control group.

Group Differences in Perceived Adolescent Psychopathology

The data indicate no differences in mothers' mean scores on any of the CBCL subdimensions between the suicide and control groups. This nondifference runs

---

[2] The presence of so many mixed parental patterns (one healthy partner and one pathological partner) was not expected by the theory. Nevertheless, the findings are clear with regard to healthy versus pathological couples.

against findings showing predictive affects for suicide of affective disorder, substance abuse, and conduct disorder, either alone or in combination (e.g., Brent et al., 1988; Fowler, Rich, & Young, 1986; Garfinkel & Golombek, 1983; Rich, Young & Fowler, 1986; Shafii, Carrigan, Whittinghill & Derrick, 1985). Other studies have pointed to the role of bipolar disorder, affective disorder with comorbidity, and psychosis (e.g., Brent et al., 1988; Otto, 1972), though some studies have shown negative results (Black, Winokur, & Nasrallah, 1987).

Parental Marital Pathology and Perceived Adolescent Psychopathology

Interestingly, a number of these CBCL dimensions do discriminate pathological versus healthy marital styles (IAQ) when we collapse across suicide and control groups. Pathological couples produce adolescents judged by their mothers to be more somatic (62.4 to 56.2, $p = .038$), more uncommunicative (65.8 to 56.7, $p = .06$), more obsessive–compulsive (68.8 to 56.3, $p = .023$), and more hostile (65.6 to 56.4, $p = .043$). These effects are summarized in Table 8-4.

These findings are quite interesting. They suggest that the IAQ marital pathology score differentiates adolescent psychopathology independent of suicide and adolescent suicide independent of psychopathology (see Figure 8-2). Yet adolescent suicide and psychopathology are unrelated in the study. Some pathological defensive behaviors on the part of the adolescents growing up in disturbed families (e.g., hostile withdrawal) actually may serve a suicide-preventive function by removing the adolescent from the pathological family dynamics.

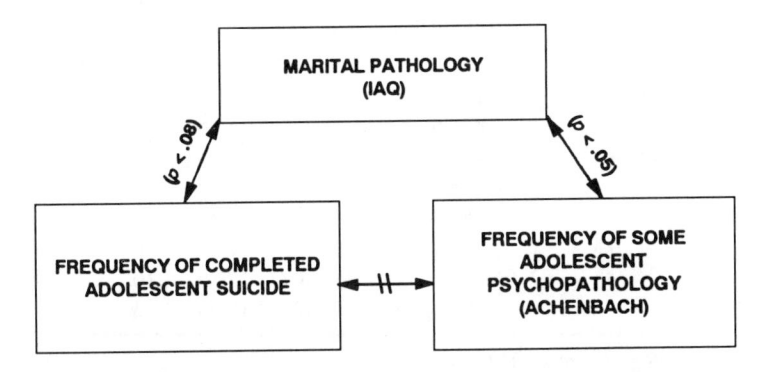

Figure 8-2 Marital pathology, adolescent suicide, and adolescent psychopathology.

Table 8-4
Adolescents' Achenbach Pathology by parents
Individuation–Attachment Questionnaire (IAQ) marital style

Achenbach path	IAQ path	Mean	SD	N	Sig.[a]
Somatic	Healthy	56.20	2.69	10	.038*
complaints	Mixed	64.30	8.98	10	
	Pathological	62.40	7.26	5	
Schizoid	Healthy	55.40	.51	10	.143
	Mixed	62.30	11.05	10	
	Pathological	63.40	11.84	5	
Uncommunicative	Healthy	56.70	3.46	10	.060
	Mixed	62.60	6.89	10	
	Pathological	65.80	12.07	5	
Immature	Healthy	57.70	3.19	10	.245
	Mixed	63.20	10.22	10	
	Pathological	63.40	9.12	5	
Obsessive–	Healthy	56.30	3.43	10	.023*
compulsive	Mixed	63.20	7.16	10	
	Pathological	68.80	14.13	5	
Hostile	Healthy	56.40	2.54	10	.043*
withdrawal	Mixed	60.90	6.45	10	
	Pathological	65.60	10.71	5	
Delinquency	Healthy	57.40	2.06	10	.402
	Mixed	59.40	5.16	10	
	Pathological	60.00	4.24	5	
Agressive	Healthy	56.10	2.80	10	.121
	Mixed	62.00	9.95	10	
	Pathological	62.30	6.87	5	
Hyperactive	Healthy	56.70	2.94	10	.084
	Mixed	64.00	11.18	7	
	Pathological	66.75	11.08	4	
Internalizing	Healthy	49.50	6.85	10	.129
	Mixed	59.70	12.79	10	
	Pathological	60.20	17.81	5	
Externalizing	Healthy	50.40	7.63	10	.305
	Mixed	56.60	12.19	10	
	Pathological	58.40	12.93	5	

[a] *-Significant at .05 level.

IMPLICATIONS FOR TILT

A number of findings of interest to TILT can be highlighted in the previously discussed study: (1) Parents of suicides are significantly older than control parents. (2) Parents of suicides have more pathological marital styles as revealed by the IAQ (incongruity between individuation and attachment) than do control parents. No such differences between suicide and control groups emerge on the unidimensional FACES measure. (3) There are no differences between suicide and control groups in maternal perception of their adolescents on any of the CBCL dimensions. (4) However, pathological families do perceive their adolescents as more uncommunicative, more obsessive–compulsive, and more hostile than do healthy families when the data is collapsed across the suicide and control groups. Each of these findings will be discussed briefly in turn.

Age of Parents and Adolescent Suicide

The average age of both of the index parents was higher than that of the control parents. Are older parents less able to cope with the adolescent's emotional needs? That is, does the accentuated age difference sharpen the generation gap between parent and child? An alternative explanation is also possible. The age discrepancy between the index parents and those in the control group may indicate that the suicided adolescent may be a younger sibling (thus having an older parent), whereas the control is more likely to be an older sibling (thus having a younger parent). This pattern raises research questions regarding effects between adolescent suicide and birth order.

Marital Pathology and Adolescent Suicide

To begin with, the IAQ assessment of marital pathology discriminates the suicide and control groups, whereas the assessment based on FACES does not. This is probably due to the different assumptions between the two measures. FACES is based on a unidimensional view of cohesion. Attachment represents the bipolar opposite of individuation. Thus, the FACES cohesion scales are anchored at one end by enmeshment and at the other by disengagement. The IAQ, in contrast, makes no such assumption, allowing independent measures of individuation and attachment. Thus, subtle nuances in congruencies or incongruencies between individuation and attachment can be measured. Another difference is that FACES as well as the FES and DAS measure the parent's perception of the marriage and/or family. The IAQ, in contrast, measures the parent's self-perceptions. Marital types are classified through combinations of self-perceptions of the two partners. This latter procedure may provide a more sensitive and less guarded indicator of parental dysfunction.

These findings support the predictions developed in the beginning of this chapter. Children from clinical AC families are more likely to be suicidal than those from developmentally BED families.[3] The adolescent, like the earlier child, needs secure parenting to develop his or her own identity. This involves parents themselves congruent between individuation and attachment. Parents incongruent between individuation and attachment, in contrast, withdraw support for the adolescent's necessary stage-appropriate attempts at individuation. Perhaps they see such attempts by the adolescent as disloyal to the family agenda. Thus, Neal Perry's desire to be an actor in the film *Dead Poets' Society* is seen by his father as betrayal of the family agenda that Neal follow his father's footsteps and be a doctor. The adolescent in such an incongruent family is caught between the unlivable alternatives of enmeshment and disengagement. Like Neal Perry, such a child may attempt to find a solution to this problem through suiciding.

Maternal Perceived Adolescent Psychopathology and Adolescent Suicide

There were no differences between suicide and control groups in terms of maternal perception of their adolescents on any of the CBCL dimensions. These results are somewhat surprising in light of the findings of some other studies (e.g., Garfinkel & Golombek, 1983; Kaplan & Harrow, 1996, 1998; Shaffer, 1974; Shaffi et al., 1985; Westermeyer and Harrow, 1989), all of which report that adolescents who committed suicide have significant psychiatric conditions, such as affective disorders, schizophrenia, antisocial behavior, and alcohol and substance abuse. It is

---

[3] These results indicate a linkage between parental marital pathology and completed adolescent suicide. Further, certain adolescent psychiatric disturbances may actually buffer the adolescent from suicidogenic family forces. Nevertheless, any retrospective study of suicide and family structure obscures the causality question. Do pathological family patterns contribute to adolescent suicide or does adolescent suicide, indeed any loss, contribute to pathological family patterns? A number of studies, for example, have pointed to the all-pervasive effects of loss, whether by suicide or not, on the family (cf., Cain & Fast, 1965; Jacobs, 1971; Jacobs & Teicher, 1967; Morrison & Collier, 1969; Moss & Hamilton, 1957; Rieger, 1971; Richman, 1981). Disentangling this question requires the inclusion in future studies of a second control group involving adolescents who have died in accidental deaths rather than suicides. Soutre (1988) suggests employing passengers killed in automobile accidents. Forward effects of family pathology (i.e., parental pathology contributes to adolescent suicide) should show uniquely in the suicide group, the accident control group being no different than the control. Forward effects of adolescent loss (i.e., adolescent loss, whether by suicide or not, contributes to parental pathology) should emerge in both the accident and suicide groups, which should both be different from the control group.

tempting to dismiss the present results by pointing to the limitations of employing only parental informants. The accuracy of a particular informant varies with the diagnosis. Children and adolescents tend to be better sources for assessment of conduct disorder and substance use, whereas parents more accurately report oppositional disorder and attention deficit disorder, although they tend to underreport the presence of internalizing disorders. Both parental and child informants are typically used to assess mood and thought disorders. There is no real reason, however, to assume that these biases should differ between mothers in the suicide and control groups. It is possible that internalizing disorders did exist among the adolescent suicides but that they were underreported by their mothers. However, such an interpretation remains conjecture in the present study.

Marital Pathology and Maternal Perceived Adolescent Psychopathology

Examining the effects of marital style itself collapsing across the suicide and control groups suggests an entirely different line of interpretation. Maternal ratings of adolescent somatic complaints, obsessive–compulsive disorders, hostility, and uncommunicativeness are higher for the pathological than the healthy marriages. The presence of significant effects here leads to serious doubt whether the noneffect of the suicide versus control groups discussed immediately above can be simply dismissed in terms of biases and limitations in the method. Obviously, despite these limitations, significant effects do occur if they are strong enough.

My preference is to consider the two sets of results in tandem. Marital pathology covaries with adolescent suicide largely independent of adolescent psychiatric diagnosis (as measured by the maternal CBCL ratings) and with adolescent psychiatric diagnosis independent of suicide. In other words: some adolescents in the pathological families suicide, others withdraw. There is no such need to withdraw in the happy families. These findings have a very important implcation:

WITHDRAWAL MAY BE SUICIDE-PREVENTIVE

These findings seems to fit the view expressed in Laing and Esterson (1970) and Borst and Noam (1990) emphasizing the self-preservative functions of some behavior labeled "mentally ill." In the absence of outside intervention, some adolescents in the pathological families may actually shield themselves from the destructive family dynamics through protective behaviors labeled by mothers as obsessive–compulsive, hostile, and uncommunicative. These are the adolescents who turn out to be nonsuicidal even though they are labeled mentally ill. These adolescents may actually be erecting walls to protect fragile boundaries. They may be tilting themselves off of the clinical AC axis backward to Position B on the BED developmental axis.

IMPLICATIONS FOR SAFE

In an important article on suicide in children and adolescents, Shaffer and Fisher (1981) suggest that integration within the framework of family protects children from suicidal behavior through the reduction of isolation and the extension of social and emotional support. This is a reasonable assumption given the known correlates of adult suicide. Single adults living alone have higher suicide rates than their married counterparts (Barraclough, Bunch, Nelson, & Sainsbury, 1974). Indeed, the conventional wisdom in the suicide prevention movement is to reduce social isolation. Nevertheless, the data suggest that the pathological family itself may sometimes exacerbate rather than ameliorate the suicidal crisis. At such times, the child or adolescent may actually need to be separated temporarily from the family and provided with an alternate base of social and emotional support. In fact, the data suggest that some nonsuicidal adolescents in the pathological families withdraw on their own from the potentially suicidogenic family milieu, often without an alternate base of interpersonal support. In TILT terms, they regress off of the clinical AC axis to Position B on the developmental BED axis.

I am presently co-developing a family approach to suicide prevention based on TILT. It is titled SAFE (Staying Alive in a Family Environment) and employs many of the individuation–attachment principles developed in this book (cf., Kaplan & Selinger, 1997). There are times when temporary separation of the adolescent from the parents may be called for, being especially careful to provide alternate bases of social support during this period to protect the youth from isolation. This suggestion does not imply abandoning a family perspective. Rather, it is meant to emphasize the importance of the family as an organic functioning unit capable of both support and destructiveness, rather than as some idealized abstraction, and to employ more sophisticated techniques of family therapy.

SAFE takes the following stance with regard to families: It is critical to treat adolescents within the context of their family. However, this does not mean that the adolescents should always be seen initially in conjoint sessions with their parents. Sometimes, concurrent (separate but coordinated) treatment of family and adolescent may be called for initially. Initial concurrent therapy provides the opportunity for (a) the youth to learn to differentiate in ways that are not threatening to the family unit and (b) for the family to come to understand these differentiation behaviors as necessary requirements of adolescence rather than as threats of abandonment. The Individuation–Attachment Questionnaire (IAQ) represents an important diagnostic tool in this process. Conjoint therapy of family and adolescent may be brought into the treatment plan as part of the reintegration of the youth into the family. However, it may become helpful in a particular family only after parental support has been achieved for the youth to separate in nonabandoning ways and for the youth to learn to differentiate in ways that maintain genuine family attachment. Premature reintegration in that family may be inappropriate and actually prolong the adolescent's crisis, whether suicidal or otherwise.

PART FOUR
TILT FOR THE CLINICIAN

Chapter 9

A Developmental Guide for the Clinician[1]

This chapter returns to the application of TILT across the life span as developed in chapter 5, this time from the perspective of suicide prevention. The intent of this chapter is to provide the clinician with a developmentally sensitive guide to working with suicidal patients. The emphasis on suicide prevention may seem odd for a book called *Teaching Individuals to Live Together*; however, there is a method to my madness. It is the imbalance between individuation and attachment occurring on the AC clinical axis that I feel saps the individual's will to live. The individual is unable to be him- or herself in relationships with others, and finds the alternative resolutions of estrangement from self or from others as intolerable. Escaping the field, often through suicide, becomes in the individual's mind the only available resolution. A sensitive therapist can help alleviate this problem by helping the patient transform the psychosocial situation into one in which self-identity is not achieved at the expense of interpersonal relations. Such a resolution TILTs the individual from a situation in which suicide is an escape to one in which it becomes irrelevant. If people can truly be themselves with others, they are not faced with intolerable choices and can find freedom in ongoing relations.

THE GENERAL PROBLEM

Even an experienced clinician may become nervous when dealing with a suicidal patient. Some of this nervousness is undoubtedly functional in evoking appropriately increased caution on the part of the clinician. However, it may also lead the clinician to stigmatize and shy away from the patient, seeing him or her as somehow removed from the normal developmental issues of life. To be sure, the

---

[1] An earlier version of this chapter appeared as: Kaplan, K. J. and Worth, S. (1993). Individuation-attachment and Suicide Trajectory: A Developmental Guide for the Clinician. *Omega, 27,* 207–237. Reprinted with permission of Baywood Publishing Company, © 1993.

clinician working with a suicidal patient must be aware of the life and death issues unique to that patient. However, the clinician must do so in a way that places the suicidal crisis within the context of human development. Developmental stage theories have suggested that there is a general tendency for people to face certain issues at specific life stages. What may represent a suicidal risk for an adolescent may be a quite normal life challenge for an older adult and vice versa. "Failure to survive" may manifest itself differentially across the lifespan. Perhaps the best known of these theories has been developed by Erik Erikson (1951, 1968, 1980, 1982). As mentioned in chapter 5, Erikson describes eight different stages of life, each presenting its own psychosocial crisis. If the crisis is satisfactorily resolved, a positive quality is added to the ego. If it is unsatisfactorily resolved, a negative factor is added.

Stillion, McDowell, and May (1996) have attempted to apply Erikson's model to the identification of suicidal risk factors, both in terms of commonalities in suicide across the life span as well as differences that may occur as a result of developmental and/or age related stages. The model identifies four major categories of risk factors at the stages of school-age childhood to old age inclusively. These factors represent failure to trasverse satisfactorily a stage as expressed in the biological, psychological, cognitive, and environmental domains, and describe how. This suicide trajectory model attempts to show how these risk factors, drawn from the research literature on suicide, interact to contribute to suicide ideation. Additional elements of the model include triggering events and warning signs.

In contrast, the present chapter builds on the TILT two-axis approach to human development that has been proposed in chapter 5. Let us once again specify the assumptions of the TILT approach. Two life issues exist at each life stage, albeit in the specific forms of that lifestage: (a) attachment–detachment and (b) individuation–deindividuation. Attachment–detachment is designated in Table 9-1 by external square icons or walls and defined as the capacity to bond with external objects. Individuation–deindividuation is designated by internal circle icons or boundaries and defined as the capacity to differentiate from these same external objects. Typical interpretations of Erikson suggest healthy development is achieved by resolving each stage crisis *horizontally* in favor of the positive or syntonic, as opposed to the dystonic, ego quality. A two-axis view proposes that an individual is propelled by a life event (e.g., weaning) into the negative or dystonic position (e.g., mistrust) and must move ahead *vertically* to achieve the positive syntonic quality (e.g., trust) and to attain a stage-specific syntonic equilibrium. In turn, a subsequent life event or stressor (e.g., toilet training) *forwardly regresses* the individual into a new dystonicity (e.g., shame) with regard to the now broader social radius, parental persons.

Table 9-1
Developmental forward regression versus disintegrative suicidal trajectory at successive life stages

	Nonsuicidal integration				
Stage/age (social radius)	Psychological risk factors	Integrative nonsuicidal resolution	Core strength	Normal life event	Forward regression to next stage
(i)	B_i	D_i	CS_i	$LE_{(i+1)}$	$B_{(i+1)}$
Stage 5/ school age 6–12 years (school/ neighborhood peers)	Normal inferiority	Industry	Competence	Appropriate social identity demands	Normal identity confusion
Stage 6/ adolescence 12–22 years (peer group/ outgroups)	Normal identity confusion	Identity	Fidelity	Appropriate personal identity demands	Normal isolation
Stage 7/ young adulthood 22–34 years (intimate partners)	Normal isolation	Intimacy	Love	Appropriate marriage and family demands	Normal stagnation
Stage 8/ middle adulthood 34–65 years (household and children)	Normal stagnation	Generativity	Care	Appropriate unfulfilled & fulfilled goal evaluation	Normal despair
Stage 9/ older adulthood 65–80 years humankind/ my kind)	Normal despair	Integrity	Wisdom	Appropriate mortality awareness and physical decline	Normal incapacitation
Stage 10/ oldest old 80+ years (present/ future)	Normal incapacitation	Transgenerational continuity	Faith	Death	—

(*Continues*)

Table 9-1
(Continued)

		Suicidal disintegration		
Warning signs		Core pathology	Triggering event	Disintegrative suicidal crisis
A_i	C_i	CP_i	$LE_{(i+1)}$	$(A/C)_i$
Conformity	Peer rejection	Inertia	Premature social identity demands	Mixed conformity–peer rejection (pseudoindustry)
Affective disorders	Conduct disorders	Repudiation	Premature personal identity demands	Mixed affective–conduct disorder (psecudoidentity)
Foreclosure	Diffusion	Exclusivity	Premature marriage and family demands	Mixed foreclosure–diffusion (pseudointimacy)
Dependency-depression	Counter-dependency-separation	Rejectivity	Premature unfulfilled and fulfilled goal evaluation	Mixed depression–separation (pseudogenerativity)
Loss of independence	Social isolation	Disdain	Overwhelming morality shock and incapacitation	Mixed loss of independence–social isolation (pseudointegrity)
Overactivity	Disengagement	Doubt	Death	—

THE NEGATIVE EGO QUALITY AT EACH STAGE IS THE NATURAL CONSEQUENCE OF THE PRECEDING LIFE EVENT

Successful development involves working through a stage vertically to attain the respective stage-specific positive or syntonic ego position, followed by *forward regression* to the next advanced stage. The term *forward regression* is applied to this simultaneous regression in level (trust to shame, positive to negative, syntonic to dystonic) and advance to the next stage, where the within-stage process from dystonic to syntonic ego quality must be once more worked through.

The purpose of this approach is to provide the working clinician with a set of guidelines to distinguish at each lifestage an individual undergoing healthy stage-appropriate development from one clinically fixated. A life event introducing a more advanced stage should impact on two individuals in very different ways. The life event may be a quite normal stressor and even represent an invigorating challenge for the normally developing individual, but a potential suicidal trigger for the clinically fixated individual. The working clinician may support, encourage, and even facilitate the event for the first type of individual but must attempt to discourage, delay, or even prevent the event for the second type of individual.

FOR HEALTHILY DEVELOPING INDIVIDUALS, A LIFE EVENT IS A CHALLENGE

FOR CLINICALLY FIXATED INDIVIDUALS, A LIFE EVENT IS A RISK FACTOR

WITHIN-STAGE DYNAMICS

Two axes have been differentiated in Figures 2-1 and 2-2: a developmental BED axis (Figure 2-1) and a clinical AC axis (Figure 2-2). Let us consider the developmental BED axis first. Position B represents an immature individual who is deindividuated but detached. Deindividuation (◌) represents a low state of individual organization and definition, and detachment (□) can be thought of as defensive in structure. An impermeable wall is necessary to shield the inarticulately defined individual from external engulfment (▧). In Position E, the individual is slowly maturing. Semiindividuated and semiattached, he or she has achieved a modicum of self-definition, a semiarticulated boundary (○). Some defensive structure is necessary, a semipermeable wall (▢). The E individual can be described as semiindividuated and semiattached (◍). In Cell D, the individual is individuated and attached (⊙) and has matured to the point where he or she has achieved a high degree of self-definition, an articulated boundary (O). Here the defensive structure can be quite minimal, a permeable wall (⊡) as there is little danger of external engulfment. The logic of this developmental axis is simply that the loosening of one's defenses (i.e., greater permeability of walls) should occur in conjunction with the strengthening of one's ego (i.e., greater definition of boundaries). The specific manifestations of each of these positions should vary with the stage; however, their general form should remain invariant. Healthy development at each stage requires an ongoing congruency between individuation and attachment.

Figure 2-2, in contrast, presents the clinical AC axis. Here there is a lack of coordination between walls and boundaries. The A individual attempts to become attached to the external world before he or she is individuated (⊡). In other words, defenses are loosened (permeable walls: ⊡) while ego is still ill-defined (inarticulated boundaries: ○) The C individual, in contrast, remains detached even after becoming sufficiently individuated (◙). In other words, this individual holds onto the defenses (impermeable walls: □) even after his or her ego has become sharply defined (articulated boundaries: O). The A/C individual horizontally oscillates between these styles (⊡), first favoring attachment and then individuation. A and C individuals thus represent polarities on this clinical axis, the A individual manifesting a tendency toward enmeshment (deindividuated attachment) and the C individual a tendency toward disengagement (detached individuation). To help the individual escape the AC clinical axis and begin to develop integrated individuation and attachment, the therapist must facilitate backward regression to the B level in the same stage. From this position, the BED journey may be traversed, preparing the individual for healthy forward regression to the next stage

BETWEEN-STAGE DYNAMICS

It is this point of transition between stages that challenges the individual to achieve nonsuicidal integration or suffer suicidal disintegration. These two alternatives are portrayed as a tube leading from the D level at Stage i to the B level at Stage (i + 1). Nonsuicidal integrations (Figure 9-1) are indicated by healthy developmental progression from Level B to Level E to Level D within a specific stage. Each successive stage must be entered at Level B. In other words, progression in stage is achieved through regression in level and is precipitated by the specific life event initiating the next stage. Here the stance of the therapist should be to facilitate or encourage the life event that precipitates the next stage, $LE_{(i+1)}$, that forwardly regresses the individual from D_i to $B_{(i+1)}$. Although the individual may experience a temporary adjustment reaction ($B_{(i+1)}$) upon entering a new stage, equilibrium will be recovered ($E_{(i+1)}$) and he or she ultimately will flourish ($D_{(i+1)}$). In other words,

A Developmental Guide for the Clinician 215

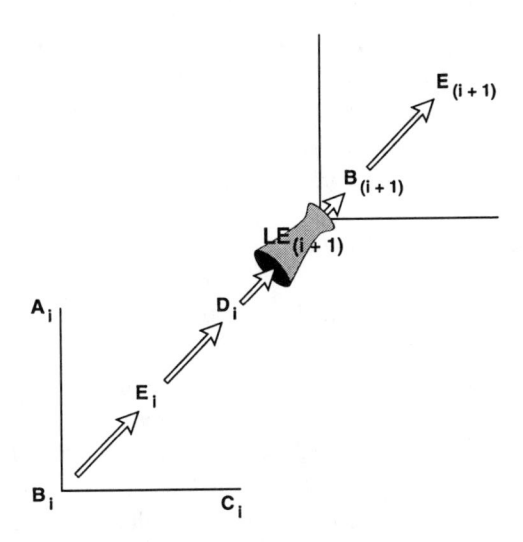

Figure 9-1 Integrative forward regression.

D REPRESENTS INTEGRATION

On the other hand, suicidal disintegrations (Figure 9-2) are indicated by clinical fixation on the AC axis. Such enmeshed–disengaged behaviors indicate that the individual may be unready for $LE_{(i+1)}$. Although an individual might have stabilized in the A (enmeshed) or C (disengaged) positions within a stage, the demands of

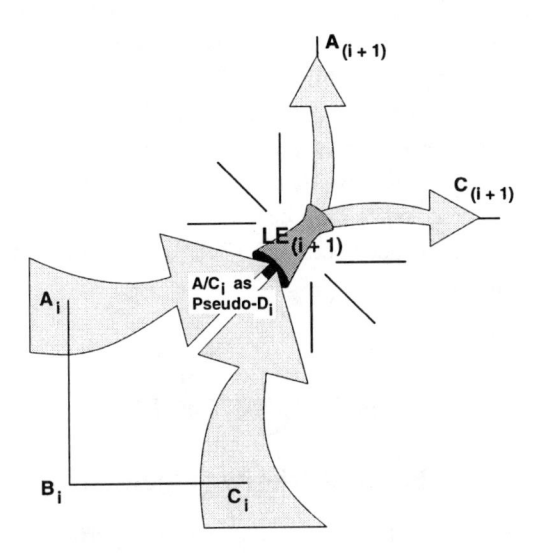

Figure 9-2 Disintegrative suicidal crisis.

$LE_{(i+1)}$ may actually prompt on AC individual at Stage i to attempt an A/C (borderline or even psychotic) resolution. This may present as a pseudo-D (pseudomature) position, which may serve to mask pathology both to self and to others. However, it does not represent any true integration between individuation and attachment and may even deepen the disintegrative process as it disguises it. In short:

A/C REPRESENTS DISINTEGRATION

Extreme distress can result from the attempt to apply A and C styles simultaneously, creating a potentially explosive level of stress as the individual tries to resolve the apparently irreconcilable opposites to cope with the unaccustomed challenges of the new life stage. The outcome of this crisis might be that the pressure of this inadequate coping style would propel the individual through the life event into the next stage on the AC axis, if not into a suicidal disintegration. Here, the therapist must attempt to delay the life event, or to protect the individual from its effects as much as possible, while facilitating backward regression to the same-stage B level. From this position, healthy development of integrated individuation and attachment may be achieved, allowing normal forward regression to the next stage.

Table 9-2 summarizes the process at each stage, listing the premature life events as triggering events and the resultant A/C reactions as suicidal behaviors. In such a situation, the stance of the therapist should be to delay $LE_{(i+1)}$ or protect the individual from its effects until the individual indicates readiness for it in terms of showing healthy resolution on the BED developmental axis.

While the pattern of development described above applies to infants, toddlers, and play-age children, suicide is an extremely rare occurrence in young children. These stages are therefore omitted from Table 9-1, which begins with Stage 5 (the school-age child) and ends with Stage 10 (the oldest). It should be noted, however, that failure to achieve healthy integration of attachment and individuation at the earliest stages may set a pattern of AC behavior that can set the stage for a suicidal crisis later in life. These stages have been discussed in detail in chapter 5. I approach them here from the perspective of a TILT (and subsequent SAFE) therapy designed to prevent suicide.

THE LIFE-STAGES

Stage 5–School Age: From Inferiority to Industry

Stage 5 (see Table 9-2) denotes Erikson's school age (approximately ages 6 to 12). It is precipitated by Life Event 5–*social evaluation*. The social radius has changed.

Table 9-2
School-age childhood

Nonsuicidal integration

	Psychological risk factors B_5	Integrative non-suicidal resolution D_5	Core strength CS_5	Normal life event LE_6	Forward regression to next stage B_6
Stage 5 school age (6–12 years) Social radius: school and neighborhood peers	Normal inferiority	Industry	Competence	Appropriate social identity demands	Normal identity confusion

Suicidal disintegration

	Warning signs		Core pathology CP_5	Triggering event LE_6	Disintegrative suicidal crisis $(A/C)_5$
	A_5	C_5			
	Conformity	Peer rejection	Inertia	Premature social identity demands	Mixed conformity-peer rejection (pseudoindustry)

It is school and neighborhood peers (SR$_5$) rather than one's own nuclear family. The demands of social evaluation forwardly regress the syntonically initiating (D$_4$) play-age child into an initially dystonic state of inferiority (B$_5$). Criticism from peers and negative social comparison can lead to a pessimistic self-definition with regard to future success and even a sense of "learned helplessness" and depression (Seligman, 1975). Withdrawal from social interaction (detachment) accompanies the self-doubt (deindividuation) for the B$_5$ child and may well provide a protective shield until the child begins to feel better about exposing (permeable wall) his or her abilities (articulated boundary).

Nonsuicidal integration. The core strength behind this BED journey is Erikson's concept of competence, and the major process is education (cf., Newman and Newman, 1987). Children can be helped to set realistic goals for themselves so they can experience success. Individuation and attachment are inextricably linked in this process. Pellegrini (1985), for example, has shown that children who display maturity in their social reasoning (individuation) are likely to be more positively evaluated by their peers (attachment). The strength of a healthy child's (D$_5$) need for success is well established by the end of the school-age stage (Atkinson and Birch, 1978). These are also the years when children can have best friends (Berndt, 1981), a process Sullivan (1949) argues is crucial for later sexual and romantic relations.

A child showing D$_5$ industry behaviors is ready to face the life event of adolescence (LE$_6$)—appropriate social identity demands. The therapist can safely facilitate this process without any fear of suicidal risk. The child will forwardly regress as a function of meeting these demands to the B$_6$ state of normal identity confusion characteristic of the early part of adolescence.

Suicidal disintegration. Calhoun and Morse (1977), for example, have shown that failure in school and the experience of public ridicule can interact with an initially negative self-concept to disrupt the above developmental process. The core pathology for Erikson at this stage is inertia, which can be expressed either in A or C pathologies. One type of A$_5$ pathology is hyperactivity (Sainz, 1966; Werry, 1968) and another is conformity (Pepitone et al., 1977). Children learn to dress, talk, and joke in ways that gain peer approval, in extreme cases showing willingness to go along with antisocial peer behavior. The A$_5$ child is quite simply afraid to be different lest he or she receive negative social evaluation. Thus, such children blend in (deindividuate) to avoid the evaluation process. They may accomplish the same goal through going to the opposite polarity, a C$_5$ (detached individuation) structure. This can be labeled peer rejection with associated feelings of loneliness. The direction of this process is not always clear. Sometimes C$_5$ children may reject (detach) to avoid being rejected. However, the result is the same—loneliness and feelings of social dissatisfaction (Asher, et al., 1984). Such children may feel left out, have trouble making friends, and feel that they are alone. These AC polarities are often reflected in suicidal behavior.

At least two studies have shown depression is more prevalent among suicidal than nonsuicidal children (Orbach, 1984; Pfeffer, Conte, Plutchik, & Jerrett, 1979). Depression among children may be manifested by both A and C behaviors. A manifestations include increased anxiety while C manifestations include antisocial behavior and aggression. One study (Kazdin, French, Unis, Esveldt-Dawson, & Sherick, 1983) finds that school-age children who contemplate suicide are likely to be depressed and to dislike themselves (A_5). Another study (Pfeffer, Plutchik, & Mizruchi, 1983) points to suicidal children of a second type. They are angry, assaultive, and tend to approach problems in an assaultive manner (C_5).

A child exhibiting these AC behaviors is not ready for the precipitating life event of adolescence—premature social identity demands—and the therapist must attempt to delay this event or protect the child from it as much as possible. If the therapist fails, the premature demands of social identity may well trigger an A/C suicidal crisis. Here the $(A/C)_5$ child would show signs of both depression and aggression in an attempt to simulate pseudoindustry and may even be at greater risk for suicide than before.

Stage 6–Adolescence: From Identity Confusion to Identity

Stage 6 (see Table 9-3) in this model describes Erikson's adolescent stage (approximately ages 12 to 22). It is initiated by the life event of *social identity demands* (LE_6), which forwardly regresses the syntonically industrious (D_5) school-age child into an initial dystonic position of normal identity confusion (B_6). The social radius at this stage is peer groups and outgroups (SR_6). The life task is to find what groups one belongs to and what groups to avoid. The adolescent may experience a sense of omnipotentiality with the resultant lack of ability to commit to any particular group.

Nonsuicidal integration. Erikson has labeled the core strength at Stage 6 as fidelity, which is realized through the integrated achievement of both individuation and attachment. A successful integrated progression along the developmental BED axis with regard to both of these life issues leads to a syntonic position of identity achievement (D_6), which for Marcia (1966, 1980) involves an individual who has both undergone exploration and made commitments.

An adolescent child showing D_6 identity behaviors is ready to face the life event of early adulthood (LE_7)—appropriate personal identity demands. The therapist can safely facilitate this process. The adolescent will forwardly regress as a function of meeting these demands to the B_7 state of normal isolation characteristic of the early part of adolescence.

Table 9-3
Adolescence

	Nonsuicidal integration			
Psychological risk factors B_6	Integrative non-suicidal resolution D_6	Core strength CS_6	Normal life event LE_7	Forward regression to next stage B_7
Normal identity confusion	Identity	Fidelity	Appropriate personal identity demands	Normal isolation

	Suicidal disintegration			
Warning signs		Core pathology CP_6	Triggering event LE_7	Disintegrative suicidal crisis $(A/C)_6$
A_6	C_6			
Affective disorders	Conduct disorders	Repudiation	Premature personal identity demands	Mixed affective-conduct disorder (pseudoidentity)

Stage 6
adolescence
(12–22 years)
Social radius:
peer group
and outgroups

Suicidal disintegration. The core pathology at this stage has been described by Erikson as repudiation, which can lead to fixation and oscillation on the clinical AC axis. Depression or affective disorders represent the clearest example of A_6 behavior and are the most common pathological symptoms of suicidal individuals of all ages (Goldberg, 1981; Linehan, 1981). The depressed adolescent who has suicidal thoughts is greatly at risk for suicide (Berman & Carroll, 1984; Clarkin, Friedman, Hurt, Corn, & Aronoff, 1984; Ray & Johnson, 1983; Tischler, McKenry & Morgan, 1981; Toolan, 1975). The work of Shaffer (1974) highlights the prevalence of depressive symptoms among adolescent suicide attempters and adolescent suicide completers. Garfinkel, Froese, and Hood (1982) report a positive correlation between level of depression and lethality of suicide attempt among 505 adolescents admitted to a hospital emergency room for suicide attempts. The importance of depression in adolescent suicide attempts has also emerged in the findings of Borst, Noam, and Bartok (1990), Pfeffer, Conte, Plutchik, and Jerret (1980), and Robbins and Alessi (1985).

The C polarity is also implicated in suicidal behavior, whether it be manifested in social isolation or antisocial behaviors. Both Seiden (1983) and Hawton (1982) have pointed to the role of social isolation in adolescent suicide. Contributing to this sense of social isolation is the pervasiveness of high degrees of family mobility. The highest degree of suicide occurs in the western region of the United States, which also has the highest degree of family relocation. The lowest incidence of suicide occurs in the northeast, which has the lowest degree of family relocation. Topol and Resnikoff (1982) have endorsed the importance of social isolation in youth suicide. They point out that adolescent suicides have a personal history of difficulty in relating to peers. Adolescent suicides rarely have close friends and are nonjoiners who are often invisible to peers and teachers. More recently, Apter, Bleich, Plutchik, Mendelsohn, and Tyonao (1988) and Borst and Noam (1989) have reported a significant number of suicidal adolescents who were not depressed, but presented with either a conduct disorder or antisocial behaviors, both representative of a C_6 position.

An adolescent child exhibiting these AC depressive–aggressive behaviors is not ready for the precipitating life event (LE_7) of early adulthood, premature personal identity demands, and the therapist must attempt to delay this event or protect the child from it as much as possible. If the therapist fails, the premature demands of social identity may well trigger an A/C suicidal crisis. Here the $(A/C)_6$ adolescent would show signs of both depression and aggression in an attempt to simulate a pseudoidentity and may even be at greater risk for suicide than before. Indeed, this is exactly the finding emerging from the work of Borst et al. (1990), who report that the majority of suicidal adolescents in their study were diagnosed with a mixed $(A/C)_6$ conduct–affective disorder. The pure conduct disorders in their sample had a much lower incidence of suicide than did the affective disorders alone, leading Borst et al. to warn against the suicidal risk inherent in premature development. They suggest that "the self-protective and externalizing qualities of the earlier developmental positions put a person at greater risk for impulsivity, acting-out problems or delinquency but may shield the adolescent from directing the aggression against the self, as the problem is viewed as mainly externally located" (p. 13).

Stage 7–Early Adulthood: From Isolation to Intimacy

Stage 7 (see Table 9-4) in this model describes Erikson's early adulthood (approximately ages 22 to 34) with a social radius of partners in friendship and sex (SR_7). It is initiated by LE_7, *personal identity demands*, which forwardly regresses a previously syntonic identity-achieving adolescent (D_6) into a dystonic state of normal isolation (B_7). The hard-won social identity emerging from group commitment and membership is no longer enough. The young adult requires a more developed personal identity but must be free of the intense peer pressures emerging from the preceding social radius (deindividuation). This confusion in personal identity (deindividuation) leads to a sense of loneliness and isolation (detachment).

Nonsuicidal integration. The core strength at this stage for Erikson is love, which allows the formation of one's own identity and respect for that of the other, essential to intimacy. Central to this journey is an establishment of a self separate from one's parents on which one can base one's own life. Peers have served the adolescent well in facilitating this separation process. But now the young adult must turn to more intimate dyadic encounters to further develop this separation.

A child showing D_7 intimacy behaviors is ready to face the life event of middle adulthood (LE_8), appropriate marriage and family demands. The therapist can safely facilitate this process. The young adult will forwardly regress as a function of meeting these demands to the B_8 state of normal stagnation characteristic of the early part of middle adulthood.

Suicidal disintegration. The core pathology in Stage 7 is for Erikson exclusivity, which blocks this healthy developmental journey. It can be expressed either in what Minuchin (1974) calls enmeshment (A_7) or disengagement (C_7). Enmeshment refers to a diffuse set of self–other boundaries (in my sense, a premature removal of walls); disengagement refers to rigid self–other boundaries (a delayed removal of walls). Marcia (1966, 1980) has labeled the A_7 polarity foreclosure (a young adult who prematurely commits to another without sufficient exploration) and the C_7 polarity diffusion (an adolescent who engages in pseudoexploration without personal commitment). The foreclosed individual is often depressed and dependent, whereas the diffuse individual is often withdrawn (Bourne, 1978b) or socially isolated and out of place (Donovan, 1975).

Table 9-4
Young Adulthood

		Nonsuicidal integration			
	Psychological risk factors B_7	Integrative non-suicidal resolution D_7	Core strength CS_7	Normal life event LE_8	Forward regression to next stage B_8
Stage 7 young adulthood (22–34 years) Social radius: intimate partners	Normal isolation	Intimacy	Love	Appropriate marriage and family demands	Normal stagnation
		Suicidal disintegration			
	Warning signs		Core pathology CP_7	Triggering event LE_8	Disintegrative suicidal crisis $(A/C)_7$
	A_7	C_7			
	Foreclosure	Diffusion	Exclusivity	Premature marriage and family demands	Mixed foreclosure-diffusion (pseudointimacy)

Both of these polarities are implicated in suicidal behaviors as well. Goldney (1981) found that depression (A_7) and the absence of a significant personal relationship (C_7) were associated with suicide attempts by 110 women aged 18–30. Also involved was hopelessness, as measured by the Beck Hopelessness Scale, and a history of parental conflict. Maris (1971) described the prototypic young adult female suicide as married, having children, suffering from depression, and enmeshed in a marriage with a history of conflict. This is clearly an A_7 pattern. Illfeld (1977) reports that job-related problems may represent a more important stressor for men than do family problems. Rygnestad (1982) found an increased incidence of separation, divorce, and unemployment in both men and women suicide attempters between the ages of 13 and 88. Other studies have pointed to the role of unemployment and downward occupational mobility in adult suicide (Breed, 1963; Maris, 1989; Powell, 1958). These all represent a C_7 pattern.

A young adult exhibiting these AC depressive–isolative behaviors is not ready for the precipitating life event (LE_8) of middle adulthood, marriage and family demands, and the therapist must attempt to delay this event or protect the person from it as much as possible. If the therapist fails, the premature demands of social identity may well trigger an A/C suicidal crisis. Here the $(A/C)_7$ young adult would show signs of both foreclosure and diffusion in an attempt to show pseudointimacy. This individual would be isolated within an enmeshed relationship and may even be at greater risk for suicide than before.

Stage 8–Middle Adulthood: From Stagnation to Generativity

Stage 8 (see Table 9-5) in the present model corresponds to Erikson's middle adulthood (approximately ages 34 to 65) with a social radius of household and children (SR_9). It is initiated by LE_8, *marriage and family demands*, which forwardly regresses a syntonic intimacy-achieving younger adult (D_7) into the dystonic stage of stagnation (B_8). Here a middle adult feels overwhelmed by the demands of marriage and family (deindividuated) and finds him- or herself in a state of confused withdrawal. Indeed, the very intimacy that has been achieved with a particular partner in Stage 7 must make room for the expanded social radius of household and children in Stage 8.

Nonsuicidal integration. Erikson defines the core strength at this stage as care, which propels the stagnating middle adult forward along the developmental BED axis into a syntonic state of generativity (D_8). Withdrawal to personal resources has freed the generative middle adult to get in touch with an individual sense of creativity (individuation), enabling him or her to enter the role of a mentor for the next generation (attachment), whether in a home or work environment, in a way that integrates care for self and care for others.

Table 9-5
Middle Adulthood

	Nonsuicidal integration			
	Psychological risk factors B_8	Integrative non-suicidal resolution D_8	Core strength CS_8	Normal life event LE_9	Forward regression to next stage B_9
Stage 8 middle adulthood (34–65 years) Social radius: household and children	Normal stagnation	Generativity	Care	Appropriate unfulfilled and fulfilled goal evaluation	Normal despair

	Suicidal disintegration			
	Warning signs		Core pathology CP_8	Triggering event LE_9	Disintegrative suicidal crisis $(A/C)_8$
	A_8	C_8			
	Dependency–depression	Counter dependency–separation	Rejectivity	Premature unfulfilled and fulfilled goal evaluation	Mixed depression–separation (pseudogenerativity)

A middle adult showing D_8 generativity behaviors is ready to face the life event of older adulthood (LE_9), appropriate unfulfilled and fulfilled goal evaluation. The therapist can safely facilitate this process. The middle adult will forwardly regress as a function of meeting these demands to the B_9 state of normal despair characteristic of the early part of older adulthood.

Suicidal disintegration. The core pathology for Erikson at this stage is rejectivity, which can be expressed either in what Gutmann et al. (1982) have called dependency (an A_8 structure) or counterdependency (a C_8 structure). Stewart and Salt (1981) have reported that single "agentic" (C_8) working women exhibited ill health in response to stress. In contrast, homemakers with a traditional "communal" (A_8) orientation responded to stress with depression. However, working wives combining agentic and communal (D_8) orientations experienced no negative effects in response to stress.

Slater and Depue (1981) found that exit events (e.g., separation, divorce, and death) differentiate suicidal depressed individuals from nonsuicidal depressed individuals more than any other kind of loss. The suicidal middle-aged adult is likely to have been recently divorced or separated, to have lost a parent, or to have had a child leave home. Several studies show the important role of early parental loss on middle-adult suicides (Adam, Bouckoms, & Streiner, 1982, Richman, 1981; Warren & Tomlinson-Keasey, 1987). These all represent C_8 behaviors. The A_8 polarity is manifested in depression. Depression has been shown repeatedly to be the most common psychiatric diagnosis associated with suicide among adults. Numerous studies have reported a diagnosis of affective disorder among suicidal individuals, with rates running from as low as 35% to as high as 80% (Borg & Stahl, 1982; Dorpat & Ripley, 1960; Guze & Robins, 1970; Weissman, 1974). Pfeffer (1986) concludes in her review of these studies that suicide is 30 times more prevalent among adults with affective disorder than among those not so diagnosed.

A middle adult exhibiting these AC depressive–isolation behaviors is not ready for the precipitating life event (LE_9) of older adulthood, premature unfulfilled and fulfilled goal evaluation, and the therapist must attempt to delay this event or protect the middle adult from it as much as possible. If the therapist fails, the premature demands of mortality shock may well trigger an A/C suicidal crisis. Here the $(A/C)_8$ middle adult may attempt to achieve a pseudogenerativity through alcoholism. Specifically, alcoholism may blur nagging feelings of unfulfillment but at the expense of increasing both depression (A_8) and aggression and/or isolation (C_8). Male alcoholics who drink in bars may be more likely to experience alcohol-related interpersonal problems than women who are inclined to drink alone at home. Further, males are more vulnerable to alcohol-related job stress and to the stress of losing their jobs. Roy and Linnoila (1986) reported the results of a group of studies that show the risk of suicide among alcoholics to be 58 to 85 times higher than that for nonalcoholics. The suicide rate for alcholics has been estimated to be as high as 270 per 100,000 population (Miles, 1977). Several studies have shown that comorbidity of depression and alcoholism represents a greater risk for suicide than either alone (Berglund, 1984; Murphy, Armstrong, Hermele, Fisher, & Clendenim, 1979). Premature exposure of the AC middle adult to goal evaluation (LE$_9$) has only exacerbated the suicidal crisis.

Stage 9–Older Adulthood: From Despair to Integrity

Stage 9 (see Table 9-6) in this model refers to Erikson's older adulthood (approximately ages 65 to 80). The social radius (SR$_9$) for the older adult has become humankind/my kind—a differentiation of universalistic and particularistic affiliations. It is initiated by the life event (LE$_9$) of *unfulfilled goals* (or perhaps *now meaningless fulfilled goals*), a stressor that forwardly regresses the previously syntonic generative (D$_8$) middle adult into a profound dystonic state of despair (B$_9$). All of one's previous achievements have proved meaningless, and many of one's dreams are now out of grasp. The B$_9$ individual has lost the meaning in life (deindividuation) and so withdraws from social involvements (detachment).

Nonsuicidal integration. Erikson defines the core strength at this stage as wisdom, which guides the older adult forward along the developmental BED axis to a position of both individuation and attachment. Such a syntonic D$_9$ individual finds a self-integrity (articulated self–other boundary) based on something more profound than simple fulfilled personal goals and is thus able to reintegrate into humankind (permeable interpersonal walls) with a particularistic affirmation of his or her own kind.

An older adult showing D$_9$ integrity behaviors is ready to face the life event of the oldest old (LE$_{10}$), appropriate mortality awareness and physical decline. The therapist can safely facilitate this process. The older adult will forwardly regress as a function of meeting these demands to the B$_{10}$ state of normal incapacitation characteristic of the early part of oldest old age.

Suicidal disintegration. Erikson describes the core pathology at this stage as disdain, which can lead to fixation and oscillation on the clinical AC axis. This can be expressed either in social isolation (C$_9$ personalities) or in passive-dependence (A$_9$ individuals who have strong dependency needs and seek responsiveness from others). Darbonne (1969) found that suicide notes of the elderly included more references to loneliness and isolation than those of any other age group. Miller (1979) found that older men who committed suicide were three times less likely to have a confidante than those who died of natural causes. Widowhood has been shown to increase the risk of suicide, especially among elderly males during

Table 9-6
Older Adulthood

Nonsuicidal integration

	Psychological risk factors B_9	Integrative non-suicidal resolution D_9	Core strength CS_9	Normal life event LE_{10}	Forward regression to next stage B_{10}
	Normal despair	Integrity	Wisdom	Appropriate morality awareness and physical decline	Normal incapacitation

Suicidal disintegration

	Warning signs		Core pathology CP_9	Triggering event LE_{10}	Disintegrative suicidal crisis $(A/C)_9$
	A_9	C_9			
Stage 9 older adulthood (65–80 years) Social radius: humankind and my kind	Loss of independence	Social isolation	Disdain	Overwhelming morality shock and incapacitation	Mixed loss of independence social isolation (pseudointegrity)

228

the first 6 months of bereavement (Benson & Brodie, 1975; Berardo, 1968; Bock & Weber, 1972; McMahon & Pugh, 1965; Miller, 1978). Bock and Webber (1972) found that suicidal and widowed elderly people were more socially isolated than those who were nonsuicidal.

The A_9 polarity, in contrast, represents passive dependence often accompanying chronic illness. One study found that 85% of a group of suicide completers over age 60 were physically ill at the time they killed themselves (Dorpat, Anderson, & Ripley, 1968). Miller (1979) found extreme illness to be associated with 60% of the cases in his study of suicide among elderly men. Further evidence of the role of physical deterioration can be gleaned from studies indicating that over 70% of elderly suicides have visited a physician within the past month and that as many as 10% have consulted a physician on the actual day of the suicide (Barraclough, 1971; Miller, 1978; Rockwell & O'Brien, 1973). Losses are a natural part of old age, often occurring in a relatively short period of time. Depression in such a situation may become chronic and indeed is the most common of all illnesses among the aged (Butler & Lewis, 1982). Many researchers have estimated that a large majority of elderly suicides, perhaps as many as 80%, involve significant depression (also an A_9 structure) and cumulative loss (Benson & Brodie, 1975; Lyons, 1984; McIntosh, Hubbard, & Santos, 1981).

An older adult exhibiting these $(A/C)_9$ dependent–isolated behaviors is not ready for the precipitating life event $(LE)_{10}$ of oldest old adulthood, overwhelming mortality shock and incapacitation, and the therapist must attempt to delay this event or protect this type of older adult from it as much as possible. If the therapist fails, the $(A/C)_9$ adult is likely to become alcoholic or dependent on drugs in an attempt to elevate his or her spirits and ease aches, pains, and fears of death. Such an attempt at pseudointegrity is unfortunately extremely disintegrative. The interactive effects of alcohol abuse with over-the-counter and prescription drugs may result in a clouding of consciousness and increase the likelihood of depression and suicidal behavior (Butler & Lewis, 1982). Miller (1979) found that approximately 25% of a group of elderly male suicides were alcoholic or had significant drinking problems, and that 35% of this group was addicted to or heavily dependent on drugs.

Stage 10–The Oldest Old: From Incapacitation to Generational Continuity

Stage 10 (see Table 9-7) in this model, the oldest old (approximately 80+), has not been covered specifically by Erikson nor has it been studied as extensively as some of the earlier adult stages. Peck (1968) represents a classic attempt to extend Erikson's thinking to the oldest old, offering finer distinctions in the second half of life than he felt were made by Erikson. Issues of old age as distinct from those

Table 9-7
Oldest Old

Stage 10 oldest old (80 years) Social radius: present/future	Nonsuicidal integration				
	Psychological risk factors B_{10}	Integrative non-suicidal resolution D_{10}	Core strength CS_{10}	Normal life event LE_{11}	Forward regression to next stage B_{11}
	Normal incapacitation	Transgenerational continuity	Faith	Death	—
	Suicidal disintegration				
	Warning signs		Core pathology CP_{10}	Triggering event LE_{11}	Disintegrative suicidal crisis $(A/C)_{10}$
	A_{10}	C_{10}			
	Overactivity	Disengagement	Doubt	Death	—

of middle age, which have been offered by Peck, are ego-differentiation versus work-role preoccupation, body transcendence versus body preoccupation, and ego transcendence versus ego preoccupation. Newman and Newman (1987) have tried to extend Erikson's thinking to the oldest old, suggesting the life issue here is "immortality versus extinction." In other papers, Levin (1963) has emphasized depression among the aged, Berger and Zarit (1978) have studied later life paranoid states, and Cath (1966) has differentiated depression and depletion among the elderly.

Nonsuicidal integration. The TILT model sees the oldest old stage as initiated by the staggering life event or stressor of *physical decline and awareness* of *mortality and life-finiteness* (LE_{10}). Gutmann et al. (1982) have labeled it "life cycle shock" or "existential stress," which upsets the syntonic equilibrium (D_9) achieved by the integrity-achieving older adult (Birren et al., 1971) and forwardly regresses the now oldest old into the helpless dystonic position of incapacitation (B_{10}). A previously healthy older adult may now need a cane or a walker, or even a wheelchair. Memory may fail, as may kidneys. Previously reliable social supports may themselves have died, and the individual may become aware of his or her own limited time. In short, the now oldest old individuals may find themselves both enfeebled (deindividuated) and isolated (detached). What is critical here is how they manage to transcend the present-centered integrity of humankind/my kind to deal with a once again expanded social radius (SR_{10}) of present versus future generations. Lifton (1973) has called for a "sense of immortality" that overcomes a preoccupation with one's own ego, body, and generation through a faith, a vested interest if you will, in future generations. This sense of a transgenerational continuity is deepened by the oldest old taking on the role of transmitter of history to the next generation and helps to prepare the individual for his or her own death, the final life event (LE_{11}).

An oldest old adult showing D_{10} transgenerational continuity behaviors is ready to face the final life event (LE_{11}), appropriate personal death. The therapist can safely facilitate this process by calling on the individual's sense of himself as a link between the generations.

Suicidal disintegration. The core pathology at his stage is what Newman and Newman have labeled doubt, a profound uncertainty that there is anything beyond the present ego, body, and life-finiteness. It tends to truncate the individual's sense of time in the present and may be expressed in one of two forms. One expression is what Cumming and Henry (1961) have labeled disengagement (a C_{10} structure), which is indicated by increased preoccupation with the self and decreasing emotional investments in persons and objects in the environment. This structure may also have a paranoiac aspect to it (Berger & Zarit, 1978), which may involve suspicions and accusations of others. The second expression is paraphrased from the work of Havighurst et al. (1968) and may be labeled overactivity (an A_{10}

structure), where the individuals trivialize themselves through mindless activities designed to numb them to their terminal position in the life cycle. While Lawton (1980) has reported that residents of institutions for the aged seek out areas of high activity, Lemon et al. (1972) find that activity per se was not found to be significantly related to life satisfaction among new residents of a retirement community.

An oldest old adult exhibiting these AC overactivity–disengagement behaviors is not ready to face *death* openly and may disintegrate (A/C) if the realization is imposed on him or her. In this case, the therapist must attempt to protect the individual from death awareness as much as possible. If the therapist fails, the individual may fall apart, attempting to simulate a sense of transgenerational continuity through a fusing of the irreconcilable polarities of disengagement and overactivity $(A/C)_{10}$. My own research indicates that many of the "preemptive" physician-assisted suicides conducted by Drs. Jack Kevorkian and Georges Reding in Michigan fall into this category (cf., Kaplan et al., In press).

SUMMARY

This chapter has developed the TILT model for the working clinician. Specifically, TILT provides the clinician with a developmental guide to recognize suicide risk across the lifespan. For an individual developing normally on the BED axis, a new life event at the appropriate time offers the potential for integrated development and forward regression from one stage to the next. Here, the therapist should encourage or facilitate the new life event. For an individual on the AC clinical axis, a new life event may be overwhelming, pushing the individual into an A/C attempt to simulate D-level integration. The pseudo-D position is highly disintegrative, and here, the life event may become a triggering event for suicide. In other words,

**IN NORMAL DEVELOPMENT, A LIFE-EVENT
REPRESENTS A CHALLENGE FOR INTEGRATION**

**IN CLINICAL FIXATION, A LIFE-EVENT
REPRESENTS A TRIGGER FOR DISINTEGRATION**

This chapter has offered the clinician a guide for differentiating BED versus AC behaviors across successive life stages. Hopefully, it has demonstrated to the reader the utility of the TILT model for a psychotherapy helping an individual assert his identity in relationship with others. I have argued that this integration reduces suicidal and self-disintegrative processes and provides a life-affirming and self-integrative process. In the concluding section of the book, I will briefly summarize the assumptions of the TILT model and suggest its applications into other settings. Finally, I will attempt to discuss the implications of TILT to the new millennium.

Chapter 10
Conclusion: Applications to Other Areas

TILT offers a unique model of conceptualizing human relationships. To begin with, it distinguishes walls from boundaries and as a result of this, attachment from deindividuation and individuation from detachment. Healthy development is described as healthy integration of individuation and attachment across the lifespan as opposed to pathological fixation between enmeshment and disengagement. Further, different positions in the TILT model, both healthy and pathological, express themselves in different distancing positions. The aim of TILT is to teach individuals to live together.

The TILT model has almost unlimited areas of application. We have focused on the individual and his/her family. Nothing can be more important in the modern world than to develop models of the family which integrate space for creative individual growth and care for others. The issue of care for aging parents/family is critical in modern society and more appropriate models must be found than those that are currently on the scene.

Consider next the area of international relations, specifically, the relationship of developing or third world nations to the powers of the first world (America and her allies) and the second world (Russia and her allies). From the point of view of TILT, the problem of the developing nation is quite similar to that of the developing adolescent: how to accept aid from a power figure while maintaining one's own identity. Developing nations often express the feeling of being patronized by the very countries that are helping them. These nations often perceive a choice between becoming a client state of a major power or remaining estranged from the modern world. Such states often behave inconsistently and often self-destructively. TILT can be very usefully applied to this arena to enable first and second world powers to help developing nations in a way that does not destroy the latter's identities.

Consider a third area of application for TILT: political economics. In the process of comparing communism and capitalism (or more generally, left-wing versus right-wing movements), we have often thought in a unidimensional distance framework. Communism emphasizes collectivity at the expense of the individual while capitalism emphasizes individual rights and freedom at the expense of the community. TILT suggests that the solutions of both communism and capitalism are inadequate; that societies must develop a political–economic structure that integrates individual and social needs and responsibilities, and it must do this through graduated stages of development.

A fourth area of application lies in the role of social organizations in the modern world. TILT asks the question of how a member of an organization can be committed to the larger organizational goal in a way that enhances the individual's sense of personal creativity and self-worth rather than diminishes it. TILT approaches this issue from a developmental frame of reference, suggesting that at each stage of the process, there must be a balance between the individual's self-expression and his or her attachment to the company values. Leaders of various units in organizations can profitably apply TILT to their training procedures.

A final potential application of TILT lies in the realm of modern medicine, specifically in respect to doctor–patient relations. In an intriguing paper, Emanuel and Emanuel (1992) have distinguished four types of doctor–patient relations: paternalistic, informative, interpretive, and deliberative. In the paternalistic model, the patient's autonomy is minimal; the informative model minimizes the degree of doctor involvement in looking after the patient's welfare. The interpretive and deliberative models lie somewhere in the middle, on what seems to be a unidimensional axis. From the perspective of TILT, the doctor's degree of protectiveness cannot be judged independently of the degree of patient autonomy. Early in the course of a disease, a patient may be overwhelmed and confused (i.e., exhibiting an inarticulated boundary), and is likely to feel lost without structured medical guidance (i.e., a firm and stable wall). However, later in the disease the patient may be able to make his or her own decisions (i.e., exhibiting an articulated boundary), and is likely to find the earlier relationship too restrictive.

The applications of TILT seem boundless in a world that has thrown away many of the "isms" by which our ancestors have lived. What seems to be needed more than ever is a comprehensive philosophy and application that teaches individuals to be themselves with others. All of these applications grow from the basic manifesto of TILT articulated in chapter 1:

WALLS EXIST TO KEEP THE OTHER OUT;
BOUNDARIES EXIST TO KEEP THE SELF IN

All the rest is commentary.

References

Abelin, E. L. (1971). The role of the father in the separation individuation process. In J. B. McDevitt & C. F. Settlage (Eds.), *Separation–individuation: Essays in honor of Margaret S. Mahler* (pp. 229–253). New York: International Universities Press.

Achenbach, T. M., & Edelbrock, C. (1983). *Manual for the child behavior profile.* Burlington, VT: University of Vermont.

Adam, K. S., Bouckoms, A., & Streiner, D. L. (1982) Parental loss and family stability in attempted suicide. *Archives of General Psychiatry, 39,* 1081–1085.

Ainsworth, M. D. S. (1972). Attachment and dependency: a comparison. In J. Gerwirtz (Ed.), *Attachment and dependency* (pp. 97–137). Washington, DC: V. H. Winston & Sons.

Ainsworth, M. D. S. (1973). The development of infant-mother attachment. In B. M. Caldwell & H. N. Ricciuti (Eds.), *Review of child development research* (Vol. 3). Chicago: University of Chicago Press.

Ainsworth, M. D. S. (1979). Infant-mother attachment. *American Psychologist, 34,* 932–937.

Ainsworth, M. D. S. (1982). Attachment: Retrospect and prospect. In C. M. Parkes & Stevenson-Hinde (Eds.), *The place of attachment in human behavior* (pp. 3–30). New York: Basic Books.

Ainsworth, M. D. S. (1989). Attachments beyond infancy. *American Psychologist, 44,* 709–716.

Ainsworth, M. D. S., Blehar, M. C., Waters, E., & Wall. S. (1978). *Patterns of attachment: A psychological study of the strange situation.* Hillsdale, NJ: Erlbaum.

Albert, S., Amgott, T., Krakow, M., & Marcus, H. (1977, August). *Children's bedtime rituals as a prototype rite of safe passage.* Paper presented at the annual convention of the American Psychological Association, San Francisco, CA.

Anderson, R. N., Kochanek, K. B., & Murphy, S. L. (1997). Advance Report of Final Mortality Statistics, 1995, Monthly Vital Statistics Report 45(11), Supplement 2. Hyattsville, MD: National Center for Health Statistics, DHHS Pub. No. (PHS) 97-1120, p. 65.

Andreasen, N., Endicott, J., Spitzer, R. & Winokur, G. (1977). The family history method using Research Diagnostic Criteria: Reliability and validity. *Archives of General Psychiatry, 34,* 1229–1235.

Anglin, J. M. (1977). *Word, object and conceptual development.* New York: Norton.

Anthony, E. J. (1970). The behavior disorders of children. In P. H. Mussen (Ed.), *Carmichael's manual of child psychology* (3rd ed., Vol. 2). New York: Wiley.

Apter, A., Bleich, A., Plutchik, R., Mendelsohn, S., & Tyonao, S. (1988). Suicide behavior, depression and conduct disorder in hospitalized adolescents. *Journal of the American Academy of Childhood and Adolescent Psychiatry, 27*, 696–699.

Ardrey, R. (1966). *The territorial imperative*. New York: Atheneum.

Arend, D., Gove, F., & Sroufe, L. A. (1979). Continuity of individual adaptation from infancy to kindergarten: A predictive study of ego resiliency and curiosity in preschoolers. *Child Development, 50*, 950–959.

Argyle, M., & Dean, J. (1965). Eye-contact, distance and affiliation. *Sociometry, 28*, 289–304.

Asher, S. R., Hymel, S., & Renshaw, P. D. (1984). Loneliness in children. *Child Development, 35*, 1456–1464.

Atkinson, J. W., & Birch, D. (1978). *Introduction to motivation* (2nd ed.). New York: Van Nostrand.

Augustine, W., & Kalish, R. A. (1975) Religion, transcendence and appropriate death. *Journal of Transactional Psychology, 7*, 1–13.

Bach, G. R., & Wyden, P. (1968). *The intimate enemy: How to fight in love and marriage*. New York: Avon Books.

Bader, E., & Pearson, P. (1983). The developmental stages of couplehood. *Transactional Analysis Journal, 13*, 28–32.

Bakan, D. (1966). *The duality of human existence: Isolation and communion in western man*. Boston: Beacon.

Bandura, A. (1977). *Social learning theory*. Englewood Cliffs, NJ: Prentice Hall.

Barker, R. G., & Wright, H. F., (1955). *Midwest and its children*. New York: Harper and Row.

Barraclough, B. M. (1971). Suicide in the elderly. In D. W. Kay & A. Walk (Eds.), *Recent developments in psychogeriatrics*. Kent, England: Headly Brothers.

Barraclough, B. M., Bunch, J., Nelson, B., & Sainsbury, P. (1969). A hundred cases of suicide. *British Journal of Psychiatry, 125*, 355–373.

Bartholomew, K., & Horowitz, L. M. (1991). Attachment styles among young adults: A test of a four-category model. *Journal of Personality and Social Psychology, 61(2)*, 226–244.

Baumrind, D. (1971). Current patterns of parental authority. *Developmental Psychology Monographs, 4*, 99–103.

Baumrind, D. (1975) *Early socialization and the discipline controversy*. Morristown, NJ: General Learning Press.

Beavers, W. R., & Voeller, M. (1983). Family models comparing and contrasting the Olsen circumplex model with the Beavers systems model. *Family Process, 22*, 88–95.

Bell, M., Billington, R., & Becker, B. (1986). A scale for the assessment of reality testing—reliability, validity and factorial invariance. *Journal of Clinical Psychology, 42*, 733–741.

Belsky, J. (1981). Early human experience: A family perspective. *Developmental Psychology, 17*, 3–23.

Bem, S. L. (1974). The measurement of psychological androgyny. *Journal of Consulting and Clinical Psychology, 42*, 155–162.

Benson, R. A., & Brodie, D. C. (1975). Suicide by overdose of medicines among the ages. *Journal of the American Geriatrics Society, 23*, 304–308.

Berardo, D. H. (1968) Widowhood status in the United States: Perspective on a neglected aspect of the family life-cycle. *The Family Coordinator, 17*, 191–203.

Berger, K., & Zarit, S. (1978). Late-life paranoid states: Assessment and treatment. *American Journal of Orthopsychiatry, 48(3)*, 528–536.

Berglund, M. (1984). Intervention with potential suicides. In N. Linzer (Ed.), *Suicide: The will to live vs. the will to die*. New York: Human Sciences Press.

Berman, A. L., & Carroll, T. A. (1984). Adolescent suicide: A critical review. *Death Education, 8*, 53–64.

Berndt, T. J. (1981). Relations between social cognition, nonsocial cognition, and social behavior: The case of friendship. In J. H. Flavell & L. D. Ross (Eds.), *Social cognitive development: Frontiers and possible futures*. Cambridge MA: Cambridge University Press.

Berne, E. (1961). *Transactional analysis in psychotherapy*. New York: Grove Press.

Berne, E. (1964). *Games people play*. New York: Grove Press.

Birren, J. E., Butler, R. N., Greenhouse, S. W., Sokoloff, L., & Yarrow, M. R. (1971). *Human aging I: A biological and behavior study*. (DHEW Publication No. ADM77-123). Washington, DC: U.S. Government Printing Office.

Black, D. W., Winokur, G., & Nasrallah, A. (1987). Suicide in subtypes of major affective disorder. A comparison with general population suicide mortality. *Archives of General Psychiatry, 44*, 878–880.

Block, J. H. (1976). Issues, problem and pitfalls in assessing sex differences: A critical review of The Psychology of Sex Differences. *Merrill Palmer Quarterly, 22*, 283–308.

Block, S. M., & Block, J. (1980). The role of ego control and ego-resiliency in the organization of behavior. In W. A. Collins (Ed.), *Minnesota Symposium on Child Psychology (Vol. II)*. Hillsdale, NJ: Lawrence Erlbaum Associates.

Bock, E. W., & Webber, I. L. (1972). Suicide among the elderly: Isolating widowhood and mitigating alternatives. *Journal of Marriage and the Family, 34*, 24–31.

Borg, S. E., & Stahl, M. (1982). A prospective study of suicides and controls among psychiatric patients. *Acta Psychiatrica Scandinavica, 65*, 221–232.

Borst, S., & Noam, G. (1990, March). *A clinical-developmental approach to suicidality in adolescence*. Presented at the Biennial Meeting of the Society for Research in Adolescence, Atlanta, GA.

Borst, S. R., Noam, G. G., & Bartok, J. (1990). *Adolescent suicidality: A clinical-developmental study*. Unpublished manuscript.

Boszormenyi-Nagy, I., & Spark, G. D. (1973). *Invisible loyalties: Reciprocity in intergenerational family therapy*. New York: Harper and Row.

Bourne, E. (1978a). The state of research and ego identity: A review and appraisal (Part 1). *Journal of Youth and Adolescence, 7*, 223–251.

Bourne, E. (1978b). The state of research on ego identity: A review and appraisal (Part 2). *Journal of Youth and Adolescence, 7*, 371–392.

Bowen, M. (1960). The family as the unit of study and treatment. *American Journal of Orthopsychiatry, 31*, 40–60.

Bowen, M. (1978). *Family therapy in clinical practice*. New York: Jason Aronson.

Bowlby, J. (1969). *Attachment and loss.* (Vol. 1): *Attachment*. New York: Basic Books.

Bowlby, J. (1973). *Attachment and loss.* (Vol. 2): *Separation, anxiety and anger*. New York: Basic Books.

Bowlby, J. (1977). The making and breaking of affectional bonds: Etiology and psychopathology in the light of attachment theory. *British Journal of Psychiatry, 130*, 201–210.

Brazelton, T. B., Koslowski, B., & Main, M. (1974). The origins of reciprocity: The early mother-infant interaction. In M. Lewis & L. A. Rosenblum (Eds.), *The effects of the infant on its caregiver.* New York: Wiley.

Breed, W. (1963). Occupational mobility and suicide among white males. *American Sociological Review, 28,* 179–188.

Brent, D. A., Perper, J. A., Goldstein, C. E., Kolko, D. J., Allan, M. J., Allman, C. J., & Zelenak, J. P. (1988). Risk factors for adolescent suicide: A comparison of adolescent suicide victims with suicidal inpatients. *Archives of General Psychiatry, 54,* 581–588.

Brilliant, A. (1979). *I may not be totally perfect, but parts of me are excellent.* Santa Barbara, CA: Woodbridge Press.

Brilliant, A. (1984). *I feel much better, now that I have given up hope.* Santa Barbara, CA: Woodbridge Press.

Brilliant, A. (1990). *We've been through so much together, and most of it was your fault.* Santa Barbara, CA: Woodbridge Press.

Brilliant, A. (1992). *Be a good neighbor, and leave me alone.* Santa Barbara, CA: Woodbridge Press.

Brofenbrenner, U. (1960). Freudian theories of identification and their derivatives. *Child Development, 31,* 15–40.

Buber, M. (1957). Distance and relation. *Psychiatry, 20,* 97–104.

Buber, M. (1970). *I and thou,* New York: Charles Scribner's Son.

Burnkrant, R. E., & Page, T. J. (1984). A modification of the Fenigstein, Scheier and Buss self-consciousness scales. *Journal of Personality Assessment, 48,* 629–637.

Butler, R. N., & Lewis, M. I. (1982). *Aging and mental health: Positive psycho-social and biomedical approaches* (3rd ed.). St. Louis: Mosby.

Cain, A. C., & Fast, I. (1966). Children's disturbed reaction to parent suicide. *American Journal of Orthopsychiatry, 36,* 873–880.

Calhoun, G., Jr., & Morse, W. C. (1977). Self-concept and self-esteem: Another perspective. *Psychology in the Schools, 14,* 318–322.

Cappella, J. N. (1981). Mutual influence in expressive behavior, adult-adult and infant-adult dyadic interaction. *Psychological Bulletin, 39,* 101–132.

Carr, D. H., & Gedeon, M. (1977). Population cytogenetics of human abortuses. In E. G. Hook & I. M. Porter (Eds.), *Population cytogenetics: Studies in humans.* New York: Academic Press.

Cassorla, R. (1984). Family characteristics of youngsters who attempted suicide in the city of Campinas. *Acta Psiquiatrica Y Psicologica de America Latina, 30,* 125–134.

Cath, S. (1966). Beyond depression—the depleted state: A study in ego psychology in the aged. *Canadian Psychiatric Association Journal, 11* (Suppl.), 329–339.

Check, J. M., & Buss, A. H. (1981). Shyness and sociability. *Journal of Personality and Social Psychology, 41,* 330–339.

Chia, B. H. (1979). Suicide of the young in Singapore. *Annals of the Academy of Medicine, 8,* 262–268.

Chwast, J. (1972). Sociopathic behavior in children. In B. B. Wolman (Ed.), *Manual of child psychopathology.* New York: McGraw-Hill.

Cicirelli, V. G. (1976). Effects of evaluating task competence on the self-concept of children from different socioeconomic status levels. *Journal of Psychology, 94,* 217–223.

Clark, A. L. (1976). Application of psychological concepts. In A. L. Clark & D. D. Alfonso (Eds.), *Childbearing: A nursing perspective* (pp. 239–262). Philadelphia: F. A. Davis.

Clarkin, J. F., Friedman, R. C., Hurt, S. W., Corn, R., & Aronoff, M. (1984). Affective and character pathology of suicidal adolescents and young adult inpatients, *Journal of Clinical Psychiatry, 45(1)*, 19–22.

Coie, J. D., & Krehbiel, G. (1984). Effects of academic tutoring on the social status of low-achieving socially rejected children. *Child Development, 55*, 1465–1478.

Cole, M., & D'Andrade, R. (1982). The influence of schooling on concept formation: Some preliminary conclusions. *Quarterly Newsletter of the Laboratory of Comparative Cognition, 4*, 19–26.

Corder, B. B., Page, P. V., & Corder, R. F. (1974). Parental history: Family communication and interaction patterns in adolescent suicide. *Family Therapy, 1*, 285–290.

Costanzo, P. R. (1970). Conformity development as a function of self-blame. *Journal of Personality and Social Psychology, 14*, 366–374.

Cowan, E. P., Cowan, P. A., Coie, L., & Coie, J. D. (1978). Becoming a family: The impact of a first child's birth on the couple relationship. In W. Miller & L. Newman (Eds.), *The first child and family formation* (pp. 296–324). Chapel Hill, NC: Carolina Population Center and University of North Carolina.

Crandall, V. C. (1963). Reinforcement effects of adults reactions and nonreactions of children's achievement expectations. *Child Development, 34*, 335–354.

Cranley, M. S. (1981). Development of a tool for the measurement of maternal attachment during pregnancy. *Nursing Research, 30*, 281–284.

Cross, H., & Allen, J. (1970). Ego identity status, adjustment and academic achievement. *Journal of Consulting and Clinical Psychology, 34*, 288.

Cumming, E., & Henry, W. E. (1961). *Growing old.* New York: Basic Books.

Dabrowski, K. (1973). *The dynamics of concepts.* London: GRYF Publications.

Darbonne, A. R. (1969). Suicide and age: A suicide note analysis. *Journal of Consulting and Clinical Psychology, 33*, 46–50.

Davis, M. H. (1983). The effects of dispositional empathy on emotional reactions and helping: A multidimensional approach. *Journal of Personality, 51*, 167–184.

Davison, G. C., & Neale, J. M. (1982). *Abnormal psychology: An experimental clinical approach* (3rd. ed.). New York: Wiley.

Deutch, H. (1948). *Psychology of women* (Vol. 11). New York: Grune & Stratton.

Diagnostic and statistical manual of mental disorders, 4th ed. (1994). Washington, DC: American Psychiatric Association.

Donovan, J. M. (1975). Identity status and interpersonal style. *Journal of Youth and Adolescence, 4*, 37–55.

Dorpat, T. L., Anderson, W. F., & Ripley, H. S. (1968). The relationship of physical illness to suicide. In H. L. P. Resnik (Ed.), *Suicide: Diagnosis and management* (pp. 209–219). Boston: Little, Brown.

Dorpat, T. L., & Ripley, H. S. (1960). A study of suicide in the Seattle area. *Comprehensive Psychiatry, 1*, 349–359.

Durkheim, E. (1951). *Suicide.* New York: Free Press (Original work published 1897).

Dweck, C. S., & Licht, G. G. (1980). Learned helplessness and intellectual achievement. In J. Gerber & M. E. P. Seligman (Eds.), *Human helplessness: Theory and applications.* New York: Academic Press.

Dyer, E. (1963). Parenthood as crisis: A restudy. *Journal of Marriage and Family Living, 25*, 196–201.

Edwards, A. L. (1957). *The Edwards Personality Preference Schedule.* New York: The Psychological Corporation.

Egeland, J. A., & Sussex, J. N. (1985). Suicide and family loading for affective disorder. *Journal of American Medical Association, 254*, 915–918.

Emanuel, E. J., & Emanuel, L. J. (1992). Four models of the physician–patient relationship. *Journal of the American Medical Association, 267*, 2221–2226.

Epstein, I. (Ed.) (1961). *The Talmud*. London: Soncino Press.

Erikson, E. (1951, revised 1963). *Childhood and society*. New York: W. W. Norton.

Erikson, E. (1968). *Identity: Youth and crisis*. New York: W. W. Norton.

Erikson, E. (1980). *Identity and the life cycle*. New York: W. W. Norton.

Erikson, E. (1982). *The life cycle completed*. New York: W. W. Norton.

Ernst, F. (1971). The OK corral: The grid for get-on with. *Transactional Analysis Journal, 1(4)*, 33–42.

Falbo, T., & Peplau, L.A. (1980). Power strategies in intimate relationships. *Journal of Personality and Social Psychology, 38*, 618–628.

Farberow, N. L., & Simon, M. D. (1969). Suicides in Los Angeles and Vienna—An intercultural study of two cities. *Public Health Reports, 84*, 389–402.

Feldman, S., & Ingham, M. (1975). Attachment behavior: A validation study in two age groups. *Child Development, 46*, 319–330.

Fenigstein, A., Scheier, M. F., & Buss, A. M. (1975). *Journal of Consulting and Clinical Psychology, 43*, 522–527.

Fey, W. F. (1955). Acceptance by others and its relation to acceptance of self and others. A revaluation. *Journal of Abnormal Social Psychology, 50*, 274–276.

Figurski, T., & Kaplan, K. J. (1989 August). The IAQ, self-consciousness and interpersonal reactivity. Presented at the meeting of the American Psychological Association, New Orleans, LA.

Finch, S. M., & Poznanski, E. O. (1971). *Adolescent suicide*. Springfield, IL: Charles G. Thomas Publishers.

Firestone, I. J. (1977). Reconciling verbal and nonverbal models of dyadic communication. *Environmental Psychology and Nonverbal Behavior, 2*, 30–44.

Firestone, I. J., Kaplan, K. J., & Russell, C. J. (1973). Anxiety, fear, and affiliation with similar-state versus dissimilar-state others. *Journal of Personality and Social Psychology, 26*, 490–515.

Fiske, M. (1980). Tasks and crisis of the second half of life. The interrelationship of commitment, coping and adaption. In J. E. Birren & R. B. Sloan (Eds.), *Handbook of mental health and aging*. Englewood Cliffs, NJ: Prentice Hall.

Forehand, R., Roberts, M. W., Doleus, D. M., Hobbs, S. A., & Resick, P. A. (1976). An examination of disciplinary procedures with children. *Journal of Experimental Child Psychology, 21*, 109–120.

Fowler, R. D., Rich, C. L., & Young, D. (1986). San Diego suicide study. II. Substance abuse in young cases. *Archives of General Psychiatry, 43*, 962–965.

Freud, A. (1936). *The Ego and the Mechanisms of Defense*. New York: International Universities Press.

Freud, S. (1953). Three essays on the theory of sexuality. In J. Strachey (Ed. and Trans.), *The standard edition of the completed psychological works of Sigmund Freud, 7*, 130–243. London: Hogarth Press (Original work published 1905).

Freud, S. (1957a). Mourning and melancholia. In J. Strachey (Ed. and Trans.), *The standard edition of the completed psychological works of Sigmund Freud, 14*, 237–258. London: Hogarth Press. (Original work published 1917).

Freud, S. (1957b). On narcissism: An introduction. In J. Strachey (Ed. and Trans.), *The standard edition of the completed psychological works of Sigmund Freud, 14*, 73–102. London: Hogarth Press. (Original work published 1914).

Freud, S. (1958). The disposition to obsessional neurosis: A contribution to the problem of choice of neurosis. In J. Strachey (Ed. and Trans.), *The standard edition of the completed psychological works of Sigmund Freud, 12*, 313–326. London: Hogarth Press. (Original work published 1913).

Freud, S. (1964). New introductory lectures in psychoanalysis. In J. Strachey (Ed. and Trans.), *The standard edition of the complete psychological works of Sigmund Freud, 22*, 3–182. London: Hogarth Press (Original work published 1933).

Friedman, R. C., Corn, R., Hurt, S. W., Fibel, B. Schalick, J., & Swirsky, S. (1984). Family history of illness in the seriously suicidal adolescent: A life-cycle approach. *American Journal of Orthopsychiatry, 54*, 390–397.

Gagnon, J. H. (1977). *Human sexualities*. Glenview, IL: Scott-Foresman.

Galenson, E. (1971). A consideration of the nature of thought in childhood play. In J. B. McDevitt & C. F. Settlage (Eds.), *Separation–individuation: Essays in Honor of Margaret S. Mahler* (pp. 41–60). New York: International Universities Press.

Garfinkel, B. D., Froese, A., & Hood, J. (1982). Suicide attempts in children and adolescents. *American Journal of Psychiatry, 139*, 1257–1261.

Garfinkel, B. D., & Golombek, H. (1983). Suicidal behavior in adolescence. In H. Golombek & B. D. Garfinkel (Eds.), *The adolescent and mood disturbance*. New York: International University Press.

Gibran, K. (1968). *The Prophet*. New York: Alfred A. Knopf.

Gilbert, J. (1985). A response to a bidimensional distancing approach to transactional analysis. *Transactional Analysis Journal, 15*, 142–143.

Gobes, L. (1985). Abandonment and engulfment issues in relationship therapy. *Transactional Analysis Journal, 15*, 216–219.

Goldberg, E. L. (1981). Depression and suicide ideation in the young adult. *American Journal of Psychiatry, 138*, 35–40.

Goldberg, N. (Ed.) (1966). *Passover Haggadah*. New York: KTAV Publishing Company.

Goldney, R. D. (1981). Attempted suicide in young women: Correlate of lethality. *British Journal of Psychiatry, 139*, 382–390.

Gottman, T. M. (1979). *Experimental investigation of marital interaction*. New York: Academic Press.

Gould, R. L. (1972). The phases of adult life: A study in developmental psychology. *American Journal of Psychiatry, 129*, 521–532.

Gouldner, A. W. (1960). The norm of reciprocity: A preliminary statement. *American Sociological Review, 25*, 161–178.

Greenacre, P. (1966). Problems of overidealization of the analyst and of analysis: Their manifestations in the transference and countertransference relationships. *The Psychoanalytic Study of the Child, 22*, 193–212.

Greenspan, S. I., & Pollock, G. H. (Eds.) (1980). *The course of life: Psychoanalytic contributions toward understanding personality and development (Vol. 20). Latency, adolescence and youth* Washington, DC: U. S. Government Printing Office.

Grusec, J. E., & Abramovitch, R. (1982). Imitation of peers and adults in a national setting: a functional analysis. *Child Development, 53*, 636–642.

Gutmann, D. (1975). Parenthood: A key to the comparative psychology of the lifecycle. In N. Datan & L. Ginsberg E. (Eds.), *Life span developmental psychology: Normative life crises.* New York: Academic Press.

Gutmann, D. (1980a). The post-parental years: Clinical problems and developmental possibilities. In W. Norman & T. Scaramella (Eds.), *Midlife: Developmental and clinical issues* (pp. 38–52). New York: Brunner/Mazel.

Gutmann, D. (1980b). Psychoanalysis and aging: A developmental view. In S. I. Greenspan & G. M. Pollock (Eds.), *The course of life: Psychoanalytic contribution toward understanding personality and development* (Vol. 3). *Adult years and the aging process* (pp. 489–517). Washington, DC: U.S. Government Printing Office.

Gutmann, D. (1987). *Reclaimed powers: Toward a new psychology of men and women in later life.* New York: Basic Books.

Gutmann, D. L., Griffin, B., & Grunes, I. (1982). Developmental contributions to the late–onset affective disorders. *Life-Span Development and Behavior, 4,* 244–261.

Guze, S. B., & Robins, E. (1970). Suicide and primary affective disorder. *British Journal of Psychiatry, 117,* 437–438.

Haim, A. (1970). *Adolescent suicide.* New York: International Universities Press.

Hall, E. T. (1966). *The Hidden dimension.* New York: Doubleday.

Hansburg, H. G. (1980). *Adolescent separation anxiety: A method for the study of adolescent separation problems.* Huntington, NY: Krieger Publishing Company.

Harris, T. (1969). *I'm okay, you're okay.* New York: Harper and Row.

Hartmann, H. (1964). *Essays on ego psychology: Selected problems in psychoanalytic theory.* New York: International Universities Press.

Havighurst, R. J., Neugarten, B., & Tobin, S. (1968). Disengagement and patterns of aging. In B. Neugarten (Ed.), *Middle age and aging* (pp. 161–172). Chicago: The University of Chicago Press.

Hawkins, J. L., Weisberg, C., & Ray, D. W. (1980). Spouse differences in communication style preference, perception, behavior. *Journal of Marriage and the Family, 42,* 585–593.

Hawton, K. (1982). Annotation: Attempted suicide in children and adolescents. *Journal of Child Psychology and Psychiatry, 23,* 497–503.

Hayes, S. M. (1977). *Ego identity and moral education development in male college students.* Unpublished doctoral dissertation. The Catholic University of America.

Heillig, R. J. (1980). Adolescent suicidal behavior: A family systems perspective. *Dissertation Abstracts International, 40(12),* 5813–B.

Hesiod (1914). *Hesiod, the Homeric hymns and Homerica* (H. E. Evelyn-White Trans.) London: Loeb Clasical Library.

Hill, K. T., & Sarason, S. B. (1966). The relation of test anxiety and defensiveness to tests and school performance over the elementary school years: A further longitudinal study. *Monographs of the Society for Research in Child Development, 31,* 1–76.

Hill, M. N. (1970). Suicidal behavior in adolescents and its relationship to the lack of parental empathy. *Dissertation Abstracts International, 31,* 472.

Hoffman, L. (1978). Effects of the first child on the woman role. In W. Miller & L. Newman (Eds.), *The first child and family formation* (pp. 340–367). Chapel Hill, NC: Carolina Population Center and University of North Carolina.

Hoffman, L. W., & Manis, J. D. (1979). Influences of children on martial interaction and parental satisfactions and dissatisfactions. In R. W. Lerner & G. B. Spanier (Eds.), *Child influences on marital and family interaction.* New York: Academic Press.

Hoffman, M. L. (1977). Moral internalization: Current theory and research. In L. Berkowitz (Ed.), *Advances in experimental social psychology* (Vol. 10). New York: Academic Press.

Hoffman, M. L. (1979). Development of moral thought, feeling and behavior. *American Psychologist, 34*, 958–966

Hoffman, M. L. (1980). Moral development in adolescence. In J. Adelson (Ed.), *Handbook of adolescent psychology*. New York: Wiley.

Holinger, P. (1979). Violent death among the young: Recent trends in suicide, homicide and accidents. *American Journal of Psychiatry, 139*, 302–307.

The Holy Scriptures. (1917). 2 volumes. Philadelphia: Jewish Publication Society.

Housman, R. K. (1981). The relationship between suicidal behavior in female adolescents and the lack of empathic capacity and differentiation on the part of the mothers. *Dissertation Abstracts, 42(6–8)*, 2390.

Illfeld, F. W. (1977). Current social stressors and symptoms of depression. *American Journal of Psychiatry, 134*, 161–166.

Ionesco, E. (1963). *Exit the king.* (D. Watson, Trans.) London: John Calder, Ltd.

Jacobs, J. (1971). *Adolescent suicide.* New York: Wiley-Interscience.

Jacobs, S., & Teicher, J. P. (1967). Broken homes and social isolation in attempted suicides of adolescents. *International Journal of Social Psychiatry, 13*, 139–149.

Jacobson, E. (1964). *The self and the object world.* New York: International Universities Press.

Joffe, L. S., & Vaughn, B. E. (1982). Infant–mother attachment: Theory, assessment and implications for development. In B. B. Wolman & G. Stricker (Eds.), *Handbook of development psychology* (pp. 190–207). Englewood Cliffs, NJ: Prentice Hall.

Jordan, D. (1971). *Parental antecedents and personality characteristics of ego identity statuses.* Unpublished doctoral dissertation, State University of New York at Binghamton.

Jordan, W. D. (1978). Searching for adulthood in America. In E. H. Erikson (Ed.), *Adulthood* (pp. 187–200). New York: W. W. Norton.

Josselson, R. L. (1973). Psychodynamic aspects of identity formation in college women. *Journal of Youth and Adolescence, 2*, 3–52.

Jourard, S. M. (1971). *Self-disclosure.* New York: Wiley.

Jourard, S. M., & Friedman, R. (1970). Experimenter-subject distance and self-disclosure. *Journal of Abnormal and Social Psychology, 15*, 278–282.

Jung, C. G. (1928). *Contributions to Analytical Psychology.* New York: Harcourt Brace.

Kagan, J., & Moss, H. A. (1962). *Birth to maturity.* New York: John Wiley & Sons.

Kaplan, D. L. (1995). *Self-disclosure and sexual attraction in heterosexual cross-sex platonic friendships.* Unpublished Masters Thesis, University of Illinois, Chicago.

Kaplan, D. L., & Keys, C. (1997). Sex and relationship variables as predictors of sexual attraction in cross-sex platonic friendships between young heterosexual adults. *Journal of Social and Personal Relationships, 14*, 191–206.

Kaplan, K. J. (1977). Structure and process in interpersonal "distancing." *Environmental Psychology and Nonverbal Behavior, 1 (2)*, 104–121.

Kaplan, K. J. (1985). A response to Gilbert's comments. *Transactional Analysis Journal, 15*, 144–145.

Kaplan, K. J. (1987). Jonah and Narcissus. Self-integration versus self-destruction in human development. *Studies in Formative Spirituality, 8*, 33–54.

Kaplan, K. J. (1988). TILT: Teaching individuals to live together. *Transactional Analysis Journal, 18*, 220–230.

Kaplan, K. J. (1990). TILT for Couples: Helping Couples Grow Together. *Transactional Analysis Journal, 20*, 229–244.

Kaplan, K. J., Capace, N. K., & Clyde. J. D. (1984). A bidimensional distancing approach to transactional analysis: A suggested revision of the OK corral. *Transactional Analysis Journal, 15*, 114–119.

Kaplan, K. J., Firestone, I. J., Klein, K. W., & Sodikoff, C. S. (1983). Distancing in dyads: A comparison of four models. *Social Psychology Quarterly, 46*, 108–115.

Kaplan, K. J., & Greenberg, C. I. (1976). Regulation of interaction through architecture, travel, and telecommunication. *Environmental Psychology and Nonverbal Behavior 1(1)*, 17–29.

Kaplan, K. J., & Harrow, M. (1996). Positive and negative symptoms of risk factors for later suicidal activity in schizophrenics versus depressives. *Suicide and Life-Threatening Behavior, 26*, 105–121.

Kaplan, K. J., & Harrow, M. (in press) Psychosis and functioning as risk factors for later suicidal activity among schizophrenics and schizoaffective patients: A disease-based interactive model. *Suicide and Life-Threatening Behavior.*

Kaplan, K. J., Lachenmein, F., O'Dell, J. C., & Uziel, O. (in press) Psychosocial versus biomedical risk factors in Kevorkian's first 47 "suicides," *Omega.*

Kaplan, K. J., Linky, H. B., & Jacobowitz, J. (1987, Sept.). Patterns of individuation and attachment for nonclinical men and women across the adult years. Presented at the Third Congress of the International Psychogeriatric Association, Chicago, IL.

Kaplan, K. J., & Maldaver, M. (1993). Parental marital pathology and completed adolescent suicide. *Omega, 27*, 131–154.

Kaplan, K. J., & Markus-Kaplan, M. (1979). Covenant versus contrast as two modes of relationship orientation: on reconciling possibility and necessity *Journal of Psychology and Judaism, 4*, 100–116.

Kaplan, K. J., & O'Connor, N. A. (1993). From mistrust to trust: Through a stage vertically. In S.I. Greenspan & G. H. Pollock (Eds.), *The Course of Life* (Vol. 6, pp. 153–198). New York: International Universities Press.

Kaplan, K. J., & Schwartz, M. W. (1993). *A psychology of hope: An antidote to the suicidal pathology of western civilization.* Westport, CT: Praeger.

Kaplan, K. J., Schwartz, M. W., & Markus-Kaplan, M. (1984). *The family: Biblical and psychological foundations.* New York: Human Sciences Press.

Kaplan, K. J., & Selinger, S. (1997, April). SAFE: Suicide alleviation in a family environment. Presented at the Annual Meetings of The American Association of Suicidology, Memphis, TN.

Kaplan, K. J., & Worth, S. (1993). Individuation–attachment and suicide trajectory: A developmental guide for the clinician. *Omega, 27*, 207–237.

Katz, J. (1968). *No time for youth.* San Francisco: Jossey-Bass.

Kazdin, A. E., French, N. H., Unis, A. S., Esveldt-Dawson, K., & Sherick, R. B. (1983). Helplessness, depression, and suicidal intent among psychiatrically disturbed inpatient children. *Journal of Consulting and Clinical Psychology, 51*, 504–510.

Kegan, R. (1982). *The evolving self: Problems and process in human development.* Cambridge, MA: Harvard University Press.

Kernberg, O. (1967). Borderline personalty organization. *Journal of American Psychoanalytic Association, 15*, 641–685.

Kernberg, O. (1975). *Borderline conditions and pathological narcissism.* New York: Jason Aronson.

Khan, M. M. R. (1964). Ego distortion, cumulative trauma, and the role of reconstruction in the analytic situation. *International Journal of Psychoanalysis, 45*, 272–279.

Kleeman, J. A. (1967). The peek-a-boo game. Part I: Its origins, meanings and related phenomena in the first year. *The Psychoanalytic Study of the Child, 22*, 239–273.

Klemmack, D. L., & Roff, L. L. (1984). Fear of personal aging and subjective well-being in later life. *Journal of Gerontology, 39*, 756–758.

Knowles, E. (1980). An affiliative conflict theory of personal and group spatial behavior. In P. B. Paulus (Ed.), *Psychology of Group Influence* (pp. 133–188). Hillsdale, NJ: L. Erlbaum Associates.

Kohut, H. (1966). Forms and transforms of narcissism. *Journal of American Psychoanalytic Association, 9*, 567–586.

Kohut, H. (1971). *The analysis of the self*. New York: International Universities Press.

Kosky, R. (1983). Childhood suicidal behavior. *Journal of Child Psychology and Psychiatry and Allied Disciplines, 24*, 457–568.

Laing, R. D., & Esterson, R. D. (1970). *Sanity, madness and the family*. New York: Penguin Books.

Lamb, M. E. (1978). Influence of the child on marital quality and family interaction during the prenatal, perinatal and infancy periods. In R. Lefner & G. Spanier (Eds.), *Child influences on marital and family interaction: A life-span perspective* (pp. 137–164). New York: Academic Press.

Lawton, M. P. (1980). *Environment and aging*. Monterey, CA: Brooks Cole.

Leifer, M. (1977). Psychological changes accompanying pregnancy and motherhood. *Genetic Psychology Monographs, 95*, 55–96.

Leizer, J. I., & Rogers, R. W. (1974). Effects of method of discipline, timing of punishment, and timing of test on resistance to temptation. *Child Development, 45*, 790–793.

LeMasters, E. E. (1957). Parenthood as crisis. *Marriage and Family Living, 19*, 352–355.

Lemon, B. W., Bangston, V. L., & Peterson, J. A. (1972). Activity theory and life satisfaction in a retirement community: An exploration of the activity theory of aging. *Journal of Gerentology, 27*, 511–523.

Lerner, R. M. & Shea, J. A. (1982). Social behavior in adolescence. In B. B. Wolman (Ed.), *Handbook of developmental psychology* (pp. 503–526). Englewood Cliffs, NJ: Prentice Hall.

Levin, S. (1963). Depression in the aged. In N. E. Zinberg & I. Kaufman (Eds.), *Normal Psychology of the Aging Process*. New York: International Universities Press.

Levinger, G. (1980). Toward the analysis of close relationships. *Journal of Experimental Social Psychology, 16*, 510–544.

Levinson, D. (1977). The mid-life transition: A period in adult psychosocial development. *Psychiatry, 40*, 99–112.

Levinson, D. J., Darrow, C., Klein, E., Levinson, M., & McKee, B. (1978). *The seasons of a man's life*. New York: Knopf.

Lewis, J. M., Beavers, W. R., Gosset, J. T., & Phillips, V. A. (1976). *No single thread: Psychological health in family systems*. New York: Brunner/Mazel.

Lifton, R. J. (1973). The sense of immortality: On death and the continuity of life. *American Journal of Psychoanalysis, 33*, 3–15.

Linehan, M. M. (1981). A social behavioral analysis of suicide and parasuicide. Implications for clinical assessment and treatment. In J. F. Clarkin & H. I. Glazer (Eds.), *Depression: Behavioral and directive intervention strategies*. New York: Garland Press.

Litman, R. E., & Tabachnik, N. D. (1968). Psychoanalytic theories of suicide. In

H. L. P. Resnick (Ed.), *Suicidal behaviors, diagnosis and management* (pp. 73–81). Boston: Little, Brown.

Locke, H. J. (1947). Predicting marital adjustment by comparing a divorced and happily married group. *American Sociological Review, 12*, 187–191.

Locke, H. J., & Wallace, K. M. (1959). Short marital adjustment and prediction tests: Their reliability and validity. *Marriage and Family Living, 21*, 251–255.

Loevinger, J., & Wessler, R. (1970). *Measuring ego development* (Vol. 1). San Francisco: Jossey-Bass Inc.

Long, B. H., Henderson, E. H., & Ziller, R. C. (1967). Developmental changes in the self-concept during middle childhood. *Merrill-Palmer Quarterly, 13*, 210–215.

Lorr. M. & Youniss, R. P. (1973). An inventory of interpersonal style. *Journal of Personality Assessment, 37*, 165–173.

Lowenthal, M. F. (1975). Psychosocial variations across the adult life course: Frontiers for research and policy. *Gerontologist, 15*, 6–12.

Lowenthal, M. F., Thurnher, D. C., & Associates (1975). *Four stages of life*. San Francisco: Jossey-Bass.

Lyons, M. J. (1984). Suicide in later life: Some putative causes with implications for prevention. *Journal of Community Psychology, 12*, 379–388.

Maccoby, E. E., & Jacklin, C. N. (1974). *The Psychology of Sex Difference*. Stanford, CA: Stanford University Press.

MacFarlane, J. W. (1964). Perspectives on personality consistency and changes from the guidance study. *Vita Humana, 7*, 115–126.

MacMahon, B., & Pugh, T. F. (1965). Suicide in the widowed. *American Journal of Epidemiology, 81*, 23–31.

Maehr, M. C., & Stallings, W. M. (1972). Freedom from external evaluation. *Child Development, 43*, 177–185.

Mahler, M. S. (1968). *On human symbiosis and the vicissitudes of individuation*. New York: International Universities Press.

Mahler, M. S., Pine, F., & Bergman, A. (1975). *The psychological birth of the human infant*. New York: Basic Books.

Main, M. (1973). Analysis of a peculiar form of reunion behavior seen in some day-care children who are home-reared. In R. Webb (Ed.), *Social development in daycare*. Baltimore, John Hopkins University Press.

Main, M., Kaplan, N., & Cassidy, J. (1985). Security in infancy, childhood, and adulthood: A move to the level of representation. In I. Bretherton & E. Everett (Eds.), *Growing Points of Attachment Theory and Research. Monographs of the Society for Research in Child Development, 50* (1–2, serial no. 209), 66–104.

Malley, J. (1989, August). The importance of aging and communication for well-being—Individual difference in needs and experiences. In K. Kaplan (Chair), *Individuation (Agency) and Attachment (Communion) Across the Life Span*. Symposium presented at the meetings of the American Psychological Association, New Orleans, Louisiana.

Marcia, J. E. (1966). Development and validation of ego identity states. *Journal of Personality and Social Psychology, 31*, 551–558.

Marcia, J. E. (1980). Identity in adolescence. In J. Adelson (Ed.), *Handbook of adolescent psychology* (pp. 145–161). New York: Wiley.

Marcia, J. E., & Friedman, M. L. (1970). Ego identity status in college women. *Journal of Personality, 38*, 249–263.

Maris, R. W. (1971). Deviance as therapy: The paradox of the self-destructive female. *Journal of Health and Social Behavior, 12*, 113–124.

Maris, R. W. (1989). *Pathways to suicide: A survey of self-destructive behaviors.* Baltimore: John Hopkins University Press.

Markus-Kaplan, M., & Kaplan, K. J. (1979). The typology, diagnosis, pathologies and treatment-intervention of Hellenic versus Hebraic personality styles: A proposal on the psychology of interpersonal distancing. *Journal of Psychology and Judaism, 4*, 100–116.

Markus-Kaplan, M., & Kaplan, K. J. (1984). A bidimensional view of distancing: Reciprocity versus compensation, intimacy versus social control. *Journal of Nonverbal Behavior, 8*, 315–327.

Matas, L., Arend, R. A., & Sroufe, L. A. (1978). Continuity of adaptation in the second year: The relationship between quality of attachment and later competence. *Child Development, 49*, 547–556.

McAdams, D. P. (1985). *Power, intimacy and the life story.* Homewood, IL: The Dorsey Press.

McCary, J. L. (1978). *McCary's Human Sexuality* (3rd. ed.). New York: Van Norstrand.

McCubbin, H. J., Patterson, J. M., Bauman, E., & Harris, L. H. (1981). *A-FILE.* St. Paul: University of Minnesota Press.

McIntire, M. S., & Angle, C. R. (1973). Psychological "biopsy" in self-poisoning of children and adolescents. *American Journal of Diseases of Children, 126*, 42–46.

McIntosh, J. L., Hubbard, R. W., & Santos, J. F. (1981). Suicide among the elderly: A review of issues with case studies. *Journal of Gerontological Social Work, 4*, 63–74.

McKenry, P. C., Tishler, C. L., & Kelly, C. (1982). Adolescent suicide: A comparison of attempters and nonattempters in an emergency room population. *Clinical Behavior, 21*, 266–270.

Meissner, W. W. (1984). *The borderline spectrum: Differential diagnosis and developmental issues.* New York: Jason Aronson.

Meyerowitz, J., & Feldman, H. (1966). Transition to parenthood. *Psychiatric Research Reports, 20*, 78–84.

Miles, C. (1977). Conditions predisposing to suicide: A review. *Journal of Nervous and Mental Disease, 164*, 231–246.

Miller, M. (1978). Geriatric suicide: The Arizona study. *The Gerontologists, 18*, 488–495.

Miller, M. (1979). *Suicide after sixty: The final alternative.* New York: Springer.

Minuchin, S. (1974). *Families and family therapy.* Cambridge: Harvard University Press.

Molfese, D. L., Molfese, V. J., & Carrell, P. L. (1982). Early language development. In B. B. Wolman (Ed.), *Handbook of Developmental Psychology* (pp. 302–322). Englewood Cliffs, NJ: Prentice Hall.

Moore, K. L. (1982). *The developing human: Clinically oriented embryology.* Philadelphia: Saunders.

Moos, R., & Moos, B. (1986). *Family environment scale manual* (2nd ed.), Palo Alto, CA: Consulting Psychologists Press.

Morrison, G. C., & Collier, J. G. (1969). Family treatment approaches to suicidal children and adolescents. *Journal of American Academy of Child Psychiatry, 8*, 140–153.

Moss, L. M., & Hamilton, D. M. (1957). Psychotherapy of the suicidal patient. In E. S. Shneidman & N. L. Farberow (Eds.), *Clues to suicide* (pp. 89–100). New York: McGraw-Hill.

Murphy, G. E., & Robins, E. (1967). Social factors in suicide. *Journal of the American Medical Association, 199*, 3033–3038.

Murphy, G. E., Armstrong, J. W., Hermele, S. L., Fisher, J. R., & Clendenim, W. W. (1979). Suicide and alcoholism: Interpersonal loss confirmed as a predictor. *Archives of General Psychiatry, 36*, 65–69.

Murphy, L. B., & Moriarty, A. E. (1976). *Vulnerability, coping and growth.* New Haven, CT: Yale University Press.

Napier, A. Y. (1978). The rejection-intrusion pattern: A central family dynamic. *Journal of Marriage and Family Counseling, 4*, 5–12.

Neugarten, B. (1968). The awareness of middle age. In B. Neugarten (Ed.), *Middle age and aging.* Chicago: University of Chicago Press.

Neugarten, B. L. (1973). Personality change in late life: A development perspective. In C. Eisdorfer and M. P. Lawton (Eds.), *The psychology of adult development* (pp. 311–338). Washington, DC: American Psychological Association.

Neugarten, B. L. (1979). Time, age and the life cycle. *American Journal of Psychiatry, 136*, 887–894.

Neugarten, B. L., & Gutmann, P. L. (1958). Age-sex roles and personality in middle age: A thematic appreciation study. *Psychological Monographs, 72*, (whole no. 470).

Neugarten, B. L., Harvighurst, R. J., & Tobin, S. S. (1968). Personality and patterns of aging. In B. Neugarten (Ed.), *Middle age and aging* (pp. 173–179). Chicago: The University of Chicago Press.

Newman, B. M., & Newman, P. R. (1987). *Development through life—a psychosocial approach* (4th ed.), Chicago: The Dorsey Press.

Noam, G. G., O'Connell Higgins, R., & Goethals, G. W. (1982). Psychoanalytic approaches to developmental psychology. In B. B. Wolman & G. Stricker (Eds.), *Handbook of developmental psychology.* Englewood Cliffs, NJ: Prentice-Hall, Inc.

Odom, L. Seeman, J., & Newbrough, J. R. (1971). A study of family communication patterns and personality integration in children. *Child Psychiatry and Human Development, 1*, 275–285.

Offer, D., & Offer, J. B. (1975). *From teenage to young manhood. A psychological study.* New York: Basic Books.

Olds, S. B., London, M. L., & Ladewig, P. A. (1980). *Maternal newborn nursing* (3rd. ed.). New York: Addison-Wesley.

Olson, D. H., & Craddock, A. E. (1980). Circumplex model of marital and family systems: Application to Australian families. *Australian Journal of Sex, Marriage and Family, 1*, 53–69.

Olson, D. H., & McCubbin, H. I. (1982). *Circumplex model of marital and family systems V: Application to family stress, coping, and social support.* Springfield, IL: Charles G. Thomas Publishers.

Olson, D. H., Russell, C. S., & Sprenkle, D. H. (1983). Circumplex Model VI: Theoretical update. *Family Process, 22*, 69–83.

Olson, D. H., Sprenkle, D. H., & Russell, C. S. (1979). Circumplex model of marital and family systems: I. Cohesion and adaptability dimensions, family types, and clinical implications. *Family Process, 18*, 3–28.

Orbach, I. (1984). Personality characteristics, life circumstances, and dynamics of suicidal children. *Death Education, 8*, 37–52.

Orlovsky, J. L. (1976). Intimacy status: Relationship to interpersonal perception. *Journal of Youth and Adolescence, 5*, 73–89.

Orlovsky, J. L. (1978). Identity formation, achievement and fear of success in college men and women. *Journal of Youth and Adolescence, 7*, 49–62.

Otto, U. (1972). Suicidal acts by children and adolescents. *Acta Psychiatrica Scandinavica. Supplementum, 233*, 7–123.

Ovid (1955). *The Metamorphoses.* M. Innes (Trans.). London: Penguin Classics.

Papalia, D. E., & Olds, S. W. (1982). *A child's world: Infancy through adolescence* (3rd ed.). New York: McGraw Hill.

Park, R. E., Burgess, E. W., & McKenzie, R. D. (1925). *The city, Chicago.* Chicago: University of Chicago Press.

Parkes, C. M. (1972). *Bereavement: Studies of grief in adult life.* London: Tavistock.

Parnitzke, C., & Regel, H. (1973). Self-destruction of minors caused by social disintegration. *Psychiatrie, Neurologie and Medizinische Psychogie, 25*, 606–614.

Parton, D. A. (1976). Learning to imitate in infancy. *Child Development, 47*, 14–31.

Passman, R. H., & Longeway, K. P. (1982). The role of vision in maternal attachment: Giving 2 year olds a photograph of their mother during separation. *Developmental Psychology, 18*, 530–533.

Patterson, M. L. (1976). An arousal model of interpersonal intimacy. *Psychological Review, 83*, 235–245.

Patterson, M. L. (1982). A sequential model of nonverbal exchange. *Psychological Review, 89*, 231–249.

Peck, R. C. (1968). Psychological developments in the second half of life. In B. Neugarten (Ed.), *Middle age and aging* (pp. 88–92). Chicago: The University of Chicago Press.

Pellegrini, D. S. (1985). Social cognition and competence in middle childhood. *Child Development, 56*, 253–264.

Pepitone, E. A., Loeb, H. W. & Murdock, E. M. (1977, August). *Social comparison and similarity of children's performance in competitive situations.* Paper presented at the annual meeting of the American Psychological Association, San Francisco, CA.

Pfeffer, C. R. (1981). The family system of suicidal children. *American Journal of Psychotherapy, 35*, 330–334.

Pfeffer, C. R. (1986). *The suicidal child.* New York: Guilford Press.

Pfeffer, C. R., Conte, H. R., Plutchik, R., & Jerrett, I. (1980). Suicidal behavior in latency-age children: An outpatient population. *Journal of the American Academy of Child Psychiatry, 18*, 703–710.

Pfeffer, C. R., Plutchik, R., & Mizruchi, M. S. (1983). Suicidal and assaultive behavior in children: Classification, measurement, and intervention. *American Journal of Psychiatry, 140*, 154–157.

Phillips, D. (1984). The illusion of incompetence among academically competent children. *Child Development, 55*, 2000–2016.

Piaget, J. (1954). *The construction of reality in the child.* New York: Basic Books. (Original work published 1937).

Pines, A., & Aronson, E. (1981). *Burnout: From tedium to personal growth.* New York: Free Press.

Pitts, F., & Winokur, G. (1964). Affective disorder: III. Diagnostic correlates and incidents of suicide. *Journal of Nervous and Mental Disease, 139*, 176–181.

Podd, M. M. (1972). Ego identity status and morality: The relationship between two developmental constructs. *Developmental Psychology, 6*, 497–527.

Poppen, P. J. (1974). *The development of sex differences in moral judgement for college males and females.* Unpublished doctoral dissertation. Cornell University.

Powell, E. H. (1958). Occupation, status, and suicide. Toward a redefinition of anomie. *American Sociological Review, 23*, 131–139.

Rank, O. (1936). *Will therapy.* New York: Knopf.

Ray, L. Y., & Johnson, N. (1983), Vol. 62 Adolescent suicide. *The Personnel and Guidance Journal, 62*, 131–135.

Recklitis, C. J., Noam, G. G., & Borst, S. R. (1989). *Adolescent suicide and defensive style.* Unpublished manuscript.

Rich, C. L., Young, D., & Fowler, R. C. (1986). San Diego Study: I. Young versus old subjects. *Archives of General Psychiatry, 43*: 577–582.

Richman, J. (1978). Symbiosis, empathy, suicidal behavior, and the family. *Suicide and Life-Threatening Behavior, 8*, 139–149.

Richman, J. (1981). Suicide and the family affective disturbances and their implications for understanding, diagnosis and treatment. In M. R. Laneky (Ed.), *Family therapy and major psychopathology.* New York: Grune & Stratton.

Rieger, W. (1971). Suicide attempts in a federal prison. *Archives of General Psychiatry, 24*, 532–535.

Robbins, D. R., & Alessi, N. E. (1985). Depressive symptoms and suicidal behavior in adolescents. *American Journal of Psychiatry, 142*, 588–592.

Robins, L. N. (1966). *Deviant children grown up.* Baltimore: Williams & Wilkins.

Robins, L. N. (1978). Childhood predictors of adult antisocial behavior: Replications from longitudinal studies. *Psychological Medicine, 8*, 611–622.

Rockwell, D., & O'Brien, W. (1973). Physicians' knowledge and attitudes about suicide. *Journal of the American Medical Association, 225*, 1347–1349.

Rosenberg, M. (1965) *Society and the adolescent self-image,* Princeton, NJ: Princeton University Press.

Rossi, A. (1968). Transition to parenthood. *Journal of Marriage and the Family, 30*, 26–39.

Rowe, I. (1978). *Ego identity status, cognitive development and levels of moral reasoning.* Unpublished master's thesis. Simon Fraser University.

Roy, A. (1980). Early parental loss in depressive neurosis compared with other neurosis. *Canadian Journal of Psychiatry, 25*, 503–505.

Roy, A. (1983). Family history of suicide. *Archives of General Psychiatry, 40*, 971–974.

Roy, A., & Linnoila, M. (1986). Alcoholism and suicide. In R. Maris (Ed.), *Biology of suicide.* New York: Guilford Press.

Rubin, R. (1975). Maternal tasks in pregnancy. *Maternal–Child Nursing Journal, 4*, 143–153.

Rubin, Z. (1980). *Children's friendships.* Cambridge, MA: Harvard University Press.

Ruble, D. N. (1983). The development of social comparison processes and their role in achievement-related self-socialization. In E. T. Higgins, D. N. Ruble, & W. W. Hartup (Eds.), *Social cognition and social behavior: Developmental issues.* New York: Cambridge University Press.

Russell, C. (1974). Transition to parenthood: Problems and gratifications. *Journal of Marriage and the Family, 36*, 294–303.

Ryff, C. D., & Heincke, S. G. (1983). Subjective organization of personality in adulthood and aging. *Journal of Personality and Social Psychology, 44*, 807–816.

Rygnestad, T. K. (1982). A prospective study of social and psychiatric aspects of self-poisoned patients. *Acta Psychiatrica Scandinavica, 66*, 139–153.

Sainz, A. (1966). Hyperkinetic disease of children: Diagnosis and therapy. *Diseases of the Nervous System, 27*, 48–50.

Sangiuliano, I. (1978). *In her time.* New York: Morrow.

Sarwer-Foner, G. J. (1969). Depression and suicide: On some particularly high risk suicidal patients. *Diseases of the Nervous System, 30*, 104–110.

Sathyavathi, K. (1975). Suicide among children in Bangalore. *Indian Journal of Pediatrics, 42*, 149–157.

Schenkel, S., & Marcia, J. E. (1972). Attitudes toward premarital intercourse in determining ego identify status in college women. *Journal of Personality, 3*, 472–482.

Schiff, J. L., & Day, B. (1970). *All my children.* New York: M. Evans Publishing Co.

Schiff, J. L., Schiff, A. W., Mellor, K., Schiff, E., Schiff S., Richman, D., Fishman, J., Wolz, L., Fishman, C., & Momb, D. (1975). *Cathexis reader: Transactional analysis of psychosis.* New York: Harper & Row.

Seiden, R. H. (1983). Death in the west: A spatial analysis of the youthful suicide rate. *Western Journal of Medicine, 139*, 783–795.

Seligman, M. E. P. (1975). *Helplessness: On depression, development and death.* San Francisco: W. H. Freeman & Co.

Shaffer, D. (1974). Suicide in childhood and early adolescence. *Journal of Child Psychology and Psychiatry, 15*, 275–291.

Shaffer, D., & Fisher, P. (1981). The epidemiology of suicide in children and young adolescents. *Journal of the American Academy of Child and Adolescent Psychiatry, 20*, 545–565.

Shaffer, D., & Gould, M. (1987). *Study of completed and attempted suicides in adolescents.* Progress Report: National Institute of Mental Health.

Shafii, M., Carrigan, S., Whittinghill, J. R., & Derrick, A. (1985). Psychological autopsy of completed suicides in children and adolescents. *American Journal of Psychiatry, 142*, 1061–1064.

Shanan, J. (1985). Personality types and culture in later adulthood. In J. Meacham (Ed.), *Contributions to Human Development* (Vol. 12). Basel, Switzerland: Karger.

Shereshefsky, P., Labenberg, B., & Lockman, R. F. (1973). Maternal adaptation. In P. Shereshefsky & L. J. Yarrow (Eds.), *Psychological aspects of a first pregnancy and early postnatal adaptation.* New York: Raven Press.

Shneidman, E. S., & Farberow, N. L. (Eds.), (1957). *Clues to suicide.* New York: McGraw-Hill Book Co.

Silber, E., Hamburg, D. A., Coelho, G. V., Murphey, E. B., Rosenberg, M., & Pearlin, L. I. (1961). Adaptive behavior in competent adolescents. Coping with the anticipation of college. *Archives of General Psychiatry, 5*, 354–365.

Singer, J. L. (1973). *The child's world of make-believe: Experimental studies of imaginative play.* New York: Academic Press.

Singer, J. L. (1975). *The inner world of daydreaming.* New York: Colophon Books.

Slater, J., & Depue, R. A. (1981). The contribution of environmental events and social support to serious suicide attempts in primary depressive disorder. *Journal of Abnormal Psychology, 40*, 275–285.

Sommer, R. (1969). *Personal space.* Englewood Cliffs, NJ: Prentice-Hall.
Sonnenberg, J., & Jacobowitz, J. (1989, August). Psychological attachment to the family and adaptation during the later years of the life span. In K. Kaplan (Chair), *Individuation (Agency) and Attachment (Communion) Across the Life Span.* Symposium presented at the meetings of the American Psychological Association, New Orleans, Lousiana.
Soutre, E. (1988). Completed suicides and traffic accidents: Longitudinal analysis in France. *Acta Psychiatrica Scandinavica, 77,* 530–534.
Spanier, G. B. (1976). Measuring dyadic adjustment. New scales for assessing the quality of marriage and similar dyads. *Journal of Marriage and the Family, 38,* 15–28.
Sroufe, L. A. (1979). The coherence of individual development: Early care, attachment, and subsequent development issues. *American Psychologist, 34,* 834–841.
Sroufe, L. A., & Rutter, M. (1984). The domain of developmental psychopathology. *Child Development, 55,* 17–29.
Sroufe, L. A., & Waters, E. (1977). Attachment as an organizational construct. *Child Development, 48,* 1184–1199.
Stein, J. (1979, August). Gender and midlife developmental processes: Commonalities and differences. In S. Cytrynbaum (Chair), *Midlife Development Influences of Gender, Personality and Social System.* Symposium presented at the meeting of the American Psychological Association, New York.
Stern, D. (1977). *The first relationship: Mother and infant.* Cambridge, MA: Harvard University Press.
Stewart, A. J., & Malley, J. E. (1987). Role combination in women: Mitigating agency and communion: In F. S. Crosby (Ed.), *Spouse, parent, worker: On gender and multiple roles.* New Haven: Yale University Press.
Stewart, A. J., & Salt, P. (1981). Life stress, life-styles, depression and illness in adult women. *Journal of Personality and Social Psychology, 210,* 1063–1069.
Stewart, M. A. (1967). Hyperactive child syndrome recognized 100 years ago. *Journal of the American Medical Association, 202,* 28–29.
Stierlin, H. (1974). *Separating parents and adolescents: A perspective on running away, schizophrenia, and waywardness.* New York: Quadrangle/The New York Times Book Club.
Stillion, J. M., McDowell, E. E., & May, J. H. (1996). *Suicide across the life span—premature exits.* New York: Hemisphere Publishing Corporation.
Sullivan, H. S. (1949). *The collected works of Harry Stack Sullivan* (Vols. 1 and 2). New York: Norton.
Terman, L. (1938). *Psychological factors in marital happiness.* New York: McGraw Hill Book Company.
Tischler, C. L., McKenry, P. C., & Morgan, K. C. (1981). Adolescent suicide attempts: Some significant factors. *Suicide and Life-Threatening Behavior, 11,* 86–92
Toolan, J. M. (1975). Suicide in children and adolescents. *American Journal of Psychotherapy, 29,* 339–344.
Topol, P., & Resnikoff, M. (1982). Perceived peer and family relationships, hopelessness, locus of control as factors in adolescent suicide attempts. *Suicide and Life-Threatening Behavior 12,* 141–150.
Tsuang, M. T. (1983). Risk of suicide in the relatives of schizophrenics, manics, depressives, and controls. *American Journal of Clinical Psychiatry, 44,* 396–400.

Vaillant, G. E. (1977). *Adaption to life*. Boston: Little, Brown.
Vaughn, B., Egeland, B., Sroufe, L. A., & Waters, E. (1979). Individual differences in infant–mother attachment at 12 and 18 months: Stability and change in families under stress. *Child Development, 50*, 971–975.
Virkuner, M. (1971). Alcoholism and suicides in Helsinki. *Psychiatric Fenn*, 201–207.
Warren, L. W., & Tomlinson-Keasey (1987). The context of suicide. *American Journal of Orthopsychiatry, 57*, 41–48
Weissman, M. M. (1974). The epidemiology of suicide attempts, 1960 to 1971. *Archives of General Psychiatry, 30*, 737–746.
Wells, L. E., & Marwell, G. (1976). *Self-esteem: Its conceptualization and measurement*. Beverly Hills, CA: Sage.
Wenz, F. W. (1978). Economic status, family anomie, and adolescence suicide potential. *Journal of Psychology, 98*, 45–47.
Wenz, F. W. (1979). Family constellation factors, depression and parent suicidal potential. *American Journal of Orthopsychiatry, 49*, 164–167.
Werry, S. S. (1968). Developmental hyperactivity. *Pediatric Clinics of North America, 15*, 581–599.
Westermeyer, J. F., & Harrow, M. C. (1989). Early phases of schizophrenia and depression: Prediction of suicide. In R. Williams & T. Dalby (Eds.), *Depression in schizophrenia* (pp. 153–169). New York: Plenum Publishing Company.
White, R. W. (1960). Competence and the psychological stages of development. In M. R. Jones (Ed.), *Nebraska symposium on motivation* (Vol. 8), Lincoln, NE: University of Nebraska Press, *Archives of General Psychiatry, 18*, 16–27.
Willi, J. (1982). *Couples in collusion*. New York: Jason Aronson.
Windle, M., & Sinnott, J. D. (1985). A psychometric study of the Bem Sex Role Inventory with an older adult sample. *Journal of Gerontology, 40*, 336–343.
Winnicott, D. W. (1965). *The maturational processes & the facilitating environment*. New York: International Universities Press.
Winnicott, D. W. (1971). *Playing and reality*. New York: Basic Books.
Wold, C. I. (1968, August). Some syndromes among suicidal people: The problem of suicide potentiality. Presented at the Annual Meeting of the American Psychological Association, San Francisco.
Wold, C. I. (1970). Characteristics of 26,000 suicide-prevention center patients. *Bulletin of Suicidology, 6*, 24–28.
Yalom, I., Lunde, D. T., Moos, R. H., & Hamburg, D. A. (1968). Post-partum "blues" syndrome: A description and related variables. *Archives of General Psychiatry, 18*, 16–27.

Index

AA couple (neurotic enmeshed)
   clinical case, 164, 166–167, 168
   description, 141, 144
   flip to CC couple, 149
   TILT goals for, 150–151
$(A/C)_{ATT}$. (*See* Borderline pathology, paranoid position)
AC axis. (*See* Clinical axis)
$(A/C)_{IND}$. (*See* Borderline pathology, depressed position)
Adolescence
   description of, 106–108
   suicide. (*See* Suicide, adolescent)
Adulthood
   early
      description of, 108–110
      suicidal contemplation and, 222–224
   middle
      description of, 110–112
      suicidal contemplation and, 224–227
   older
      description of, 112–114
      suicidal contemplation and, 227
   oldest-old
      description of, 114–116
      suicidal contemplation and, 229–232

Advanced reciprocal relationship, 138, 140
Age
   adult life stages. (*See under Adulthood*)
   of parents, adolescent suicide and, 197, 201–204
Altruistic suicide, 193
Anomic suicide, 193
Attachment
   ambivalence, 51, 52
   autonomy and
      mutual exclusiveness, 119–121
      not mutual exclusive, 121–126
   definition of, 6, 8–9, 17
   deindividuated, 106
   dismissing, 39–42
   exploration, 97
   fear of, 33–34
      developmental axis and, 47–49
      self-confidence, sociability and, 39–42
   individuation and, 6–11
      congruency of, 22, 23
      incongruency of, 22, 24
   nearness and, 9
   need for, 33–34, 47–49
   preoccupied, 38–42
   secure

Attachment (*Continued*)
    description of, 38–42
    from normal infantile autism, 92, 96–98
    styles, 38–42
    in TILT approach, 210
    walls and, 17–18
Autonomy/individuation
    attachment and, 6–11, 119–121
        congruency of, 22, 23
        incongruency of, 22, 24
        independence of, 12–13
        mutually exclusive, 119–121
        not mutually exclusive, 121–126
    boundaries and, 13, 17–18
    definition of, 6–7, 9, 17
    detached. (*See* Disengagement)
    farness and, 9–10
    fear of, 33–34, 35, 47–49
    indifference toward, 51, 52
    life stage resolution and, 86
    need for, 33–34, 35, 47–49
    vs. attachment, 6*n*
    vs. shame, 100–102
Avoidant personality disorder, 22

BB relationship. (*See also* Regression)
    couple
        from AC, 150–151
        clinical illustration of, 155–157
    family, 189
BED axis. (*See* Developmental axis)
Bidimensional perspective, for couple therapy, 145
Binding, adolescent, 108
Blastocyst (zygote), 94–95
Bonding. (*See* Attachment)
Borderline pathology
    conflicts, 53
    depressed position (A/C)$_{IND}$, 56–57, 60
        couples, 129, 134, 142–143, 172, 174–176
        description of, 24–25
        family, 190
    mixed position
        couples, 130, 136, 144–145, 178, 180–181, 182
        family, 190–191
    paranoid position (A/C)$_{ATT}$
        couples, 78, 80, 81, 143, 144, 175–179
        description of, 25, 57–58, 61
        family, 190
Boundaries
    amorphous, 55
    description of, 12–15
    diffuse *vs.* rigid, 12
    in disengaged families, 119
    in enmeshed families, 119
    establishing, 15
    extradyadic, 119–120
    individuation and, 17–18
    losing, 15
    maturation and, 49
    mixed, 57–58, 61
    moderate, 55
    purpose of, 13, 15
    withdrawal responses and, 54–58

CBCL-P (Child Behavior Checklist-Parent Version), 197
CC couple. (*See also* Disengagement/isolation)
    description of, 141, 144
    TILT goals for, 151
Child Behavior Checklist-Parent Version (CBCL-P), 197
Children. (*See also* Parent-child relationship)
    implications of couple therapy for, 185

Index 257

play-age, 92, 102–104
school-age
   developmental tasks of, 92, 104–106
   suicidal contemplation, 216–219
toddlers, 92, 100–102
Clinical axis (AC axis). (*See also* Borderline pathology; Neurosis)
   couples
      development and, 124–126
      distancing patterns and, 141–144
   description of, 50–53
   family
      adolescent suicide and, 189–191
      cohesion and, 123–126
   growth and, 147–148
   incongruency of individuation and attachment, 22, 24
   moving off of, 59–60
   parenting and, 187–188
   positions on, 17–18, 19, 122
      A, 56, 58
      (A/C)$_{ATT}$. (*See* Borderline pathology, paranoid position)
      (A/C)$_{IND}$. (*See* Borderline pathology, depressed position)
      (A/C)$_{TOT}$. (*See* Psychotic position)
      C, 56, 59
      of couples, 141–142
   between stage dynamics, 214–216
   suicidal disintegration. (*See* Disintegration, suicidal)
   TILT types and, 21, 22
   vs. developmental axis. (*See* Developmental axis, *vs.* clinical axis)
   within-stage dynamics, 213–214
Clinician, dealing with suicidal patients, 209–210
   adolescent, 219–222
   early adulthood, 222–224
   forward regression *vs.* disintegrative suicidal trajectory, 210–213
   school-age children, 216–219
   between stage dynamics, 214–216
   TILT approach assumptions and, 210
   within-stage dynamics, 213–214
Compensatory distancing pattern, 5, 7
Confident expectation, 99
Coordination, 152–153
Couples
   advanced, 193
      adolescent suicidal behavior and, 194
      clinical illustration, 159–162
   borderline pathology
      depressive, 172, 174–175, 176
      mixed, 178, 180–181, 182
      paranoid, 175, 177–178, 179
   CC, 141
   disengaged, 128, 132
   DB, clinical illustration, 163–164, 165
   DD, 142
      clinical illustration, 159–162
      developed, 126, 129
   depressive-borderline, 129, 134
   development, 124, 125
      AC axis and, 124–126
      BED axis and, 124, 125
   disengaged, 128, 132, 193
   distancing patterns, 138, 140–141, 140–144
      clinical axis and, 141–144
      developmental axis and, 138, 140–141
   emerging EE

Couples (*Continued*)
    clinical illustration, 158–159, 160
    description of, 126, 128
    enmeshed AA
        adolescent suicidal behavior and, 193, 194, 195
        description of, 127–128, 131
    healthy developmental types, 192–193
    isolated, adolescent suicidal behavior and, 194
    mixed
        borderline, 130, 136
        DB, 126, 130
        parent-child, 163–164, 165
    need and fear energy in, 126–131
    paranoid-borderline, 129–130, 135
    psychotic, 130, 137
    regressed
        BB, 126, 127
        clinical illustration, 155–157
        reciprocal, adolescent suicidal behavior and, 194
    rejection-intrusion, 193
        AC, 128–129, 133
        adolescent suicidal behavior and, 194
    TILT model for
        description of, 145–150
        goals of, 150–153

DB couple (mixed parent-child), clinical illustration, 163–164, 165
DD couple, clinical illustration, 159–162
Death, fear of, 120
Deindividuation
    definition of, 6–7, 9, 17
    life stage and, 87
    nearness and, 9
    in older adulthood, 112–114

Demographics Questionnaire, 40
Depressive-borderline pathology. (*See* Borderline pathology, depressed position)
Despair, 86
Detachment
    definition of, 6, 17
    farness and, 9–10
    in older adulthood, 112–114
    in TILT approach, 210
    walls and, 12
Developed position (D), case illustration, 69–70
Developmental axis (BED axis)
    congruency of individuation and attachment, 22, 23
    couples. (*See under couples*)
    description of, 17–18
    family
        adolescent suicide and, 188–189
        cohesion and, 122–123
    parenting and, 187–188
    positions on
        B, 54–55
        D, 55–57
        E, 55, 56
        regressed B, 65–67
    between stage dynamics, 214–216
    TILT types and, 21, 22
    vs. clinical axis
        stage 0–prebirth, 92, 94–96
        stage 1–early infancy, 92, 96–98
        stage 2–later infancy, 92, 98–100
        stage 3–toddlerhood, 92, 100–102
        stage 4–play-age childhood, 92, 102–104
        stage 5–school age childhood, 92, 104–106
        stage 6–adolescence, 92, 106–108

Index

stage 7–early adulthood, 93, 108–110
stage 8–middle adulthood, 93, 110–112
stage 9–older adulthood, 93, 112–114
stage 10–oldest old, 93, 114–116
within-stage dynamics, 213–214
Developmental process, ontogenetic view of, 86–87
Disclosure intimacy, 4
Disengagement/isolation
   couples, 141, 145
   definition of, 222
   description of, 141, 144
   life stage resolution and, 86
   TILT goals for, 151
   unidimensional view, 5, 8
   vs. intimacy, 108–110
   displaying, 24
   family, 120
   unidimensional view, 5, 8
Disintegration, suicidal, 215, 216
   adolescent, 221–222
   early adulthood, 222, 224
   middle adulthood, 226–227
   older adulthood, 227–229
   oldest-old, 230, 231–232
   school-age children and, 218–219
   TILT representation of, 215, 216
D position (developed), case illustration, 69–70

Edwards Personal Preferences Schedule (EPPS), 34–37
EE couple, clinical illustration, 158–159
E (emerging)
   case illustration, 67–68
   development of, 141
Ego
   defense, 12
   negative or dystonic qualities, 85
   qualities, 85–87
   resilience, 104
   strength, 12
Egoistic suicide, 193
Elderly, 114–116. (*See also* Adulthood, oldest-old)
Electra complex, 102
Embedded relationship. (*See* Enmeshed relationship)
Embryo, 95
Emerging reciprocal relationship
   couples, 138, 158–159
   family, 189
Enmeshed relationship
   couples, 141
   definition of, 222
   family, 120
   unidimensional view, 5, 8
Eriksonian life stages
   description of, 85–87
   expansion/reconceptualization of, 89–91
Existential stress, 115
Expelling, adolescent, 108

FACES (Family Adaptability and Cohesion Evaluation Scales), 197
"Falling in love" state, 138
Family
   boundaries in, 12
   clinical axis, 189–191
   cohesion. (*See* Family cohesion)
   developmental axis, 188–189
   disengaged or underinvolved, 12
   factors, in adolescent suicide, 191–193
   neurotic enmeshed, 190
   supportive, 192
Family Adaptability and Cohesion Evaluation Scales (FACES), 197

Family cohesion
  bidimensional model of, 121–126
  couple type and, individual distancing patterns and, 132–137
  unidimensional model, 119–121
Farness, interpretation of, 9–10
Fear energy
  in couples, 126–131
  developmental axis and, 47–49
Fetal development, 95–96
Fey Self-Acceptance Scale, 40
Forward regression
  conception of, 87, 89
  couples, 124, 152
  definition of, 85, 213
  integrative, 215–216
  vs. disintegrative suicidal trajectory, 210–213
Friendship Questionnaire, 40

Generativity, vs. stagnation, 86, 110–112
Growth, healthy, 61–62
Guilt, vs. initiative, 86, 102–104

Hall, Edward, 4
The Hidden Dimension, 4
Holding relationship, 138

IAQ. (*See* Individuation-Attachment Questionnaire)
Identity
  assertion, by AA couple, 150–151
  confusion, 86
  life stage resolution and, 86
  vs. identity confusion, 106–108
Immaturity, vs. pathology, 187
I'M OK-I'M NOT OK, 11n
Individual distancing patterns
  clinical axis, 134–137
  couples/families, 132–137
  description of, 54–58
  developmental axis, 132–134
Individual psychological model, extension to couples/families, 131–132
Individuation. (*See* Autonomy/individuation)
Individuation-attachment dilemma, 88
Individuation-Attachment Questionnaire (IAQ), 17, 18, 42–43
  administration directions, 19
  couples
    advanced, 159–161
    borderline depressive, 174
    borderline mixed, 180
    emerging, 158–159
    mixed parent-child, 163–164
    neurotic disengaged, 167, 169–170, 171
    neurotic enmeshed, 166–167
    neurotic rejection intrusion, 172
    psychotic, 183
    regressed, 156
  cutoff norms, 26–21
  developmental axis and, 47, 49
  interpersonal reactivity, 38, 39
  interpretation of scores, 21–25
  parental marital pattern in adolescent suicide, 197
  personality scales, 34–37
  reliabilities, 31, 32
  scoring, directions for, 19–21
  self-consciousness, 38, 39
  self-report, clinical perception and, 34, 35
  subscales, 47
  validities
    divergent and convergent, 31–34
    external, 34–42
Industry, vs. inferiority, 86, 104–106

Index

Infancy
  early, 92, 96–98
  later, mistrust *vs.* trust, 98–100
  normal autism, move to secure attachment, 92, 96–98
Inferiority, *vs.* industry, 86, 104–106
Inhibition, childhood, 104
Initiative, *vs.* guilt, 86, 102–104
Integrated stage progression, 151–152
Integration, nonsuicidal, 215–216, 218
  adolescent, 219–220
  early adulthood, 222, 223
  middle adulthood, 224–226
  older adulthood, 227, 228
  oldest-old, 230, 231
Integrity, 86
International relations, TILT applications, 233
Interpersonal distance
  bidimensional view, 9–11, 14
  compensatory pattern, 5, 7
  definition of, 3–4, 54
  "far" end of, 5
  "near" end of, 5
  patterns of, 4–6
  reciprocal pattern, 5, 8
  unidimensional view, 5–6, 8, 10
  unitary theory of, 5
Interpersonal reactivity, 38, 39
Interpersonal Style Inventory (ISI), 35, 37
Interpersonal walls. (*See* Walls, interpersonal)
Intimacy, *vs.* isolation, 86, 108–110
Intimate distance, 4
ISI (Interpersonal Style Inventory), 35, 37
Isolation. (*See* Disengagement/isolation)

Jourard, Sidney, 4

Kaplan, Daniel, 4

Life, fear of, 120
Life cycle shock, 115
Life stages
  advancement, 63
Life stages, Eriksonian. (*See also specific life stages*)
  descriptions of, 85–87
  developmental *vs.* clinical axis. (*See* Developmental axis, *vs.* clinical axis)
  TILT and, 87–89
Loneliness, 5
Love, 109
Love withdrawal discipline technique, 102

Marital pathology, adolescent suicide and, 201–204
Maturity
  DD family, 189
  levels, over life span, 123
  replacing walls with boundaries, 49
Medicine, TILT applications, 234
"Mid-life crossover" effect, 112
Minuchin, Salvatore, 12
Mistrust
  basic, 86
  vs. trust, 98–100
Mixed position
  borderline couples, 143–144, 178, 180–181, 182
  boundaries, 57–58, 61
  interpersonal walls, 57–58, 61
  parent-child couples, 163–164, 165
Mother
  perceived adolescent psychopathology, adolescent suicide and, 202–204
  relationship with infant, 97, 123

Narcissism
  idealizing, 123–124, 141, 142
  mirroring, 124
Narcissistic collusion, 148–149
Nearness
  bidimensional view, 10
  interpretation of, 9
  to others, 9
  to self, 8–9
Need-dominated person, 55–57
Need energy
  in couples, 126–131
  developmental axis and, 47–49
Needs, maturity and, 47
Neurosis
  couples
    disengaged, 167, 169–170, 171
    enmeshed, 164, 166–167, 168
    rejection intrusion, 170–172, 173
  disengaged position C, case illustrations, 72, 74–75, 76
  enmeshed
    couple. (*See* AA couple)
    disengaged, imbalanced, 50
    family, 190
  enmeshed position A, case illustration, 70–73
  family
    disengaged (CC), 190
    enmeshed, 190
    rejection-intrusion position (AC), 190
  individuation-attachment and, 53

Object constancy, 99–100
Object permanence, 99–100
Oedipal conflict, 102

Paranoid borderline pathology. (*See* Borderline pathology, paranoid position)

Parent-child relationship
  BD position, 189
  DB position, 140–141
Parenting
  AC axis, 187–188
  BED axis, 187–188
  developmental patterns, adolescent suicide and, 192
  in middle adulthood, 112
Parents. (*See also* Parent-child relationship)
  age of, adolescent suicide and, 197, 201–204
  discipline, in toddlerhood, 102
  marital pathology, adolescent suicide and, 197–198
  marital pattern, adolescent suicide and, 195–197
  marital types, adolescent suicide and, 193–195
  of suicides, 201
Passive-dependent personality, 113–114
Pathological axis. (*See* Clinical axis)
Patient-therapist distance, disclosure intimacy and, 4
Personal distance, 4
Personal space, 4
Political economics, TILT applications, 233
Power assertion discipline technique, 102
Prebirth period, 92, 94–96
Progression in stage, 89
Proxemics, 4
Psychotic position (A/C)$_{TOT}$
  case illustration, 81–84
  couple, 144, 181, 183–185
    completely trapped, 150
    TILT therapy goals, 183, 185
  description of, 53, 122, 124
  family, 191
Public distance, 4

Index

Reciprocal distancing pattern, 5, 8
Regression
  couple
    from AC to BB, 150–151
    clinical illustration, 155–157
  family, 189
  forward. (*See* Forward regression)
  to less advanced stage, 60
  in level, 89
  normal, 63
  position B
    case illustration, 65–67
    description of, 54–55
  positive, 60–61
  reciprocal relationship, 138
Rejection-intrusion relationship
  description of, 141–142
  neurotic couples, 170–172, 173
Rejectivity, 111–112
Reversals, 149–150
Rosenberg Self-Esteem Inventory, 40

Self-confidence, attachment styles and, 38–42
Self-consciousness, 38, 39
Self-disclosure, 4
Separation, 120
Separation-individuation process, 123
Shadowing, 123–124
Shame, *vs.* autonomy, 86, 100–102
Sociability, attachment styles and, 38–42
Sociability Scale, 40–41
Social distance, 4
Social interactions, spatial zones in, 4
Socialization, stereotyped feminine and masculine, 60*n*
Social symbiosis, 97
Stagnation, *vs.* generativity, 86, 110–112
Suicidal behavior
  adolescent. (*See* Suicide, adolescent)
  dealing with, 209–210
  middle adulthood, 224–227
  older adulthood, 227
  oldest-old, 229–232
  risk factors, 210
  school age children, 216–219
Suicide, adolescent
  age of parents and, 197, 201–204
  altruistic, 193
  anomic, 193
  clinical implications, 204–205
  disintegration, 221–222
  egoistic, 193
  family factors in, 191–195
  modes of death, 196
  nonsuicidal integration, 219–220
  parental marital pathology
    nature of, 197–198
    perceived adolescent pathology and, 199–200
  parental marital pattern and, 195–197
  perceived adolescent pathology and
    group differences in, 198–199
    parental marital pathology and, 199–200
  suicidal disintegration, 221–222
  taxonomy of family factors, 193–195
  TILT implications, 201
Symbolic play, 99

Territoriality, 3–4
TILT model, 232. (*See also specific aspects of*)
  across life stages, 87–89
  applications to other areas, 233–234
  assumptions, 59–63
  extension into prebirth, logic for, 94*n*

TILT model (*Continued*)
    goals, 63
        for couples, 150–153
        for psychotic couple, 183, 185
    logic of, 58
    model for couples, 145–150
    types. (*See also specific TILT types*)
        of children of different TILT couple types, 188
        description of, 21, 22, 25*n*
Toddlerhood, 100–102
Trust
    basic, 86
    fecal embarrassment and, 87
    vs. mistrust, 98–100

Unidimensional perspective, for couple therapy, 145–147
Union, 120

Verbal intimacy, 5

Walls, interpersonal
    attachment and, 17–18
    description of, 12–15, 54–58
    erecting, 15
    graduated/integrated replacement of, 61–62
    loosening, 15, 50, 51
    maintained unneccesarily after boundaries are established, 51–53
    maturation and, 49
    mixed, 57–58, 61
    moderate, 55
    purpose of, 13, 15
    replacement of, 148
    rigid, 55
    taking down prematurely, 62–63, 148
World social organization, TILT applications, 234

Zygote (blastocyst), 94–95